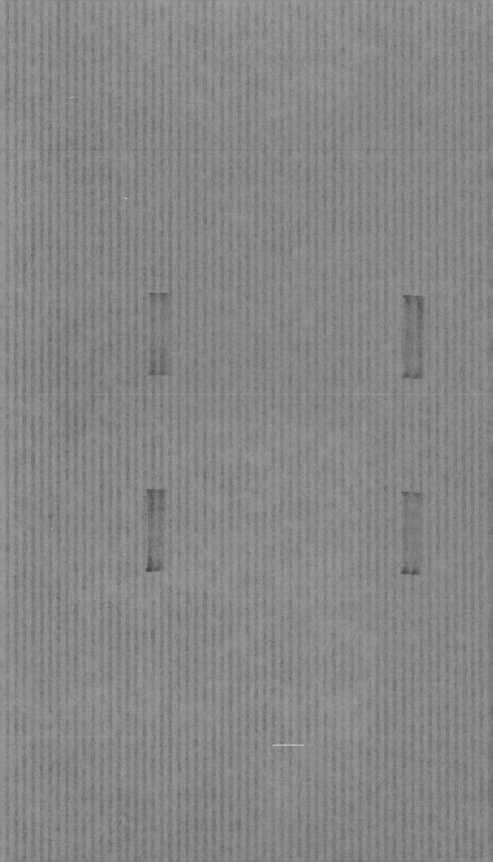

DEAR BROTHER WALT

Thomas Jefferson Whitman in his early fifties, at the height of his career as a civil engineer (c. 1885). Courtesy of the Missouri Historical Society.

Dear Brother Walt

The Letters of
THOMAS JEFFERSON WHITMAN

edited by

DENNIS BERTHOLD *and* KENNETH M. PRICE

The Kent State University Press

Copyright © 1984 by The Kent State University Press, Kent, Ohio 44242
All rights reserved
Library of Congress Catalog Card Number 83-26775
ISBN 0-87338-297-8
Manufactured in the United States of America

Library of Congress Cataloging in Publication Data

Whitman, Thomas Jefferson, 1833–1890.
    Dear brother Walt.

    Includes index.
    1. Whitman, Walt, 1819–1892—Correspondence. 2. Poets, American—19th
century—Correspondence 3. Whitman, Thomas Jefferson, 1833–1890. 4. Civil
engineers—United States—Correspondence. I. Whitman, Walt, 1819–1892.
II. Berthold, Dennis. III. Price, Kenneth M.   IV. Title.
PS3231.A48   1984   624'.092'4   [B]   83-26775
ISBN 0-87338-297-8

To our parents

Contents

Illustrations

Foreword

Of all Walt Whitman's five brothers, "Jeff" (Thomas Jefferson), was plainly his favorite. Walt tutored him, played ball with him, encouraged his interest in music by buying a piano for him, introduced him to civil engineers who gave him his first employment, and finally wrote his obituary for the *Engineering Record* when he died in 1890, two years before Walt.

These facts, of course, are known to all students of Whitman. But the editors of *Dear Brother Walt* have turned up some hitherto unpublished letters and unearthed important new information about Jefferson Whitman's career in St. Louis as superintendent of waterworks. Walt wrote that Jeff planned and built the waterworks and remained "superintendent and chief for nearly 20 years," but the poet did not give any details of his brother's ingenuity in building new systems of storing and delivering water. Editors Dennis Berthold and Kenneth M. Price have discovered that Jeff was actually a pioneer in the field and received national recognition for his achievements. In brief, Thomas Jefferson Whitman was a far more important person on his own merits than biographers of Walt Whitman have realized.

Certain of these biographers, notably Jean Catel, have argued for a streak of physical degeneracy in the poet's boasted ancestry; and it is true that three of his brothers and one of his sisters did have serious health problems. But Walt also had two remarkably healthy and able brothers—George, who survived four years as an infantryman in the Civil War and later became a successful city inspector in Camden, N.J., and Jeff, who was even more successful in St. Louis, as we now know.

This edition of Jeff's letters not only fills out the record of Walt's close friendship with his younger brother, but it also makes a contribution to American history, including municipal and state politics. There are, perhaps, insufficient materials for a book-length biography of Thomas Jefferson Whitman, though his accomplishments deserve one, but the able Introduction to this well-edited collection of his letters is a worthy substitute. I recommend *Dear Brother Walt* to all students of Walt Whitman and suggest that historians of Ameri-

can municipal development will find useful and interesting
information in it.

GAY WILSON ALLEN
JANUARY 10, 1984

Preface

This annotated edition includes all of the extant letters of Thomas Jefferson Whitman (1833–90), a younger brother of the poet Walt and a civil engineer of considerable importance. We draw our title from the most common salutation in the correspondence: seventy-seven of these letters were written to the poet. The additional letters also shed light on Walt and the Whitman family: three were addressed to the poet's friend William Douglas O'Connor and twenty-six went to other family members. Over the years a small number of Whitman scholars have referred to the holographs of these letters. We now make them readily available for literary scholars and for those interested in the Civil War, the rise of technology and engineering, and nineteenth-century American social history. Our notes have been written with these various audiences in mind.

While we of course divided the tasks on this project, each editor submitted all his copy to his collaborator for corrections and suggestions. For the merits and the flaws in the book we claim equal responsibility.

Of the many people who helped us, two deserve special mention: Charles E. Feinberg and Jerome Loving. We thank Mr. Feinberg for his broad-ranging support of Whitman studies and for gathering most of the "Jeff" Whitman letters edited here. We thank Professor Loving, who once planned to edit these letters himself, for obtaining photocopies of many of the holographs, for urging us to undertake this project, and for providing sound advice. We are also grateful to Gay Wilson Allen for both criticism and encouragement; his timely aid was far more important to us than he realizes. Randall Waldron read the entire work and criticized it with the specialized knowledge that only an editor of Whitman family correspondence could be expected to have. Roger Asselineau, Robert A. Ferguson, and Marsden Price read and improved our introduction. Help with information and materials was provided by Walter Eitner, Henry C. Johnson, Edwin H. Miller, and William White.

Our project was advanced by the support of David H. Stewart, head of the Department of English, Texas A&M University, and by research grants from the College of Liberal Arts and the University Mini-grant Committee, Texas A&M University.

Many curators and librarians helped us in our research, and we are indebted to them all. Special thanks, however, go to Beverley Bishop and Deborah W. Bolas, Missouri Historical Society; Ellen S. Dunlap, formerly research librarian of the Humanities Research Center, the University of Texas at Austin; James H. Hutson, former chief, and his staff in the Manuscript Division, Library of Congress; Edward Machowski, Archival Library, City of St. Louis; R. Russell Maylone, Northwestern University Library; Timothy D. Murray, Washington University in St. Louis; Dr. John L. Sharpe III, Duke University; E. A. Siegerist, Engineers' Club of St. Louis; Lola Szladitz, New York Public Library; and William Worthington, the Smithsonian Institution.

For permission to publish original material, we thank the custodians of the Trent Collection, William R. Perkins Library, Duke University; the Library of Congress; the Missouri Historical Society, St. Louis; the Pierpont Morgan Library; the Henry W. and Albert A. Berg Collection, New York Public Library, Astor, Lenox, and Tilden Foundations; the Special Collections Department, Northwestern University Library; the Walt Whitman Collection, Barrett Library, University of Virginia; Special Collections, Washington University in St. Louis; the Collection of American Literature, the Beinecke Rare Book and Manuscript Library, Yale University.

For careful and expeditious handling of the manuscript, we thank all those involved at The Kent State University Press, especially Paul H. Rohmann, director, and Jeanne M. West, copy editor, whose sharp eye saved us from a number of errors.

Finally, for their daily insights and constant support throughout the work on this edition, we thank our warmest advisers and helpmates, Pamela R. Matthews and Renée A. Price.

ABBREVIATIONS

Allen	Gay Wilson Allen, *The Solitary Singer: A Critical Biography of Walt Whitman* (New York: Macmillan, 1955; rev. ed., New York Univ. Press, 1967).
Berg	Henry W. and Albert A. Berg Collection, New York Public Library, Astor, Lenox, and Tilden Foundations.
Correspondence	Edwin Haviland Miller, ed., *Walt Whitman: The Correspondence*, 6 vols. (New York: New York Univ. Press, 1961–77).
DN	William White, ed., *Walt Whitman: Daybooks and Notebooks*, 3 vols. (New York: New York Univ. Press, 1978).
Faint Clews	Clarence Gohdes and Rollo G. Silver, eds., *Faint Clews & Indirections: Manuscripts of Walt Whitman and His Family* (Durham, N.C.: Duke Univ. Press, 1949).
Faner	Robert D. Faner, *Walt Whitman & Opera* (Carbondale: Southern Illinois Univ. Press, 1951).
Feinberg	Charles E. Feinberg Collection, Library of Congress.
Heyde—LC	Heyde, Hannah (Whitman) Collection, Library of Congress.
Loving	Jerome M. Loving, ed., *Civil War Letters of George Washington Whitman* (Durham, N.C.: Duke Univ. Press, 1975).
LVVW	Louisa Van Velsor Whitman
Molinoff	Katherine Molinoff, *Some Notes on Whitman's Family*, Monographs on Unpublished Whitman Material, no. 2 (Brooklyn: Comet Press, 1941).
Morgan	The Pierpont Morgan Library.
Prose Works 1892	Floyd Stovall, ed., *Walt Whitman: Prose Works 1892*, 2 vols. (New York: New York Univ. Press, 1963–64).
Rubin	Joseph Jay Rubin, *The Historic Whitman* (University Park: Pennsylvania State Univ. Press, 1973).
Traubel	Horace Traubel, *With Walt Whitman in Camden*, I (Boston: Small Maynard, 1906); II (New York: D. Appleton, 1908); III (New York: Mitchell Kennerly, 1914); IV (Philadelphia: Univ. of

	Pennsylvania Press, 1953); V and VI (Carbondale: Southern Illinois Univ. Press, 1964 and 1982, respectively).
Trent	Trent Collection, William R. Perkins Library, Duke University.
UPP	Emory Holloway, ed., *The Uncollected Poetry and Prose of Walt Whitman*, 2 vols. (Garden City, N.Y.: Doubleday, Page, 1921).
Waldron	Randall H. Waldron, ed., *Mattie: The Letters of Martha Mitchell Whitman* (New York: New York Univ. Press, 1977).
WW Papers	Walt Whitman Papers, Library of Congress.
WW	Walt Whitman

Introduction

The letters written by Walt Whitman's favorite brother, Thomas Jefferson Whitman, or "Jeff" as he was commonly called, fall naturally into two groups: first, the New Orleans and Brooklyn letters which illuminate the relationship between the two brothers and the nature of the Whitman family as a whole, and second, the St. Louis letters which focus mainly on Jeff's career. The four letters written in 1848 provide key information about the three-month visit of the two brothers to New Orleans, a crucial period in the poet's development. Jeff's fifty-five Brooklyn letters, written from 1860–67, constitute the most vivid record of the Whitman family as a functioning unit, the clearest picture of the personal relationships and circumstances that shaped America's greatest poet. The remaining forty-seven letters, most of them written in St. Louis from 1867–89, paint a full portrait of Jeff as an engineer; they trace in detail the significant career of the only Whitman other than Walt to achieve national renown in his profession.

Walt, Jeff, and the Whitman Family

Walt Whitman was fourteen when Jeff was born in the summer of 1833, and the future poet soon took responsibility for the child: "I . . . had much care of him for many years afterward, and he did not separate from me. He was a very handsome, healthy, affectionate, smart child, and would sit on my lap or hang on my neck half an hour at a time."[1] It was characteristic of Walt to take this parental role: the younger children were often "in his charge"[2] and he gradually assumed a greater and greater responsibility for the family finances. The father, Walter Whitman, Sr., suffered numerous financial reverses, and by 1847 it was young Walt who was buying boots for his brothers and who held the title to the family home.[3] In

1. *Prose Works 1892*, II, 693.
2. "Notes from Conversations with George W. Whitman, 1893," *In Re Walt Whitman*, ed. Horace L. Traubel et al. (Philadelphia: David McKay, 1893), p. 38.
3. Charles E. Feinberg, "A Whitman Collector Destroys a Whitman Myth," *The Papers of the Bibliographical Society of America*, 52 (1958), 75, 77.

the 1840s Walt also explored the surrogate parent role in his fiction. As his brief sketch "My Boys and Girls" indicates, he considered as his "children" sisters Mary and Hannah, and brothers George, Andrew, and Jeff.[4] Interestingly, he avoided mentioning Jesse, his only older sibling, and Edward, the youngest Whitman, both of whom already showed signs of mental disorders.

Walt was especially fond of Jeff: "He was of noble nature from the first; very good-natured, very plain, very friendly. O, how we loved each other!" Other family members noted their special intimacy: for example, Hannah once commented on Jeff's "close bond of friendship" with Walt, "closer as it were than a brother."[5] And Walt himself described Jeff as his only "real brother" and "understander."[6] In 1848, when Walt was offered a post on the *New Orleans Daily Crescent*, the fourteen-year-old Jeff accompanied him to serve as office boy on the paper. One imagines that here, over a thousand miles away from home, with Jeff suffering from dysentery and homesickness, the bond between the brothers grew even stronger.

Beyond emotional ties, common tastes linked the brothers. Jeff played the guitar and sang pleasantly, and Walt encouraged such musical inclinations by purchasing a piano for Jeff in 1852.[7] About this time Walt introduced his brother to Italian opera and frequently took him across the East River to the new opera houses in New York. Jeff also took a knowledgeable and sympathetic interest in Walt's career as both poet and journalist. On April 3, 1860, he wrote to Walt in Boston about the forthcoming edition of *Leaves of Grass*: "I quite long for it to make its appearance. What jolly times we will have reading the notices of it wont we." He warned his older brother: "you must expect the 'Yam Yam Yam' writer[s] to give you a dig as

4. *Walt Whitman: The Early Poems and Fiction*, ed. Thomas L. Brasher (New York: New York Univ. Press, 1963), p. 249. For brief sketches of the various members of the Whitman family, see Loving, pp. 8–17, and Waldron, pp. 6–16.

5. For WW's comment, see *Prose Works 1892*, II, 693; for Hannah's, see the letter from Charles L. Heyde to WW, December 3, 1890 (Trent).

6. See Traubel, III, 541, and Justin Kaplan, *Walt Whitman: A Life* (New York: Simon and Schuster, 1980), p. 235.

7. Hannah to LVVW, October [1858?] (Heyde—LC).

often as possible but I dont suppose you will mind it any more than you did in the days of your editorship of the B.[rooklyn] Eagle when the Advertiser['s] Lees used to go at you so roughly" (Letter 5).[8] Later in life, when Walt's relationship with Jeff was less close, the poet exaggerated his family's indifference toward his literary career just as he exaggerated his poor reception in American literary circles: in both cases the poet was shaping the myth of the neglected, misunderstood genius. A fair assessment of the family's attitude would indicate that his mother, George, and Hannah followed Walt's career as a poet. Jeff, on the other hand, took an informed interest in the poetry itself.[9]

Perhaps because of their shared interests, Walt attempted to guide Jeff into career lines that resembled his own, urging him to become a printer. But even in adolescence Jeff seems to have been drawn toward engineering, once remarking in a letter to his parents on the canals and poor drainage of New Orleans (Letter 4). Walt's description of Jeff's vocational choice again reveals the paternal role that the older brother had assumed: "he learn'd printing, and work'd awhile at it; but eventually (with my approval) he went to employment at land surveying, and merged in the studies and work of topographical engineer."[10]

8. The 1840s in American journalism were notorious for the scurrilous manner in which competing editors attacked one another. For example, in an editorial in the *Brooklyn Daily Advertiser* of November 4, 1846, Henry A. Lees apparently responded to WW's characterization of him as "an English cockney of fifty-sixth mental calibre" by accusing the future poet of "bad grammar." See Thomas L. Brasher, *Whitman as Editor of the Brooklyn Daily Eagle* (Detroit: Wayne State Univ. Press, 1970), pp. 33-34.

9. WW once commented that "A man's family is the people who love him. You know for the most part I have always been isolated from my people—in certain senses have been a stranger in their midst. . . . Who of my family has gone along with me? Who? Do you know? Not one of them" (Traubel, III, 525). Although none of the family understood WW as deeply as he wished, there was widespread family pride and interest in his work. When "Personalism" was published in *The Galaxy*, LVVW wrote to the poet: "george has got the galaxy   just come with it   walt i suppose you see that little peice in thursdays times about your being the only American poet i cut it out and was going to send it to Jeff   if you haven't seen it i will send it to you" (April 25, 1868 [Trent]).

10. *Prose Works 1892*, II, 693.

That Walt would support Jeff's decision to pursue engineering is not surprising when one recalls the poet's enthusiastic response to the completion of the Croton Aqueduct in 1842, a water system for New York which had taken five years to build. Walt recognized the thirty-eight-mile-long aqueduct as one of the engineering triumphs of the century, hailing this "performance which all Europe cannot parallel."[11] Instead of water polluted by seepage from graveyards and privies, the city now enjoyed pure water; many hoped that New Yorkers would adopt water as the preferred beverage over beer. (Not coincidentally, Walt's temperance novel *Franklin Evans* was published a month after the opening of the aqueduct.) After Jeff chose engineering as a career and began work for the Brooklyn Water Works in the late 1850s, Walt remained interested in problems of municipal water supply, but now his opinions were buttressed by an insider's knowledge. As editor of the *Brooklyn Daily Times* he "bent the whole weight of the paper steadily in favor of the McAlpine plan [for the new waterworks], as against a flimsy, cheap and temporary series of works that would have long since broken down, and disgraced the city."[12] No doubt, Jeff informed the poet-editor of the superiority of the McAlpine plan and provided information to help Walt write such essays as "A Visit to the Water Works," "A City Sweet and Clean," and "Important Questions in Brooklyn."[13]

Although Jeff seems to have influenced Walt's journalism in 1858 and 1859, the relationship between the brothers was perhaps not as close as it had been. On February 23, 1859, Jeff married Martha E. Mitchell ("Mat" or "Mattie") and brought her into the family home.[14] The poet liked the new bride and

11. Quoted in Kaplan, p. 112.

12. *Correspondence*, III, 386.

13. The first two pieces are reprinted in Walt Whitman, *I Sit and Look Out: Essays from the Brooklyn Daily Times*, ed. Emory Holloway and Vernolian Schwarz (New York: Columbia Univ. Press, 1932), pp. 140, 144–45. The manuscript pages of "Important Questions in Brooklyn" can be found in the Alderman Library at the University of Virginia. This essay advocates what WW called "a grand system of Sewerage" for Brooklyn. WW develops a detailed and sensible argument for a more expensive "permanent closed brick conduit" rather than "a temporary open ditch or earthen canal."

14. Biographers of WW have thought that Jeff and Mattie had a place of their own in 1859 because *Lain's Brooklyn Directory* for 1858/59 lists a

later concluded that she was one of the two finest women he had ever known, yet Walt's relationship with Jeff was now fundamentally altered.

Unfortunately, no letters that were written by either Walt or Jeff in 1858 or 1859 survive, thus making it nearly impossible to reconstruct how Jeff's marriage might have affected Walt at the time. What seems clear is that the marriage deprived Walt of his ward and companion and changed the poet's understanding of male friendship. As Justin Kaplan has recently argued, when Walt began shifting affection to those who were not kin, manly love lost the sanctions of brotherly love. Significantly, Walt wrote a number of important crisis poems—"Out of the Cradle Endlessly Rocking," "As I Ebb'd with the Ocean of Life," the "Calamus" group—about the time of Jeff's marriage.[15]

Only in 1863, when Walt began to work in the hospitals in Washington tending wounded soldiers, did he again find emotional relationships as fulfilling as the primal relationship with Jeff. Walt himself commented on the nature of his response to the soldiers: he found them "appealing to me most profoundly. . . . Often they seem very near to me, even as my own children or younger brothers. I make no bones of petting them just as if they were."[16] Walt's relationship with Jeff might be seen as the prototype for the "Calamus" relation-

---

"Whitman, J city surveyor" with a home on Fifth Avenue near Twelfth Street (Allen, p. 216; Kaplan, p. 236). However, an examination of the directories from the preceding and following years reveals this J. Whitman to be Jarvis rather than Jefferson Whitman.

Recently, Randall Waldron has noted that Mattie's life "prior to 1859 remains almost entirely a mystery" (Waldron, p. 1). Fortunately, on October 18, 1939, Garrett Newkirk interviewed Mattie's daughter, Jessie, who explained: "Her full name before marriage was Martha Emma Mitchell. She was an orphan, her father who had married a second time being dead. Her stepmother was her guardian and while mother was a minor, had charge of her money, which amounted to several thousand dollars. [When] Mother announced to her, her intentions of marrying father after she came of age . . . the stepmother skipped out with all the funds, simply vanished, and mother was left penniless. She and father were terribly hard-up for years" (Fansler Collection, Northwestern Univ.).

15. Throughout this paragraph we are indebted to Kaplan, esp. pp. 235–36.

16. *Correspondence*, I, 125.

ships the poet developed during his work in the hospitals (and indeed for his relationships after the war with Peter Doyle and Harry Stafford).[17] Although Jeff's marriage complicated the context of manly love for the poet, Walt still found familial terms for expressing male love: the poet sent soldiers impassioned, ambiguous signals suggesting that he was friend, comrade, and lover while insistently addressing them as "sons" and "brothers."[18] Once again Walt assumed the tender, protective, and nurturing role that he had first taken with Jeff. And as in the relationship with Jeff, he seems to have helped a number of the young men he befriended grow to heterosexual maturity and marriage.[19]

For Walt, the older brother–younger brother relationship eventually became a metaphor that conveyed a sense of love and deep understanding. Late in his career, when Walt wanted to stress his final consanguinity with his literary mentor, he explained that "What made, and ever makes the argument of Emerson, in that walk on the Common, so dear and *holy to me, was the personal affectionateness* of it, as of an elderly brother to a younger." Separation from and a desired reunion with the brother became for Walt a theme laced with personal emotion. When William Stansberry, a former soldier, wrote Walt and

17. Edwin Haviland Miller comments on the nature of WW's relationships: "These young men were . . . emotionally insecure, and desirous of establishing a dependent relationship with an older man. Whitman instinctively understood them. . . . He was both father and mother. This bisexual role, safely removed from the threats of literal paternity and of mature sexuality, he fulfilled in 'Calamus' friendships, the only relationships that were emotionally satisfying to him or for that matter possible" (*Correspondence*, III, 3–4).

18. See, for example, *Correspondence*, I, 93, 94, 106, 120, 139, 149, 160, 186.

19. The emotional cost of this was high. WW had to struggle to accept the marriages of the young men he befriended. As late as 1890, he still pointed to Jeff's marriage as a transforming event in their relationship: Jeff "was very much with me in his childhood & as big boy. [We were] greatly attached to each other till he got married." WW seems to have had a similarly negative response to the marriage of Benton Wilson, a former soldier. On January 27, 1867, Wilson observed, "I wrote to you a year and more ago that I was married but did not receive any reply, so I did not know but you was displeased with it." And in 1884, when WW's comrade Harry Stafford mentioned his marriage plans to the poet, Whitman ignored these plans in his return letter. See *Correspondence*, V, 123; I, 322–23, n. 63; III, 371, n. 40.

recalled the days in Armory Square Hospital, the poet responded: "I send you my love, & to your dear children & wife the same. As I write, you seem very dear to me too, like some young brother, who has been lost, but now found." Perhaps it is not surprising, then, that when the poet of "Passage to India" contemplates encountering God, the embrace of brothers is the central image:

> the aim attain'd,
> As fill'd with friendship, love complete, the Elder Brother found,
> The Younger melts in fondness in his arms.[20]

In 1863, while George fought as part of the Union army and Walt worked in Washington caring for the nation's wounded, Jeff in Brooklyn concerned himself with the deteriorating health of his other brothers and Hannah. He assumed many of the financial burdens of the household that he, Mattie, and their two daughters shared with Mother Whitman, Jesse, and Edward. At the Portland Avenue home, Jesse, perhaps syphilitic, suffered from bouts of raging insanity in which he threatened his closest relatives (he would be institutionalized a year later). Edward, physically and mentally retarded, remained largely helpless. In his own nearby home in Brooklyn, yet another brother, Andrew, battled without success against alcoholism and a throat disease which would claim his life by the end of the year. The news from farther afield was not cheering either: letters from Vermont, where Hannah had moved when she married Charles Heyde, indicated that she now suffered from stomach illness along with chronic marital problems. And although George was a model of health, his life as a soldier caused anguished concern for the entire clan, including the oldest sister Mary Elizabeth, who lived on Long Island. Not surprisingly, Jeff longed for Walt's opinions during this year of turmoil: "I do so wish that I could see you and have a good talk abt family affairs." And he added, "I think you would see and think as I do" (Letters 40 and 37).

The thirty-seven letters Jeff wrote to Walt in 1863 shed light on the character of many members of the family, includ-

---

20. See *Correspondence*, III, 285; II, 299; and *Leaves of Grass: Comprehensive Reader's Edition*, ed. Harold W. Blodgett and Sculley Bradley (New York: New York Univ. Press, 1965), pp. 419–20.

ing the mother. Although Jeff loved his mother and admired
her stability and strength, he was—unlike Walt—willing to
see her failings. Jeff complained of her excessive frugality,
what he called her "mistaken notion" of economy (Letter 37).
He felt that Andrew's health could only be salvaged by moving
him into the Portland Avenue home (where Mattie could cook
and care for him) and away from Nancy, his slovenly wife. Jeff
noted that Jesse, too, was failing rapidly because he lacked
nourishing and palatable food: "Mother seems to think that
she ought to live without spending any money. Even to day she
has 25 or $30 in the house and I will bet that all they have for
dinner will be a quart of tomats and a few cucumbers, and then
Mother wonders why Jess vomits up his meals" (Letter 35).

Poor health, emotional stress, close quarters, shared
finances—all these contributed to some fierce family quarrels.
Jeff's wife, Mattie, attempted to be a peacemaker: she offered
to nurse George if he should return home wounded, and she
actually cared for Andrew in his illness, cleaning the blisters on
his neck and cooking him rice pudding many nights.[21] Despite
these efforts, Jeff and Mattie did not find it easy to make their
home within the mother's home. There was petty bickering
over money and tension over Jeff's children. Although Mother
Whitman generally liked Jeff's wife, she grew impatient with
the couple's oldest child Manahatta ("Hattie"). Andrew's attitude toward Hattie went beyond impatience to a real threat of
violence. Mother Whitman remarked in a letter to Walt (after
a series of other complaints), "then add to that i have hattey of
coarse and she is very obstropolous and her uncle Andrew says
if she was his hed break her neck   so you see walt what we go
through every day sundays and all."[22]

Andrew's death in December 1863 did not end the danger
of violence. Jesse, apparently overwrought at his brother's
death, became irritated when Hattie pushed a chair, on which a
diaper was hanging, across the floor. When Hattie failed to
stop on command, Jesse burst into rage and repeated Andrew's
threat to break Hattie's "dam'd neck." Naturally, Mattie defended her three-year-old. Jesse then "turned from the child to
Mat and swore that he would kill her." When Jeff heard about

21. Letter from LVVW to WW, October 21, 1863 (Trent).
22. October 30 (?), 1863 (Trent).

this he was furious. He waited ten to twelve days before writing Walt, "because I was afraid to think about it":

> Probably had I been home he [Jesse] would not have done anything of the kind but if he had, so help me God I would have shot him dead on the spot—And I must confess I felt considerably like it as it was. I love Mat as I love my life—dearer by far—and to have this infernal pup—a perfect hell-drag to his Mother—treat her so—threaten to brain her—call her all the vile things he could think of—is a little more than I will stand   He says he dont know any better   he lies—he does know better. I wish to God he was ready to put along side of Andrew. (Letter 43)

The incandescent anger displayed here has led biographers and editors to characterize Jeff as volatile.[23] At first glance, other evidence from the letters seems to support this characterization. For example, after estimating that four hundred people—mostly Irishmen—had died in the New York draft riots of July 1863, Jeff wrote: "The only feeling I have is that I fear that they did not kill enough of 'em Walt. I'm perfectly rabid on an Irishman" (Letter 32). In letters to the poet, Jeff voices the darkest impulses of his nature, impulses which he never seems to have acted upon. It is as if he purged his bile by writing to Walt. Some of Jeff's letters *are* volatile, but as his St. Louis career will show, the public Jeff always remained a poised, controlled, politically astute engineer.

Even in 1863 when Jeff's emotions were in turmoil because of both family and national crises, he still managed to control his external life. Beyond maintaining his employment at the Brooklyn Water Works, he helped sustain Walt's work in the hospitals by channelling a steady stream of money toward his brother (at least thirty-six installments totalling over $326.00 and perhaps much more).[24] So far as can be determined, Jeff

---

23. See, for example, Allen, p. 307, and *Correspondence*, I, 189, n. 75.

24. The specific amounts given by Jeff and his associates in thirty-one known instances total $281.20. No record survives of the amounts given for the five additional contributions mentioned; assuming the $9.00 average for these instances gives the figure of $326.00.

No doubt, this total estimate is low because some of the Whitman family correspondence from this period is lost and because promised payments (e.g., Moses Lane's indication that he would contribute $5.00 per month for an unspecified period of time) are not included.

and his friends at the Brooklyn Water Works began before and continued after other contributors to Walt's work. From January 12, 1863, until at least December 24, 1866, Walt served as the unofficial and only agent of what Jeff called "The B. Watr Works soldiers Aid society" (Letter 20).

Jeff's capacity to involve himself imaginatively in the welfare of strangers, demonstrated first by his support of the hospital work, surfaces again in a letter he wrote shortly after moving to St. Louis. Here Jeff displays his gentler side:

> On the street to-day I saw a very interesting yet somewhat painful sight—twas that of a family moving in from the plains—An old woman—I shoud judge all of eighty—another woman of about 35—a young man and his wife abt 25 a boy of 12 two children 8 and 6 and a little babe—all but the young man and his wife were in the wagon drawn by 4 oxen—the wagon covered with dirty white canvass—The boy had leading with a rope a fine old cow—a young cow and calf were alongside—under the wagon was a large white dog and inside by the old woman was a small black terrier—They had met with an accident in the way of b[r]eaking one of the hind wheels and were therefore hard up— The faces of all were a study—but particularly of the young man and his wife—neither of them was at all handsome but yet I shall remember their faces for a long time—The old woman had that peculiar look of crazy stupidity that you can hardly tell whether they are really stupid or thinking of by-gone life. (Letter 61)

There are rudiments of literary power in this passage, and one is struck by the similarities between this and the poet's own portrayal of "A Specimen Tramp Family," written thirteen years later:

> We pass'd quite a number of tramps, singly or in couples—one squad, a family in a rickety one-horse wagon, with some baskets evidently their work and trade—the man seated on a low board, in front, driving—the gauntish woman by his side, with a baby well bundled in her arms, its little red feet and lower legs sticking out right towards us as we pass'd—and in the wagon behind, we saw two (or three) crouching little children. It was a queer, taking, rather sad picture. . . . But on our return nearly two hours afterward, we found them a ways further along the same road. . . . The freed horse was not far off, quietly cropping the grass.

The man was busy at the wagon, the boy had gather'd some dry wood, and was making a fire—and as we went a little further we met the woman afoot. . . . Eyes, voice and manner were those of a corpse, animated by electricity. She was quite young—the man she was traveling with, middle-aged. Poor woman—what story was it, out of her fortunes, to account for that inexpressibly scared way, those glassy eyes, and that hollow voice?[25]

Each brother presents a catalogue of individuals which begins with adults and proceeds to children, conveys the sympathy felt in the presence of a sad scene, and expresses a final desire to understand the death-in-life of these women. The parallel passages evidence a mental affinity between the brothers, a common ground of sensibility such as Walt shared with no other sibling.

Jeff's Professional Career

When Jeff was offered a post in St. Louis in 1867, Walt responded enthusiastically: it is "a great work—a noble position—& will give you a good big field."[26] Jeff's appointment as chief engineer of the Board of Water Commissioners testifies to the value of his training in Brooklyn. In the antebellum days of engineering, few schools offered more than one or two courses in surveying and topography, and except for the military institutes, only six colleges had organized programs in civil engineering.[27] Many civil engineers, including experts in the profession with whom Jeff worked—James P. Kirkwood and Julius W. Adams, for example—learned their profession without benefit of a college education, coming up through the ranks as laborers, apprentices, and surveyors, usually attached to the military or the railroads. Although no record exists for the earliest part of Jeff's career, we do know that he first worked as a land surveyor and then became an assistant to a Lewis L. Bartlett who was engaged in harbor improvements

25. *Prose Works 1892*, I, 168–69.
26. *Correspondence*, I, 326.
27. J. Elfreth Watkins, "The Beginnings of Engineering" (1891; rpt. *The Civil Engineer: His Origins* [New York: American Society of Civil Engineers, 1970]), p. 76.

for New York City.[28] In 1856 or 1857 he became an assistant engineer on the construction of the Brooklyn Water Works under Kirkwood, who had just completed five years as chief engineer of the Missouri Pacific Railroad. With Kirkwood, Jeff helped build the first scientifically engineered system of coordinated sewer and waterworks in the country. In 1863 Jeff was appointed chief assistant engineer under Moses Lane, who had succeeded Kirkwood in 1862. Soon Jeff was supplementing his income by running surveys in upstate New York and Massachusetts, including one in Springfield for W. E. Worthen, a leading hydraulic engineer and a future president of the American Society of Civil Engineers (1887).[29] Experiences and contacts like these placed Jeff at the center of the developing profession of civil engineering. The Brooklyn Water Works was a virtual training ground for the nation's future hydraulic and sanitary engineers, a school perhaps more valuable than any academic institute of the time.

Brother Walt surely admired such self-education, a remarkable family example of the opportunities available to diligent young Americans of practical scientific bents. Perhaps under the tutelage of Lane, Jeff cast a wide net for engineering information and asked Walt to send him useful government publications to further his professional development. Displaying that desire for new ideas and broad vistas that Walt admired in the national character, Jeff showed particular interest in the West. He was especially eager to read the twelve lavish volumes of the *Reports of Explorations and Surveys . . . for a Railroad From the Mississippi River to the Pacific Ocean* (1855–60).[30] He also wanted the *Report on the Construction of a Military Road From Fort Walla-Walla to Fort Benton*

28. Robert Moore and Henry Flad, "Thomas Jefferson Whitman, M. Am. Soc. C. E.," *Proceedings of the American Society of Civil Engineers*, 18 (April 1892), 103.

29. For information on Worthen, consult *A Biographical Dictionary of American Civil Engineers* (New York: American Society of Civil Engineers, 1972), pp. 131–32.

30. U.S. War Department, prepared under the supervision of the U.S. Engineer Department, Topographical Bureau, 12 vols. (Washington, D.C.: A. O. P. Nicholson, 1855–60). Jeff received the later, quarto edition of this

(1863) by Captain John Mullan,[31] a pioneering military surveyor whom Walt knew and admired. Both Walt and his friend William Douglas O'Connor encouraged Jeff's pursuit of knowledge by sending him the books and pamphlets he requested, some of which were expensive technical publications representing the latest developments and newest information in the field. Jeff considered using his knowledge to gain a position on the Pacific Railroad: "I've no doubt but I could get a place at once on it, yet I think that in the end I will make more by staying where I am but its rather pleasant to have that to fall back on" (Letter 41).

Jeff was right. His years in Brooklyn had prepared him for far larger responsibilities than he could have assumed as a railroad surveyor. By maintaining contact with Lane and the influential professionals at the Brooklyn Water Works, he would later be in a perfect position to "make more" by moving to the "Future Great City of the World," a city touted as the next capital of the United States, St. Louis.[32] In May 1867, his former boss and mentor Kirkwood recommended him for the position of chief engineer of the Board of Water Commissioners, a body created in 1863 by the Missouri State Legislature to construct a modern waterworks for St. Louis. Kirkwood, who had drawn up plans for the project, thought enough of Jeff's ability to entrust him with primary responsibility for constructing a much-needed waterworks for a city of nearly 300,000 inhabitants. For the next twenty years, Jeff would oversee the water supply of the nation's fastest-growing large city.

The demands of the job were great, and Jeff met them well. He was paid a good annual salary, perhaps as much as four thousand dollars, and was considered the resident expert on

---

important publication with the supplementary twelfth volume added in 1860.

31. U.S. Topographical Bureau (Washington, D.C.: GPO, 1863).

32. The city's most enthusiastic promoter was L. U. Reavis who, during the 1870s, wrote several speeches, pamphlets, and books with the title *St. Louis: The Future Great City of the World*. See esp. the 3rd ed. (St. Louis: The St. Louis City Council, 1871).

municipal water supply.[33] As one of his initial tasks, Jeff composed an eight-thousand-word manuscript history of the waterworks from 1829 to 1868, giving a detailed report of his first year on the job and explaining his professional view of the new system.[34] To help build the waterworks Jeff brought his old friend Joseph P. Davis down from Brooklyn and made him principal assistant engineer. (Davis, a graduate of Rensselaer Polytechnic Institute, later became city engineer of Boston in 1880 and chief engineer of the American Telephone and Telegraph Company in 1900.)[35] Jeff completed the waterworks in 1871 and supervised numerous additions to it over the next sixteen years, including the 190-foot granite and red brick water tower which he discussed with Walt (Letter 98). This water tower and another one designed as a Corinthian column which Jeff built in 1871 still mark the city skyline and stand as fitting monuments to this pioneering era in municipal water supply.

While working in St. Louis, Jeff also developed a busy consulting practice. During the 1870s and 1880s he contributed plans for waterworks in Kansas City (Missouri), Leavenworth, St. Joseph, Little Rock, and Galveston. For a time (1875–77) he worked as a consulting engineer in Henry Flad's firm, a leading engineering company in St. Louis. After concluding his career as water commissioner in 1887, Jeff set up his own business specializing in "Designing and Superintendence of Water Works." As an independent consultant he played a major role in planning the Milwaukee sewer system, incorporating the designs E. S. Chesbrough had developed for Chicago which

33. J. T. Scharf, *History of St. Louis City and County* (Philadelphia: Everts & Co., 1883), p. 783, lists Jeff's annual salary in 1867 as $4,000.00. The more reliable and precise *Journal of the City Council*, April 27, 1877, lists his salary as $312.50 per month, or $3,750.00 annually. This was a nationally competitive salary during this period.

34. Thos. J. Whitman, "A History of the Water Works of St. Louis from Their Inception in the Year 1829 to the Year 1868," ed. Thos. E. Flaherty, in the *Water Commissioner's Report* (St. Louis, 1924), pp. 209–34. A separately bound copy of this work is located in the Missouri Historical Society. A longer and more recent account which incorporates much of Jeff's material is John C. Pritchard, "The Saint Louis Water Works: Being a History of a Century of Service," TS, Missouri Historical Society (St. Louis, 1933).

35. *The National Cyclopedia of American Biography* (New York: James T. White & Co., 1878–), XXV, 51.

safely and efficiently coordinated sewage disposal and water consumption in lakefront cities. And in 1888 Jeff was appointed chief engineer of the Memphis Water Works, a progressive system of deriving municipal water supplies from artesian wells instead of rivers.

Unlike any other Whitman, Jeff gradually advanced into the new technocratic and managerial class that developed after the Civil War. In St. Louis, he became a strong advocate of the movement to professionalize engineering in the United States, and was among the earliest members of the American Society of Civil Engineers. Though founded in 1852, the society did not prosper until it was reorganized under its second president, James P. Kirkwood, in October 1867.[36] Jeff joined the revitalized organization about as early as anyone, on January 29, 1868, and remained a member for the rest of his life. He attended many national meetings (perhaps giving him opportunities to see George and Walt), officially invited the society to meet in St. Louis in 1880, sat on the local arrangements committee, and served one year as national vice-president (1885).[37] Jeff was the friend and colleague of some of the most important civil engineers of the day and moved in the mainstream of those professional, political, and economic groups that were transforming the nation.

Among Jeff's closest associates in St. Louis was an energetic German immigrant and civil engineer named Henry Flad. An early photograph shows a jaunty Jeff posing with Flad in a local beer garden, and several of Mattie's letters to Mother Whitman recount visits between the Flads and Jefferson Whitmans.[38] Although Jeff only mentions Henry Flad once in the correspondence (Letter 104), it is clear that from Jeff's first days in St. Louis he was close to this important local figure. Flad had assisted Kirkwood in planning the waterworks and had met with widespread public approbation for his contribution in building the Eads Bridge. (This structure cap-

36. Watkins, p. 77.

37. Jeff's activities are mentioned in the following volumes of the *Proceedings of the American Society of Civil Engineers*: 4 (1878), 45; 5 (1879), 46; 6 (1880), 46; 8 (1882), 112; 11 (1885), 5–6, 32; 13 (1887), 112; 15 (1889), 37.

38. Waldron, pp. 49, 61, 64.

tured the imagination of Walt Whitman on his visit to St. Louis in 1879.)[39] It was probably Flad who, as a member of the Board of Water Commissioners, invited Jeff on a Mississippi River cruise attended by such local dignitaries as Carl Schurz, who was soon to be elected United States senator from Missouri (1869–75). It was probably Flad, too, who helped Jeff survive the tumultuous shift to home rule in St. Louis in 1877, since by this time Jeff was a consulting engineer in Flad's firm.[40] When Jeff's position at the waterworks was suddenly abolished in July, he feared he might be passed over for appointment to the newly created city Board of Public Improvements; Henry Flad, however, was the mayor's and the municipal assembly's choice for president of the board; surely Jeff's appointment in August as the board's water commissioner owed something to Flad's influence and position.

Both Jeff and Flad helped create the Engineers' Club of St. Louis, a local professional society that remains active today. They were charter members and cofounders, with Flad serving as the first president (1868–80) and Jeff as the second president (1881, when one-year terms began). This large group of young engineering professionals met bimonthly to read and discuss technical papers. Although we have no record of Jeff's having presented a paper to the group, we know that meetings were frequently held in his office and that, in addition to his year as president, he served one year as secretary and three years as vice-president. Selected papers from the "Transactions" of the club were published along with similar material from other regional groups in the *Journal of the Association of Engineering Societies.* Jeff's name appears regularly in the published material as a proposer, discussant, and occasional speaker (for example, his eulogy of his colleague Charles Pfeiffer on February 28, 1883).[41]

39. Walter H. Eitner, *Walt Whitman's Western Jaunt* (Lawrence: Regents Press of Kansas, 1981), pp. 76–77.

40. For an account of these difficulties, see Thomas S. Barclay, *The St. Louis Home Rule Charter of 1876: Its Framing and Adoption* (Columbia: Univ. of Missouri Press, 1968).

41. For the published "Proceedings of the Engineers' Club of St. Louis," see the *Journal of the Association of Engineering Societies,* 1 (1881/82) to 6 (1886/87), passim. After January 1886, Jeff's activities with the club dimin-

Jeff's career was not entirely smooth. A continuing frustration for him and for civil engineers in general was the often corrupt political systems with which they had to work. As early as April 16, 1860, Jeff wrote Walt about the state legislature's interference with appointments at the Brooklyn Water Works: "I think it will be a dark day for the B. W. W. if he [Welles, a local contractor] succeeds, but I suppose to the victor belongs the spoils. I know I ain't going to worry, if it does go through." This philosophical attitude toward the realities of the "spoils system" contributed as much to Jeff's success in St. Louis as did his technical training at the Brooklyn Water Works. His original appointment in St. Louis was at least partly the product of petty political squabbling between the city council and the state Board of Water Commissioners. Kirkwood, acting for the board, had recommended that the new waterworks be located at the Chain of Rocks, a site on the Mississippi River about 12 miles north of city hall; the council preferred a less costly location at Bissell's Point, only 3½ miles upstream. When Jeff arrived in St. Louis, he saw that Kirkwood was correct; but, perceiving the controversial nature of the issue and powerless to change the council's mind, he did his best to satisfy the conflicting demands of politics and his profession while proceeding with the Bissell's Point project.[42] Perhaps better than technical planners like Kirkwood, Jeff understood the practical poli-

---

ished considerably. In March 1888, he was nominated to a three-man committee to prepare an obituary for a member, but when the brief notice appeared a month later, his name was not among the signers. In February 1888, he had begun meeting with the "St. Louis Association of Members of the American Society of Civil Engineers," apparently a short-lived rival group ("Minutes," Missouri Historical Society), and on December 4, 1889, he submitted his resignation to the Engineers' Club. Although his declining interest in the club may have simply been a product of his frequent absence from St. Louis on consulting trips, other members with similar obligations maintained their memberships. Some political controversy stemming from his failure to be reappointed as water commissioner in 1887 may have led to his resignation from the club.

42. The story of city council opposition to a first-rate waterworks is recorded in many contemporary versions, most of them defensive and apologetic. A reasonably fair and concise account that acknowledges Jeff's wisdom and foresight is in James Cox, *Old and New St. Louis* (St. Louis: Central Biographical Pub. Co., 1894), pp. 108–10.

tics that municipal engineers had to master in order to survive. That he headed the waterworks longer than any previous administrator testifies to his political acumen. Even a person as competent as Jeff could not last forever in such a demanding and controversial position. As the city grew, the Bissell's Point works proved inadequate, just as Kirkwood had predicted. Furthermore, river water was becoming increasingly polluted with city sewage, causing periodic outbreaks of typhoid to which Jeff himself was exposed (Letter 96). Although Jeff continued to argue for an extension at the Chain of Rocks, the municipal assembly viewed his efforts as self-aggrandizing and refused to heed his pleas. The lower house of the assembly even passed a resolution condemning the quality of the water and held Jeff personally responsible. When Jeff came up for his third term as water commissioner in 1887, he was passed over in favor of M. L. Holman, one of his young assistants and a fellow member of the Engineers' Club.[43] Shortly after Jeff left office, the assembly approved the Chain of Rocks extension, and today St. Louis still draws much of its water from this location.

The other difficulties besetting Jeff in St. Louis came from the same source as they had for so many other Whitmans—the family. Mattie's death in February 1873, after a long and painful illness, left him with two daughters, thirteen and ten, needing more attention and time than a person in his position could offer. He gave up the private home the family had lived in for four years and moved into a boarding house where he remained until 1878. It was fortunate he could afford to send his daughters to school in the East, yet separation from them must have made him lonely. He had pleaded with his mother to visit St. Louis, but she died just three months after Mattie

---

43. The reasons that Jeff was not reappointed are obscure. He may simply have been tired of the job and declined reappointment, desiring to devote more time to his consulting; or, he may have been ill and wanted to escape the political pressures of the position. It seems likely, however, that he had become such a controversial figure that Mayor David R. Francis decided to appoint a new water commissioner to avoid a confrontation with the municipal assembly, whose support was crucial if the waterworks was to be expanded. According to E. D. Meier, M. L. Holman was "one of T. J. W's boys" (letter to WW, December 19, 1890 [Feinberg]).

without ever seeing her son's professional accomplishments. He made similar pleas with Walt during the late 1860s and 1870s. The poet finally visited him for three months in the winter of 1879–80, and Jeff saw him during his own trips east. When Jeff read newspaper accounts of Walt's illnesses and brushes with death, he sent hurried telegrams inquiring about his brother's condition and wrote letters expressing deep concern (Letters 97 and 101). Jeff's most heartbreaking personal loss in these later years must have been the sudden death of his older daughter, Hattie, in early September 1886. Such experiences help to explain the occasional signs of loneliness and depression in his later correspondence. Nonetheless, while enduring a rugged snowstorm in Milwaukee, he expressed a characteristic family belief in the importance of a positive outlook: "I hope, dear Walt, that you will keep in good spirits during the bad weather . . . . I often think that the only fellow that knows how to live is the wild-goose   He makes the world his own and follows the climate he likes—and no question of business can keep him either" (Letter 102).

Contributing to Jeff's melancholy was the gradual weakening of his ties with Walt. In 1863 Jeff had written the poet more than three letters per month. But after April 5, 1869, Jeff wrote to Walt infrequently, averaging less than one letter a year; during the same period Walt averaged slightly over one letter per year to Jeff. Why the correspondence declined remains unclear. One explanation may be that Walt was at his best with those who were emotionally dependent; but by the late 1860s Jeff was strong and progressing well on his own. Also there may have been friction because Walt regularly paid for Edward's board while both George and Jeff were making more money than the poet. Further, Jeff had gained the recognition of his peers at a time when Walt remained only partially accepted. The poet was too large-minded to begrudge his brother's success, but Walt may have been discomfited by this shift in roles. If Walt felt such tensions, one way to reduce them would be to write Jeff fewer letters and refuse to visit him.

During his final three years of life Jeff worked mainly as a consultant, and while he must have enjoyed the prestige associated with his wide-ranging practice, he complained to Walt of "spending about 1/3 of my time on Rail Road trains" (Letter 102). Fatigue may have contributed to his early death from typhoid pneumonia in St. Louis on November 25, 1890. The reaction of friends and colleagues to this unexpected loss underscored his prominence in the engineering profession and his popularity as a person. On November 28, M. L. Holman, water commissioner of St. Louis and one of Jeff's protégés, introduced a resolution honoring Jeff at a meeting of the Board of Public Improvements. That same afternoon, the entire board, several leading citizens, and representatives from the Engineers' Club and the American Society of Civil Engineers attended the funeral at Jeff's home on 2437 Second Carondelet Avenue. Although a newspaper account maintained that Jeff "never received full credit for all he has accomplished,"[44] at least seven obituaries of Jeff were published, including five in national engineering journals. Contributors included Henry Flad, Horace Traubel (see Appendix B), and Walt. The poet also supplied E. D. Meier, president of the St. Louis Engineers' Club, with information for a eulogy Meier presented before the club and later had printed in the *Journal of the Association of Engineering Societies* (see Appendix A).

One might argue that Walt's eulogy was, in a way, unnecessary. Two decades earlier in "Passage to India" he gave lasting expression to his feelings about Jeff and engineering. In this poem Walt praises "the strong light works of engineers": the trans-Atlantic cable, the Suez Canal, and the transcontinental railroad. These modern accomplishments are linked to the pioneering spirit, to the driving force that led men westward, and finally to the quest for God. We commented above on this poem's image of embracing brothers and it seems nearly certain that Walt was thinking of Jeff while composing this work. Jeff, as an engineer in the West who had asked Walt for publications concerning the transcontinental railroad, embodied the poem's ideals. And yet, despite Walt's praise of engineering, he insists on the greater importance of his own profession: the poet, not the engineer, stands as "the true son of God."

When Jeff's daughter Jessie died in 1957, she also recog-

44. *St. Louis Republican,* November 29, 1890.

nized her father's professional expertise with a $72,764 bequest to Washington University in St. Louis that established "The Thomas J. Whitman Engineering Library Fund."[45] The University Library still purchases engineering books with these monies and places a bookplate bearing Jeff's picture (see frontispiece) in each volume. However, Jeff's detailed correspondence and contributions to engineering constitute his most important legacy. Alone among the Whitmans, he made a name for himself in his own right, apart from the fame of Walt. It seems appropriate, then, that Jeff should have escaped the poet's final assertion of an encompassing ego. Though eight family members lie within the Harleigh Cemetery vault bearing only the name WALT WHITMAN, Jeff rests apart with his wife and children in the Bellefontaine Cemetery, St. Louis.

Editorial Note

In general, we follow the practices of other editors of the Whitman family letters by remaining as unobtrusive as possible and presenting an inclusive text representing as nearly as possible the writer's final intentions. We have not recorded cancellations, noted author's insertions, or attempted to duplicate the appearance of the original holographs, and we have silently eliminated the few internal addresses Jeff added. Since most of the letters were written on office stationery, we have also omitted letterheads. We have standardized the placement of salutations, signatures, and postscripts. Because Jeff frequently omitted terminal punctuation, rather than interpolating the missing mark we have simply left an extra space where a pause improves readability. Walt apparently marked several letters: we have silently omitted the annotation "brother Jeff" from eleven letters of 1863, but have mentioned the other markings—usually parentheses—in the footnotes. Those parentheses without a footnote, of course, are Jeff's.

Ambiguous cases of transcription inevitably arise. Because Jeff's prose is reasonably grammatical and sometimes quite sophisticated, we give him the benefit of the doubt in such

45. News Release, Washington University [in St. Louis] News Bureau, August 18, 1958.

cases and choose the more correct reading. For example, he frequently indicates the terminal letters of familiar words with a hasty single line, thus seeming to omit an *s*, an *e*, or an *ly*. We would misrepresent him if we bracketed every such ending as an editorial correction, when in fact his meaning and intended spelling are clear. On the other hand, we have retained obvious misspellings, omissions, repetitions, and grammatical errors, using *sic* as sparingly as possible to avoid unnecessary clutter. Where a confusing error or omission occurs, we supply clarifying information in brackets; when a word is illegible, we supply a reading in brackets with a question mark. In those few cases where no cogent reading suggests itself, we place a question mark alone in brackets.

Beyond supplying information necessary to a proper reading of the letters, our annotations serve two main purposes: to demonstrate Jeff's important position within the family, especially with respect to Walt, and to reveal Jeff's deep concern with local and national politics, the engineering profession, and the broader social and cultural questions of the period that also engaged his brother Walt. Instead of glossing the names of family members, we refer the reader to our Introduction and to the Genealogical Data for the Whitman Family preceding the first letter. We identify other persons when they are first mentioned and subsequently identify them with a cross-reference to the letter in which they first appear. In a few cases we have incorporated necessary information in a headnote, particularly where a major transition occurs. Abbreviations for those sources which are frequently cited in the notes—usually standard works on the Whitman family—can be found in the list of abbreviations preceding the Introduction. We generally do not cite our historical sources because we have relied on standard works concerning the Civil War and the development of engineering.

Of the 106 letters, 91 are from the Feinberg Collection, Library of Congress; letters 1 through 4 and 52, 70, and 72 are from the Berg Collection, New York Public Library; letters 16, 47, and 73 are from the Trent Collection, Duke University; letters 89 and 100 are from the Beinecke Rare Book and Manuscript Library, Yale University; letters 103 and 105 are from the Missouri Historical Society; and letter 106—the only one not transcribed from a holograph—is reprinted from *Camden's Compliment to Walt Whitman: May 31, 1889: Notes, Addresses, Letters, Telegrams,* ed. Horace L. Traubel (Philadelphia: David McKay, 1889).

GENEALOGICAL DATA FOR THE WHITMAN FAMILY

PARENTS
Walter Whitman, Sr. (1789–1855)
Louisa Van Velsor (1795–1873)

CHILDREN
Jesse (1818–70)
Walter (1819–92)
Mary Elizabeth (1821–99)
m. Ansel Van Nostrand, January 2, 1840
Hannah Louisa (1823–1908)
m. Charles Louis Heyde, March 16, 1852
Andrew Jackson (1827–63)
George Washington (1829–1901)
m. Louisa Orr Haslam, April 14, 1871
Thomas Jefferson (1833–90)
m. Martha E. Mitchell ("Mat" or "Mattie"), February 23, 1859
Edward (1835–92)

CHILDREN OF JEFFERSON AND MARTHA WHITMAN
Manahatta (1860–86) "Sis" until 1863; later, "Hattie"
Jessie Louisa (1863–1957) "Sis"

The Letters of
Thomas Jefferson Whitman

1848-1889

Very little is known about Jeff Whitman before 1848, but one can, perhaps, gather something about his early relationship with Walt on the basis of the latter's short sketch, "My Boys and Girls" (1844). Here Walt mentions many family members, but he reserves his fondest words for Jeff: "Around the waist of the sagacious Jefferson have I circled one arm, while the fingers of the other have pointed him out words to spell."

In the 1840s, while Walt experimented with fiction and poetry, he devoted his greatest efforts to journalism. He edited the Brooklyn Daily Eagle *from March 1846 until about January 21, 1848, when he was replaced because he denounced slavery and supported the Wilmot Proviso. Fortunately, a few weeks later, on February 10, 1848, J. E. ("Sam") McClure met the newly unemployed journalist in New York and offered him a job with the* New Orleans Crescent. *Walt accepted the post and also procured a position for Jeff as office boy. On February 11, the brothers began the two-week trip south described in Jeff's first letter. Once in New Orleans, Walt became a father figure in a very real sense: for three months he was Jeff's guardian, tutor, and role model.*

[New Orleans, February 18(?)-28, 1848]
[Dear Parents,]
. . .[1] Our captain though[t] he would run the risk and save the time (it takes some time longer to go through the canal) so he got a flat-boat and took out some of the freight, and we started to go over the falls.[2] Father can judge how fast we went, when I tell him it is a fall of twenty feet, within a space of three miles. And what is most dangerous, the bottom is covered with very large rock which leave a very small channel for the boat. When you get about the middle there is a large rock in this channel, and one on each side of it, the one on the right side is a little distance from the one in the middle, just room enough for a boat to pass through. So you have to take a very sudden turn, or the boat is smashed all to peices. It happened we got off with a little bump on each rock, we should not have got that (for we

1. The first page or two of this letter is missing.
2. The falls of the Ohio River, located just below Louisville. WW also described this section of the journey in "Excerpts from a Traveller's Note Book—" (*UPP*, I, 189).

had the best pilots that could be found) but one wheel would not work. The fun of the whole thing was, the <u>fright</u> we all had, some of the passengers went to bed, others walked the cabin floor, looking as gloomy as if they were going to be hung. Altho I was frightened a good deal, it was not so much as some of the <u>men</u> were. If the boat had sunk we were within a few feet of the shore, but I dont think we could have got there, the current was so swift.

Mother, you have no idea of the splendor and comfort of these western river steam-boats. The cabin is on the deck, and state rooms on each side of it, their are two beds in each room. The greatest of all these splendors is the eating (you know I always did love eating) department. Every thing you would find in the Astor house in New York, You find on these boats.

I will give you a little description of the way we live on board. For breakfast we have: coffee, tea, ham and eggs, beef steak, sausages hot cakes, with plenty of good bread sugar &c &c. For dinner: roast beef d[itt]o mutton d[itt]o veal boiled ham roast turkey d[itt]o goose with pie and puddings and for supper every thing that is good to eat.[3] . . .

Saturday noon   Last night we had a very hard storm, it rained hard and blew harder. We expect to get as far as Cairo to night on the Mississipi river. Nothing has occurred since yesterday of importance

Sunday night. We have arrived at last, at New Orleans we came in on Friday night about ten o'clock. Saturday Walter found a board in Poydrass st cor St Charles

You must dirrect your letters thus, Walter Whitman, New Orleans, La. Saturday it was a drizzely rainy day.

I hop[e] they dont have many of them

Monday. Yesterday was quite warm. I saw a good many peach trees in blossom to day. Walter will get the first number of his out on Sunday next.

Dear Mother I must bid you good bye for a little while. I will write to you again pretty soon.

Dear Father I will write to you also pretty soon   until then good bye one and all

Jefferson Whitman

Dear Mother, write often

---

3. WW noted that despite the high quality of the food "everybody gulps down the victuals with railroad speed" (*UPP,* I, 188).

New Orleans, March 14, 1848

Dear Father,

Since I wrote to Mother nothing of importance has transpired. This will be the eighth or ninth letter we have sent you,[1] and we have not received a single one from you. Mr Wilson[2] in the Eagle office sent Walter one in which he said that he called there and that you were all well. Do write to us, Father, even half a sheet would be better than nothing. I go to the post office every day so we shall get it as soon as it gets here. I have written one to Mr Brown[3] and William Devoe[4] and (as Walter said in his last letter)[5] I shall write one to you at the begining and middle of every month

Walter and myself are very well. I am now at work in the "Crescent" office at <u>five</u> dollars per week, and my work is done by three o'clock every afternoon. I dont know how long I shall stay there, but it shall be as long as I can make it.

Walter gets home much sooner than he thought he should; he is hardly ever later than eleven o'clock, and one night he was home at half past nine o'clock, he gets a few books most every day but none of them worth much.[6]

Father, you wanted me to ask how much carpenter's wages were here. I am told they are from forty to fifty dollars a month and found,[7] which I think is a pretty good sum, but every thing is so much here that you hardly know whether you get a good bargain or not.

To My Dear Mother

I do want to hear from you very, very much, do write to Walter or me and tell us how you have been getting along since

1. Only one of these letters—number 1 above—is extant.

2. Probably Peter W. Wilson, a printer.

3. Probably Henry Brown; see Letter 4. Three men with this name are listed in the 1848 Brooklyn directory: a merchant, a bookkeeper, and a well digger.

4. William Devoe, a carpenter. He corresponded with Jeff as late as 1885. See Letter 98.

5. This letter is not extant.

6. WW recommended to *Crescent* readers Cooper's *Jack Tier,* C. W. Webber's *Old Hicks, the Guide,* and Erastus Everett's *System of Versification,* but he criticized Dickens' *Dombey and Son* as "inartistical" (Rubin, p. 195).

7. Jeff means that carpenters receive additional compensation ("found") such as room and board along with their wages.

we came away and give a description of sister Mary's visit (I wrote her a letter soon after we got here). I will give you a little bit of city news.

New Orleans is a very level place and you do not dig down above two feet before you come to the water. It is also [a] very dirty place. Mother, I never wanted your cleanliness so much before as I did at our first boarding house, you could not only see the dirt, but you could taste it, and you had to too if you ate anything at all. And the rooms too, were covered with dirt an inch thick. But now we are through with all that. We are now liveing at the Tremont house, next door to the Theatre and directly opposite the office.[8]

Their has been two or three procession (and one thing or other) days since we have been here, and some rather funny ones too.

Mr. Tombs,[9] (the man that has or will give you the letter from Walter and the bundle of papers) is a brother of the foreman of the Eagle office.

He has not heard from his Father and Mother for a year and a half yet they have written to him three or four times. (Doubtful. W. W. [)][10] He has had the yellow fever three times within the passed summer. Last Sunday we took a walk in the old Cathilic cemmetery,[11] and a very beautiful place it is to. Flowers of every description were on some of the tombs, large white roses and red ones too were all along the walk from one end to the other. At night too the streets are filled with women with baskets full of flowers.

On Sunday morning we took a walk down to the old French church[12] and an old looking thing it is too. Every one would go up and dip their fingers in the holy water and then go home and whip their slaves. One old black took a bottle full home to wash the sins out of her family.

8. Jeff and WW boarded with P. Irwin on St. Charles Street at the price of nine dollars per week.

9. Andrew W. Toombs, a printer.

10. This parenthetical remark was inserted by WW, who corrected Jeff's New Orleans letters.

11. St. Louis Number One, the oldest cemetery in the city (1788), located on Basin Street between St. Louis and Toulouse.

12. The St. Louis Cathedral, located in the Place d'Armes (renamed Jackson Square in 1850).

I will write to you Mother again, you must write to me as often as you possibly can

To George and Andrew

Dear Brothers, I should like to see you very much but as I can not you must write to me too. On Saturday the 4th of March we had a grand fireman's procession[13] and I think it was larger than the one (the firemen part) in New York. the engines were very large and are drawn by horses (six or eaight). Right opposite here they are fixing it up for a balloon ascension on next Sunday. I suppose I shall see all the fun   I am going to night to see Mr Collins[14] and I expect some fun. You must write to me as soon as you can.

To Sister Hannah

Dear Sister. Your part of the letter comes on the part where their is no lines, so I think it will be pretty crooked, but you must not mind that

I beleive I promised to send you something but every thing is so d[amned] much that I cannot get it

New Orleans would be just the place for you, you could have flowers all the year round which I know you are a great lover of. Bye the Bye, Walter wants to know (and you must tell him in your letter) whether the trees and flowers he sat out are living yet. Dear Sister you must also write to me (but please pay the postage)   Among the others I must not forget my dear brother.

Eddy you must go to school and try to write and read so I can send letters to you and you can read them.

I must bid you all good bye but I will write again soon.

good bye Father, good bye Mother
good bye all
Jefferson Whitman

13. These annual parades celebrating the founding of the volunteer fire department began in 1837 or 1838 and continued for fifty years.

14. John Collins, an Irish comedian and vocalist popular on the New York stage, performed this night at Armory Hall.

[3]

Dear Mother

To day we received the first letter from you, and glad enough we were to get it too. The passage that gave me, and Walter too, the most pleasure was the one that said you were well, and that all the rest were well also. You say the weather is very cold there, here it is just the other way, that is it is pretty warm. I have now begun to wear the summer clothes sister Hannah made me which I find very comfortble.

It would have made you laugh to see me come home from the post office this morning with your letter. Eddy never was so glad when New Year's came, as I was to get your letter

You must write to us oftener than you have at least twice a month, which we are going to do

You need not be alarmed about the yellow fever[1] as that gentleman will (the folks think) not visit this place this summer. The reason they give for that is this. It does not come but once in three or four years, and last season it was very hard and killed a great many persons (I mean it does not come but once in three or four years in such a shape). Besides it is a great humbug, most every one in our office has had (some of them have had it twice) and got well. It is caused mostly (I think all of it) by the habits of the people, they never meet a freind but you have to go drink and such loose habits.

You know that Walter is averse to such habits, so you need not be afraid of our taking it[2]

Yesterday we were to have a balloon ascension, but just as it was ready to go up the balloon bursted so it did not go up, this is the third time she (it was a lady that was to go up in it) has tried it and each time failed

We are very nicely situated in our new place;—just

1. In 1847, 2,700 people died of yellow fever in New Orleans, by far the highest number recorded to that date. While Jeff is correct about the tendency of the disease to subside after severe outbreaks, it still killed nearly 900 people in 1848 and the same number in 1849. The family's fears may have been compounded by the popular view that strangers to the city were far more susceptible than natives.

2. The excessive drinking of juleps and iced ale disturbed WW: "Now you know I am not _ultra_ in these matters, but it isn't good to drink spiritous compounds at this rate in hot climates" (quoted in Rubin, p. 186).

"around the corner" is a very fine public park, which we take a walk in every night[3]

I believe I told you in my last letter that I was also at work at the "Crescent" office at five dollars a week, and I have the exchange papers for which I get twenty five cents per hundred, in a few weeks I expect to get two dollars a week for them

If you do not get the paper (the "Crescent") regular you must send Andrew or George down to the Eagle office for it, I always see that two copys go every morning. My work is good and light. I have such a part of the mail (and I can do it most over night) and then I have nothing to do for the rest of the day (I generally get through with it about two o'clock) but stay in the office.

We have (I think) got along very well for such a long journey, not a single accident occurred on the way

Dear Father, I hope you are getting along good with your work &c. Mother says it is cold so you can't work   here it is warm enough. In building houses here they do not do as they do in New York. Here they dig a hole in the ground some two feet deep and about the same width, and in length as far as the wall is to go, (they can not dig cellars here like in the north, you don't dig in the ground more than two feet before it is filled with water.) This trench they cover the bottom with boards (the ground is mostly made of quick-sand) and then build the wall on it. They cannot mak[e] good brick here, so they have to come from a distance. Carpenters wages are very high here, some forty to fifty dollars a month and found

I will write a letter to you pretty soon, but in this one I must not forget George and Andrews

Dear brothers, I should like to see you very much indeed but I suppose I cannot, you must make Mother or Hannah write to us as often as they can. Theres is nothing, I beleive, there is not any thing here you would like to hear from or of

Dear Sister,[4] I should like to see you very much indeed but I suppose you would like to hear about the ladies in N. O. They are something like the "critters" in N. Y. except they were one

3. WW and Jeff must have regularly taken long walks together in Brooklyn also. On September 22, 1852, Hannah commented: "I wish Walter and Jeffy was here [in Vermont]   they could take long walks enough" (letter to LVVW [Trent]).

4. Hannah.

or two more "flonces" and live more in the open air &c &c &c &c &c &c

to Eddy   you must got to school and learn to read and write and then you must send letters to me, besides you must be a good boy &c

And now Dear Mother I must bid you good bye for a little while but will write to you again shortly

We are both very well and the warm air argrees with Walter very much

I have had a little attack of the disentery but I am very very well now, in fact I have not been sick much at all

Dear Mother good bye

your son Jefferson Whitman

My best respects to the rest of the family[5]

[4]

New Orleans Sunday April 23th [1848]

Dear Parents,

Since I wrote to you (the night after we got your only letter) we have heard nothing from you, It is very strange you do not write oftener to us, for we have writtin to you ever so many times, now we have been from home nearly three months, and we have received only one letter from you, I beg of you to write to us often

I received a letter from Mr Brown,[1] day before yesterday, but it was a very old one, he says they are all very well, that they like Billy[2] quite well, that he sprained his back gardening at his new house, that they are building up around Prince St very fast and that I can write a letter good when I am a mind to (I do not agree with him there at all.) It is one of the greatest newsletters that I ever saw

Walter is very well indeed, he thinks this place agrees with him very much and he says he feels better than ever he did in New York. And I to feel pretty well but not so much so as I

5. WW added a paragraph-long note to his mother at the end of Jeff's letter (*Correspondence*, I, 33).

1. See Letter 2.
2. Probably William H. DeBevoise; see Letter 11.

intend to be, I have still a kind of summer complaint,[3] which does not feel very good but it is very far from being really sick

I hope you are all getting along smoothly and good, Henry[4] said Mother felt better than she had for years before, I hope she will continue to feel so, (I think I mentioned in my last letter that Walter had a letter from Henry, from Brooklyn)

Walter is trying to save up all the money he can get, and allready he has quite a sum, as soon as he gets a thousand dollars he is comeing north,[5] And I too am saveing all I can get   I give Walter five dollars (my wages) every week, and I have sold about five dollars worth of old papers, that you know is all clear gain, all the trouble it is, is to count them out and put them up in hundreds

Yesterday evening and this morning is the finest weather we have had since we have been here. Just warm and just cool enough to make it very pleasant. We took a very long walk last night, way out Camp street beyound the limits of the city. There are no hills like on old Long Island   the whole state is as level as a race course. In some of the streets they have a kind of canal or drain to let the water run off, and even then in some places there is not enough "down-hill" to make it run off good. Just a little farther up town there is a canal (of a larger kind than those in the middle of the street) where sloops &c can come up from the lake (about 7 miles westward of the city). Along by this canal (the new canal they call it) there is a road called shell road[6] where we take frequent (and very pleasant) walks, the road is nearly as hard as a brick, and on a pleasant afternoon is covered with carriages of every discription. It seems to be the fashion to drive your horse as fast as he can go.

The price of a good apple here (such a one as you could get

3. Regarding Jeff's problem with dysentery, see Letter 3.
4. Probably Henry Brown; see Letter 2.
5. Perhaps A. H. Hayes and J. E. McClure, the owners of the *Crescent*, had decided that WW's antislavery sentiments would be an embarrassment in the coming presidential elections. WW seemed puzzled at the harsh feelings that developed: "Through some unaccountable means . . . both H. and M'C, after a while, exhibited a singular sort of coldness, toward me, and the latter an irritability toward Jef., who had, at times, much harder work than I was willing he should do." When the owners refused WW's request for a salary advance on May 24, he asked to "dissolve the connection" and then headed home with Jeff on May 27 (*UPP*, II, 77–78).
6. The First District and Lake Pontchartrain were connected by Shell Road which parallelled the New Canal.

in New York for a cent and at some places two for a cent) is the small price of ten cents.

Sometimes I get thinking about you all and feel quite lonesome, but not one fifth as much as I did when we first arrived here, at first I could not make myself believe that we were so far away from home, but it is something of a distance

By this morning's mail Walter received a letter from Mr Wilson[7] of the Eagle, but there was nothing in it but what we have heard before, about the election[8] &c. He said that "Pat"[9] delivered the paper to you very regular and also that you were all well (which I liked best of all he said in his long letter of five pages). We get the Eagle and Brooklyn Star quite often, and also the New York, [:] Tribune, Mirror, Globe, Dispatch, Sunday Times, Atlas, &c, &c. The Sun and Herald seem to think the "Crescent" not worthey their exchange as we have not received theirs yet, altho we have sent to them ever since the paper began. Walter wrote them a letter[10] a few days ago and I guess we shall get them before long

You will remember that I said that we were to have a balloon ascension opposite our boarding house, the thing was tried four or five times, but as just enough persons got inside the thing would manage to burst. A few Sundays ago it was said it would go up again, they had got it all ready when it blew all to peices. The persons that had paid to see it thought it was nothing but a suck in (which I think was the case)   As soon as it touched the ground they all laid hold of it, and draging it over the fence tore it all to peices, they did not leave a peice a foot square   So ended all that

Monday April 24th

By this mornings mail I received a letter from my friend "Bill"[11] (at Mr Smiths[12] store in Fulton st)   it is a very short one however, he says nothing about you so we have not heard from you since you wrote. He said he went out on an excursion and fell overboard but his brothers got him out after a fashion

---

7. See Letter 2.
8. In New York's April elections the Whigs were victorious in Brooklyn, the Barnburners in Manhattan.
9. Unidentified.
10. This letter is not extant.
11. Perhaps William Devoe. See Letter 2.
12. At this time, four Smiths owned stores located on Fulton Street.

Walter also got a serman by Mr Johnston[13] of Brooklyn. I believe that is all we received   I am certain of one thing, that is we never got any letter from you

To day has been a very fine clear day, the ladys were out in great numbers. The city has been very lively to day

Mother. Just think what you would think of us if we had writtin you only one letter since we came away. I am afraid you would think pretty hard of us. Father and Hannah need a little "blowing up" too, but I will generously let them off if they will promise to write often in future

I have almost wrote the whole sheet out so I must stop. I shall write to you again pretty soon, untill then good bye

your son Jefferson Whitman

My love to Mary if you see her before I write again

If you do not write to us pritty soon we will do something but I don't know what.[14]

[5]

The brothers left New Orleans on May 27, 1848, and returned to the family home in Brooklyn on June 15. In the next twelve years Walt worked as a contractor, edited more newspapers, and prepared three editions of Leaves of Grass. *Jeff's development during these years is more difficult to trace; however, he did begin his engineering career with Lewis L. Bartlett, a surveyor, and in 1856 joined the Brooklyn Water Works. He also considered traveling to Utah, presumably to run surveys for the transcontinental railroad (letter from Hannah to Jeff Whitman, c. 1859 [Berg]); but perhaps because of his marriage to Martha E. Mitchell on February 23, 1859, he stayed in Brooklyn and pursued the career of a civil engineer.*

Jamaica, [New York,] April 3rd /60

Dear Brother Walt,

I have just now received yours of the 1st.[1] I should have written to you before but when I left home a week ago yester-

13. Probably Samuel R. Johnson, rector of St. John's church on Myrtle Avenue.
14. For the brief note WW added to the end of this letter, see *Correspondence*, I, 36.

1. *Correspondence*, I, 50–51. WW was in Boston reading proof for the 1860 edition of *Leaves of Grass*.

Thomas Jefferson Whitman in his early twenties, about 1855. During this period of his life, Jeff often went to Manhattan with Walt to attend the opera or spend an evening at Pfaff's beer cellar. Courtesy of the Library of Congress, Feinberg Collection.

day Mother said she would write to you that day, and I believe she did, its singular that you have not received it

Everything remains abt. as usual with us Walt. Mother has taken the house and rented the lower part to a Mr "John Brown"[2] @ $14 per month Mat and I keeping the same rooms as before.[3] Andrew has been very sick but was getting better on Sunday when I was home. His disease commenced by a very

2. A tailor and his family whom Jeff came to despise; see Letter 13.
3. For an account of the family living arrangements, see Allen, pp. 216 and 239–40.

violent pain in the side, kept up and made worse by an igno-rent Dr. and those around him.[4] Mother visited him most every day and kept his courage up

I am truly glad Walt, that you are comfortably situated and the more so that you are having things done to suit you in the way of publishing your book. I quite long for it to make its appearence. What jolly times we will have reading the notices of it wont we. you must expect the "Yam Yam Yam" writer[s] to give you a dig as often as possible but I dont suppose you will mind it any more than you did in the days of your editorship of the B.[rooklyn] Eagle[5] when the Advertiser['s] Lees[6] used to go at you so roughly Do you remember those days Walt.

I was at home as usual last Sunday but there was nothing new we miss you very much of course. Mother speaks very often of her small family now and talks of one room and bed-room &c Mattie remains the same, she has plenty to do and talks of getting a girl to do housework. I'm getting to be quite a family man aint I.[7]

When do you suppose you will get through and come home. Mother has heard from you several times and it does her a great deal of good.[8] you must write her often and let me hear from you again before long. I shall write to you again presently, now as you will perceive I am rather hard up for something to write about.

Your affectionate Brother Jeff

[6]

Jamaica April 16th 1860

Dear Brother Walt,

I was at home yesterday as usual   everything is going on about the same. Andrew has recovered in a great measure,[1] so

---

4. An alcoholic, Andrew would die of tuberculosis or perhaps throat cancer on December 3, 1863, the dupe of unscrupulous doctors.

5. WW enclosed the preceding three sentences in parentheses.

6. Henry A. Lees, publisher and editor of the *Brooklyn Daily Advertiser*, was one of several Whig editors with whom WW had feuded over political questions, especially those involving the Mexican War.

7. Jeff's first daughter, Manahatta ("Hattie"), would be born on June 9.

8. These letters are not extant.

1. See Letter 5.

that he sits up and would probably have been out-doors but the weather has been very wet and cold here for the last week. Mother herself I think is not very well. she has a bad cold that seems to pull her down. I have got one of the worst colds I ever had, and feel extremely unlike myself, still anything of that kind sits lighter on me than on one of Mother's age, and this morning Ed. seemed to be quite sick, that is he couldn't eat and complained of a bad pain in his side, however Mother put a mustard plaster on him and he felt considerably better when I left home.

Mattie and George, the rest of "the family" are well. The Mr Brown[2] who has rented the lower part of the house has sent a number of things to the house, carpets &c. Mother has let him fix the front parlor and she has emigrated and taken posession of your room. The Moore people[3] have not moved yet, and I believe do not intend to till 7 of May

The Water Works men are all trembling in our boots, the [prospects?] being that we are all going to be kicked out, neck and heels, from the chief down to the Axeman. It seems that Mr F. Spinola[4] started a bill at Albany some time last winter trying to oust the new commissioners (King, Lewis &c &c)[5] well someone made an amendment casting out the present old Com. the new Com. Chief Eng. &c all the way through, and appointing Mr McElroy[6] in place of Mr Kirkwood.[7] It has passed one house, and I guess the chances are abt

2. See Letter 5.

3. Either E. D. or John Moore, both of whom lived on Myrtle Avenue.

4. A member of the New York legislature from 1855 to 1861, Francis B. Spinola (1821–91) later became a brigadier general during the Civil War, and finally a United States congressman from 1887 to 1891.

5. The four members of the Brooklyn Board of Water and Sewer Commissioners were Gamaliel King, William B. Lewis, John H. Funk, and Daniel L. Northrup.

6. Samuel McElroy preceded Kirkwood as chief engineer of what was the Nassau Water Company (later the Brooklyn Water Works). McElroy resigned his position on June 10, 1856, at which time Kirkwood took over.

7. James P. Kirkwood (1807–77), a prominent civil engineer and co-founder of the American Society of Civil Engineers (1852), superintended the construction of the Brooklyn Water Works as chief engineer from 1856 to 1862. After his work in Brooklyn, he moved to St. Louis and designed the waterworks which Jeff would later build. Kirkwood eventually became a nationally known independent consultant and wrote the standard text on water filtration.

even for its passing the other, as Wells the Contractor[8] is helping it with all the power he can muster. I think it will be a dark
day for the B. W. W. if he succeeds, but I suppose to the victor
belongs the spoils. I know I ain't going to worry, if it does go
through.[9]

Mother wants me to be sure and tell you that you must
bring her one of those books by the authoress of "Consuelo"[10]
also Redpath's "John Brown"[11]   she says you needn't send
them as that would involve cost, but to surely remember to
bring them with you when you come home.

I read your letter at home.[12] I am glad that you are having
so good a time and that your book has such a good prospect of
success. I sincerely hope you will meet with no disappointment.

Write me again Walt. I like much to hear how you are
getting along. I shall write to you again probably next week.
Mattie sends her love.

Your affectionate Brother Jeff.

[7]

*Almost exactly a year after Jeff's last letter the Civil War
began. George Whitman responded by joining the Union
army, in which he served until the end of the war. The family's
fears and anxieties for George were the dominant theme in
Jeff and Walt's correspondence for these years, and were a
chief reason for the intense correspondence between the
brothers in 1863; in this year more than one-third of Jeff's*

8. In 1856 Henry S. Welles & Co. signed a contract with the Nassau
Water Company to build a waterworks for Brooklyn. Welles was the main
contractor for the project from its beginning to its completion in 1862.

9. Since Kirkwood and the others remained in their positions, the bill
apparently did not pass.

10. WW may have loaned LVVW his two-volume edition of George
Sand's *The Countess of Rudolstadt* (New York: William H. Graham, 1848).
These volumes were in the poet's library at his death.

11. James Redpath, *The Public Life of Captain John Brown,* a panegyric
published by Thayer and Eldridge in 1860—the same year the firm issued
the third edition of *Leaves of Grass.* LVVW acknowledged receiving the "life
of john brown" from WW on May 3 (?), 1860.

12. Jeff probably refers to a lost letter from WW to LVVW.

extant letters were written. Walt's general correspondence also increased: seventy-five letters from 1863 survive compared to only nineteen from the preceding seven years.

The immediate cause for family concern was the appearance of George's name in a list of wounded from the Battle of Fredericksburg (December 13, 1862). The poet set out on December 16 for Washington to search the hospitals for his brother. After finding George, who had sustained a superficial cheek wound, Walt decided to stay in the capital to help with the war effort by rendering aid in the city's numerous military hospitals. On January 1, 1863, Jeff wrote the poet and offered financial support, thus making Walt's hospital work a feasible project. Jeff began collecting money from his fellow engineers and sending it to Walt, who relied heavily on this source of funds. The engineers probably supported the hospital work because they were personal friends of the Whitman brothers and because their interest in engineering projects of a national scope (such as the transcontinental railroad) promoted belief in a strong federal government.

Brooklyn, N. Y. Friday Dec 19 /62

Dear Brother Walt,

We are all much worried at not hearing anything from you. I have been over to the headquarters of the 51st three or four times but could get no information about brother George. The Times of day before yesterday gave his name among the wounded thus "Lieut Whitman Co. E 51st N. Y. V. cheek" and we are trying to comfort ourselves with hope that it may not be a serious hurt. We certainly expected to hear from you before this and that you had found him. I <u>know</u> you will spare neither pains nor anything else to find him. I do hope that dear brother George is not seriously hurt. Dont fail to let us hear from you at once, even if you have not been able to learn anything about him   it would be a consolation to know certainly that you had arrived safely at Washington   Mother stands it pretty well, but begins to feel pretty bad about not hearing from you

Mat and Dolly[1] are quite well. We have been picturing to ourselves that you would bring George home with you and how nicely we would establish him in our front room with Mat

1. Probably a nickname for Manahatta ("Hattie") Whitman.

as chief nurse. Dear Brother do write immediately. Tell George how much we all love him and how badly we all feel that he should be hurt.

Your affectionate brother Jeff

[8]

Brooklyn, N. Y. Jan. 1st 1863

Dear brother Walt,

"Happy New Year" Walt, to you, is the wish and greeting of your Mother and brothers and sister in Brooklyn, and Hattie too says to send Happy new Year for her too to Uncle Walt. I received the letter that you wrote me in due time and yesterday Mother received one from you[1]   I wrote to you two letters[2] and directed [them] to the "Delevan House, cor. of Pennsylvania and West Ninth Streets.["][3] Dear Walt, what hours of trouble you must of past till you found George   Mother and Mat each had a "good cry" yesterday in reading of how you had to get along, and I myself could hardly keep the water from my face   If you had only been coming home they say, and lost your money, twould have been no matter   but to loose it when you did not know how much you might need it on Georges account, must have made you felt miserable indeed.[4] And then the damnable conduct of those "big bugs" (I believe the biggest bugs are ["] tumble turds") that you speak about must have made you feel doubly provoked.[5] But the most trying scene of all must have been your sight in front of the Hospital tent, not

1. WW's letter to Jeff of about December 28, 1862, is not extant. For WW's letter to LVVW of December 29, see *Correspondence*, I, 58–60.
2. These may be Jeff's letter of December 19, 1862, and one letter that is not extant.
3. The Delevan House, 315 West Ninth Street, was a boarding house run by Henry T. Bates.
4. WW fell victim to a pickpocket in Philadelphia while changing trains en route to Washington.
5. WW had written of his search for George among the numerous military hospitals in Washington and his frustration as he tried "to get access to big people." He complained that Moses Fowler Odell (1818–66), a member of the House of Representatives from New York, "would not see me at all" (*Correspondence*, I, 58 and 59, n. 3). "Tumble turds" is an Americanism for the common dung beetle.

knowing how severely George was wounded. I should think that it would almost have been too much for you.[6] But thank God, it has all come out right, and George was not much hurt.

I have written George, somewhat urging him to quit the army.[7] I think that it is the duty of all of us to urge this upon him, I honestly think that he has done enough and run risk enough for any one man. And too there is no judgement used in putting the old regiments in battle, they just keep throwing them in as long as there is a man left. If I belonged to one I am sure that it would look to me just as if they were bound to kill every man as long as the number of the Reg. was represented Walt do see him and talk this matter over with him Speak with him of Mother, who is getting old very old, and if anything should happen [to] him I am quite sure she could not survive it Even now I can see the effect of the weeks worry that she has already had. Certainly no one could find any falt with him, or talk of him other than the bravest of the brave if he should resign to-morrow. And another thing I certanly do not see how this immense risk and sacrifice of life is doing any good at all, it looks very much to me as if we were slowly but surely drifting towards mediation or something worse. Walt, I beg of you, do not neglect to see George and put this thing in its strongest light. Just think for a moment of the number of suckers that are gaining all the real benefits of the war (if that is not wicked to say) and think of George and thousands of others running all the risk while they are drawing all the pay. Think of Dick Butt[8] and the thousand [other?] sneaks that we know. If he wont resign see if there is no possible way in which he can be removed for a while at least from his present place to one of less danger. Dear Walt I honestly think that he is carrying the life of our Mother, dear dear Mother with his own, and

6. Shortly before finding George at the Fredericksburg battle site, WW had encountered "a heap of feet, arms, legs, &c, under a tree in front [of] a hospital, the Lacy house" (*Correspondence*, I, 59).

7. Jeff's letter of about December 30 is not extant. George replied on January 8 that he was thinking of requesting a furlough or perhaps even resigning (Loving, p. 79).

8. Richard Butt (1819–?), a Brooklyn surveyor, was appointed as a major in field and staff, First Regiment, New York Engineers, on December 3, 1861, and served until April 22, 1864. Jeff may consider him a "sneak" because his unit saw little action, spending most of its time in comparative safety at Fort Pulaski, Georgia.

therefore I say tis our <u>duty</u> to urge him to resign and his <u>duty</u> to do it. Again and again let me say that if possible accomplish it[9]

Friday 2nd. I intended to mail this to you yesterday but not having a stamp and not being able to get one could'nt do it. I have just taken dinner with Mat, Mother and Sis. on "Turkey." Knowing the locality you can imagine the whole performance to a niceity. I only wish that you and George had been with us, then the thing would have been complete. Mother is pretty well, but shows the effects of her anxiety about George, I think, quite plainly. On New Years Eve old Mr Turner[10] next door, died, quite suddenly I believe. The old man I saw out but a few days since   Otherwise I beleve things are about as usual. How about you Walt, what are you trying to get to do. How about <u>Money</u>. If you get hard pushed let me know and I will try and raise you some. I am going along as usual, earning about half time with a "constant" prospect of doing better. Of course if you can poultice any thing so as to draw a little money out of it why do so, but dont be discouraged if you cant. I would rather see you and George come home to-gether than any amt of Green-backs. I understand that our old friend Bill Hart[11] is on here, wounded in the battle of Fredricksburg—, quite badly, but will recover. Mother sends her dearest love also Mat, ditto the rest of us. Write me at once and let me know how you are getting along. I was much, very much interested by your letters and want it repeated. Good bye dear Brother

Yours very truly J.

Mother had a letter from Heyde to-day   Han is quite well. Mary writes that Fanny is married[12]

9. Jeff's continuing fears led WW to remark on January 16, 1863, "I feel that you and dearest mother are perhaps needlessly unhappy and morbid about our dear brother—to be in the army is a mixture of danger and *security* in this war which few realize—they think exclusively of the danger" (*Correspondence*, I, 68).

10. David R. Turner, a house painter.

11. William G. Hart, a captain and acting assistant adjutant general in Company K of the Eighty-eighth New York Volunteers, suffered a gunshot wound in the right forearm on December 13, 1862, and was granted twenty days sick leave on December 15.

12. Charles Heyde repeatedly informed the Whitman family of Hannah's health. Mary Elizabeth Whitman Van Nostrand, Jeff's other sister, had married in 1840 and borne five children, of whom Fanny was the oldest.

[9]

Brooklyn, N. Y. Jan 13th 1863

Dear brother Walt,

Mr Lane[1] handed me your note yesterday and I enclose the within $6, $5 from myself and $1 from Mother.[2] I wish Walt that I could do more and will try to collect a little something. I have made one or two attempts already but failed, entirely. Have you written to any of your driver friends,[3] if you could strike them I should think you might get something. Probasco[4] sent you $5 yesterday and Mr Lane would have sent you some to-day but I told him that I thought that it would be better for all concerned if we put a little time between the letters. I am in hopes to raise a few dollars more in a week or two which I will send you. I wish you would take either Lane's or Probasco['s] money and keep an exact account of what it does and send them the particulars of just the good it does. I think it would assist them (and the rest of us) in collecting more   You can understand what an effect twould have, twould give us an oportunity to show what immense good a few shillings even will do when rightly applied   besides twould please the person sending the money hugely twould bring his good deeds under his nose

We have had some two or three letters from Heyde, directed to you. He talks like a d—m fool. He says that he saw that your feelings and sympathies were excited by the things that you saw and says that he would desire to call them a little nearer home, and then follows a lot of stuff ending with the

1. Moses Lane (1823–82) served as chief engineer of the Brooklyn Water Works from 1862 to 1869. He later designed and constructed the Milwaukee Water Works and served there as city engineer.
2. In a letter of January 16 WW indicated that Jeff and his mother ought not to make personal contributions to the hospital fund since he himself was carrying the family's share of the national burden. Nonetheless, and despite his own shortage of funds, Jeff continued to contribute. See Letter 30 and the letter from Moses Lane to WW, May 2, 1863 (Feinberg).
3. Omnibus drivers in New York City and Brooklyn. One of the poet's favorite pastimes was to ride the omnibuses and sit beside the drivers whom he befriended. Occasionally, when a driver was sick, the poet would take his place without remuneration.
4. Samuel R. Probasco (1833–1910), an assistant engineer at the Brooklyn Water Works from 1856 to 1868 and principal assistant engineer on the Brooklyn Water Board from 1871 to 1875.

request that you will come on and get Han and bring her home, as he cant paint. The miserable skunk. I would like to get a fair chance at his ugly mug.[5] Mother has written to him that Mat will come on after Han, and we are now waiting a reply. The day after each letter came to you mother would get one from him, stating that he was under the influence of quinine and soda, and that he had boils, on his rump bone, and that his blood was bad (d—m his blood) and that he couldn't paint) and that charity, public charity, would have to relieve them, and a hell of a lot of other things all <u>meaning</u> that he wants to shake Han off. Undoubtedly we shall have her home before long. He says she is sick, but I think that if she was she would write home herself. It makes mother feel pretty bad. that combined with all her other troubles, I think, shows on her. She of course is with Mat and I most of the time and we try to make things as pleasant as possible   Ed and Jess are the same as usual

Mr Lane says that we ought to do something to help you to get a situation there   If we can do any thing in the way of letters let us know. Lane thinks that you might do something with Dana.[6] Can you? Did you get the papers that I sent you, I sent 15 copies.[7] Walt write me as often as possible as you cannot imagine how interesting they are to me. We all read them, Lane Probasco &c &c. They make us see things through new eyes

Mother is about as well as usual. Mattie ditto. Sis is growing more interesting than ever, and more mischiefous than the old dickens   she talks of you and Uncle George quite often Mother and Mat send their love. Mat says she is much obliged for her letter and will answer it herself soon.[8] What are you doing and how are you getting along? Things the same as usual with me. Write me soon and often   We had a long letter from George to-day   He says he thinks that he will try for a furlough and that if they wont let him have it that he may resign. I rather think Walt that he is more tired than he lets us know. I wish to God that he would come home, I think that it would

5. Heyde's treatment of Hannah frequently provoked Jeff's anger. See Letter 19 and Loving, pp. 11–12.

6. Moses Lane wrote to Captain James J. Dana on December 16, 1862, asking him to assist WW in his search for George (Feinberg).

7. These may have contained WW's article, "Our Brooklyn Boys in the War," *Brooklyn Daily Eagle*, January 5, 1863. See Letter 11.

8. This letter is not extant.

add 10 years to Mothers life. Write him. With love from all
dear brother   Good night

Jeff.

P.S. Botsford[9] also got his note and will send you something
before long. George wrote for $10. which I sent him to-day

T. J. Whitman

[10]

Brooklyn, N. Y. Feb. 6th 1863

Dear Brother Walt,
    Mr Lane[1] handed me the enclosed $11 to be sent to you for
the soldiers

$10. Contributed by Hill & Newman[2]
$1.   "   " Henry Carlow[3]

Mr Lane thinks your last letter to me was a clincher.[4]
Newman, of the above firm was in the office and upon finding
out what we were doing promised to give $10. Mr Lane, think-
ing perhaps that by sending the money immediately might
save a life or at least help to do it, advanced the money and
wished me to write you to-day.

Mother and Mat are getting along with their colds but Sis is
not so well to day. She seems to have more colds and her head
is almost stopped up

Poor little toad   I often wish that I could take it for her,
however she gets along with it quite well and is not more cross
than the law allows for a little one that has such a cold. If
mother could be persuaded to let the scrubbing of the lower
entry alone for a few days she would recover, but I believe that
she is too much afraid of Mrs Brown,[5] for this morning, and it
was one of those cold rainy ones, she went to work and

9. Charles E. Botsford, who sent WW one dollar on July 7, 1863. See
Letter 30.
    1. See Letter 9.
    2. This firm has not been identified. Henry P. Hill, James Hill, and
Warren Hill were engineers; Simon Hill, Samuel Hill, and Thomas Newman were contractors.
    3. Henry Carlow, an engineer, is listed in the Brooklyn directory for
1859/60, but not in subsequent years.
    4. This letter is not extant.
    5. See Letter 5.

scrubbed as usual. I think they all have had the worst colds that I know of. How do [you] get along about your appointment, does it come and will it. Do you hear from George. What do you think about Han?, the lot, and matters in general.[6] I think Walt, that mother has showed her age more within the last three or four weeks than I ever knew her to before

Everthing is just the same with me. I am getting along quite well, and if Mr Lane holds his position I shall eventually be all right. I think I shall be able to carry through my little "real estate" scheme without much trouble, and I think it is a good one.[7] at least I must try, for I am "in" and I suppose I shall not be a true Whitman if I dont get dis-heartened, however I do not feel at all so just now. On the "contrary quite the re-varse" You must write oftener, home, particulay Mr Lane. He likes much to hear from [you], every letter is productive of good, of course I mean those speaking of the manner of your visits to the Hospitals. Walt, you must be doing more real good than the whole sanitary Commission put to-gether[8] Mr Lane, in conversation with a gentleman in the office, said yesterday that we ought [to] raise money enough to keep a 100 Walt Whitmans, support them and pay them, (if they could be found.) and by that means take the rough edge off the War. Tis indeed true. I am thankfull that you are there. Somehow I feel that as if George, God bless him, was a little safer while you are so near him and while you are doing so much good. Oh how I wish that he could come home now, without running any more risk, and for myself, I think that he ought to. If they go to consolidating the regiments I sincerely hope that by some accident, he may be left out.[9] I really feel worried on mothers

6. In his reply to Jeff on February 13, WW did not address these questions directly but rather discussed his attempts to secure a better-paying government position (*Correspondence*, I, 73-75).

7. Apparently, Jeff hoped to build his own house in Brooklyn, a plan he never carried out. See Letter 11.

8. WW found members of the United States Sanitary Commission "incompetent and disagreeable" if not indeed "a set of foxes and wolves." He had a higher opinion of a civilian organization called the Christian Commission. See Allen, p. 289.

9. On January 8, 1863, George had written to Jeff: "I think they will have to do something with our Regt soon as we can only turn out about 160 men." Eventually the War Department issued an order to consolidate the companies in all regiments of less than 500 men. However, as George wrote on April 22, "I hear to night that Burnside has issued an order countermanding, the consolidation order" (Loving, pp. 79, 92).

account. I know that if anything should happen [to] him that she could not stand it. However I suppose we must get along the best we can.

With the exception of the colds, we are all in jolly good health Mother has taken breakfasts dinner and supper I guess, with Mat and I ever since you went away. We call her up in the morning and if it is <u>very cold</u> I go down and make her fire while she works and eats breakfast with us. Then Ed comes along just as I leave and Jess is generally getting up when I go home to dinner. so we live. all send love to you

Affectionately your brother Jeff

[11]

Brooklyn Feb. 10th—1863

Dear Brother

I received your letter of yesterday morning.[1] I am glad to hear that you are still visiting the hospitals and doing so much good. We are trying to do what little we can to furnish you with the necessary funds (in a small way to be sure) and the only thing that we are sorry about is that we cannot do more. The enclosed money is contributed by

Theo. A. Drake[2] $2.

"<u>Cash</u>" through John D Martin[3] $2.

$4

both of whom are employed on the work under Mr Lane.[4]

Mr Lane has written a letter to <u>Mr Webster</u>[5] the clerk of Seward[6] that I spoke to you about and will send you a letter of introduction to him immediately. He tells me that he (Webster) is a "politician" and that he will help you without doubt provided that he thinks that it will not interfere at all with him. Or that is about the idea of what he said.

We are all getting well at home Sis has almost entirely

1. This letter is not extant.
2. Theodore A. Drake, a waterworks inspector.
3. John D. Martin, an engineer.
4. See Letter 9.
5. For Lane's letter to E. D. Webster, see *Correspondence*, I, 72, n. 32.
6. William Henry Seward (1801–72), secretary of state under Lincoln and Johnson.

recovered Mat's throat is still quite sore and mothers cough <u>was</u> a great deal better, till she went and caught more but she is again getting well. We do not hear any more from Heyde so I presume that Han is getting better again and perhaps will soon be home. I hope so anyway

I hope that George may be successful in getting his furlough. I saw Capt. Simms[7] Sunday night, he had left George and the rest on Thursday morning. He was then well and engaged in building his hut. Simms looks very well indeed. My old friend Billy DeBevoise[8] is home sick with "weakness" I suppose you might call it. He can hardly walk alone He has been home about 2 weeks and has got so he can just get about a little. My friend J. W. Mason,[9] (used to be in my party on the Water Works) was in Brooklyn on Saturday He was then on his way to his fathers at Towando, Pa. and promised that he would call on you when he returned to the army He is now a Capt. in the regulars. (5th Cavalry)

I think I shall take a few of your letters and give them to George Wright[10] (of the ferry) and let him see if he cannot collect a few dollars from the ferry hands dont you think it would be a good idea. I think that he might be able to collect something quite handsome. I have not seen any of the ferry hands since you went away.

We often wish that you and George could pop in on us just as we were about to sit down to dinner, particulary when we have "Turk" as sis calls it. Mother eats with us at almost every meal and I think living well is about all that keeps her up through all the trouble and worry that she goes through, for

7. Samuel H. Sims, a captain in George's regiment, had been the subject in part of WW's "Our Brooklyn Boys in the War," *Brooklyn Daily Eagle*, January 5, 1863. He died on July 30, 1864, of wounds received near Petersburg, Virginia. George had to wait until March 7 for his ten-day furlough to Brooklyn.

8. Formerly a bookkeeper and clerk, William H. DeBevoise was now serving in the Union army. He was a member of a large, established family that had lived in Brooklyn at least thirty years. There was a DeBevoise Street in Brooklyn as early as 1859.

9. After working for the Brooklyn Water Works, Julius ("Jule") Mason became a career army officer. With his help Jeff and WW were later able to get provisions to George when he was a prisoner of war (Waldron, p. 37). Jeff accidentally spells "Towanda" as "Towando."

10. Unidentified. Brooklyn directories of the period list seven George Wrights.

work and worry she will and I dont think the power of man can prevent it. Mat is nearly the same as usual   she is not very well and sometimes has to give up for a little while, but she soon buckels in again. Sis of course when she is well is just as big a little scamp as ever, more mischief-making than ever, if that is possible. Jess and Ed are I guess, in every respect are just the same. I met Andrew Rome,[11] 'tother day, he wanted to know how soon you would be in Brooklyn again   I told him I did not know and asked him to write you. How would it do for you to write to Wilke,[12] detailing what you are doing, what we have contributed so that he might strike some of the big-bugs that he moves among or shall I give him the letters that you have written to us. advise me about it

Mr Lane has about finished his reports and wishes me to tell you that he will now have some time to devote and thinks he will be able to raise some more money, however he will write you himself before long, a day or two.

What about your chances for the "position" and what kind of a position do you expect to get. I sincerely hope that you might succeed and get detailed to New York.[13] Try for it Walt and dont be discouraged if you do not succeed at first

Do you write to dear brother George often, I wish he could honorably get out of it. Would'nt it be good if he was home just now to build my "house"   I should like much to have it done by him, let him get a gang of men and pay him by the day. However I suppose it cannot be done in that manner and shall have to do it in some other.

Dear Walt let me hear from you soon. All send their love to you and receive my best wishes for your health and success   I remain as ever your affectionate brother

Jeff

11. One of the members of the firm of the Rome Brothers, which printed the first edition of *Leaves of Grass.*

12. Probably George Wilkes (1820?–85), owner and editor of the New York paper, *Wilkes' Spirit of the Times* (formerly edited by William T. Porter). Wilkes was known for his strong antislavery, pro-Union views, which may be why Jeff thought he would support WW's work. Wilkes was also among the first to advocate a transcontinental railroad, having published a pamphlet, *Project for a National Railroad from the Atlantic to the Pacific Ocean,* in 1845.

13. WW did not find full-time government work until January 24, 1865, when he became a first-class clerk in the Indian Affairs Office, Department of the Interior, Washington, D.C. There is no record of his looking for work in New York.

Brooklyn, Feb. 12th 1863

Dear brother Walt,

I mailed a letter to you either last Friday or Saturday, containing $11. 10 from Hill & Newman and $1. from Henry Carlow   On Tuesday I again wrote you, sending you $4 . . . $2 from Theo. A. Drake and 2 from "Cash" through John D. Martin[1]   The enclosed $5 is from our friend Mr. E. Rae.[2] He gave it to me last night   I left him a couple of letters to read and I want you to write him one of the same kind of letters asking him to show it to some of his friends and if they have anything to devote to the purpose for him to send it directly to you or through me. Walt, I know Rae is a liberal hearted man and through his friends he could do a great deal and I am confident that he could be more earnestly interested in the matter if you write him directly. Please acknowledge the receipt of this and the others (if received) so that I may be positive that the money is reaching you. Ive no doubt we shall keep dribbling along, a few dollars at a time, for some time yet.

We are all about the same at home as when I last wrote. Mother is of course quite worried about the moving of the 9th Army Corps and very much disappointed that George will not have an opportunity to come home and see us.[3] We are all getting well of our colds, last night Mother had a very bad sore throat but I made her some "hot stuff" and she was much better this morning. Mat and Sis have nearly recovered and are all right I guess. In George's letter he speaks of wanting $20. We think of sending it to him by Capt. Simms,[4] who is now here, and I think it will be the better and safer way.

I am really much disappointed that George should have to go in the thickest of the danger. I certainly feel that he is doing

1. For Hill & Newman, Carlow, Drake, and Martin, see Letters 10 and 11.

2. Miller reads this "Rae" (*Correspondence*, I, 78, n. 46), but Loving reads "Rac" (p. 71, n. 7). We agree with Miller and believe Jeff refers to Edmund H. Rae, a notary and copyist who lived in Brooklyn but kept offices at 13 Wall Street, New York City. It is not clear why Jeff would consider having Rae build his house.

3. General Ambrose Burnside's men, including George, travelled from Falmouth to Newport News, Virginia, crossing the Rappahannock River in the infamous "mud march"—an unsuccessful attempt to capture Fredericksburg. George came home March 7.

4. See Letter 11.

wrong if there is any possible way for him to avoid it. However I try to put as good a face on the matter as possible and sincerely hope for the best   Tis too bad that he should just have got his hut done and then have to go away and leave it.[5]

How goes matters with you Walt? Mr Lane[6] will send you the letters I spoke of in a day or two. I wish you could make it so that you could visit George before they leave Fortress Monroe Do if you possibly can. I am having a plan for a small 2 Story house (22 × 32) made and shall try to get Rae to build it for me. the only question that I am not clear on and am wanting advice is the position that I shall put on the lot, front or rear. I have almost made up my mind to set it so that a 65 or 70 × 20 foot lot can at any time be made in front, and the only objection to placing it in that position is the location of the privy in the next yard, which in this case would be right abreast of the center of the house thus[7]   I do not fear that it would amount to anything unless 'twould damage the cellar in some manner. Unless I am convinced that it will be some damage via the

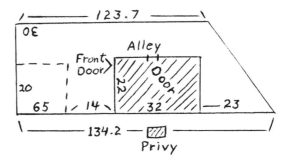

cellar I shall place it as above. Let me know what you think of it. (The above sketch is not at all in proportion, but may convey an idea to you what I mean)   The front lot will be quite ample, I think, (65 × 20) when you take in consideration that there will neither have to be a privy or cistern in the yard, and you will be able to have a gate in the ally which is quite an advantage. Mr Lane compliments me highly on my bargain and says

5. On February 1, 1863, George wrote to WW: "I have my log hut partly finished and should have had it completed long ago, but after I had cut the logs . . . orders came for us to be ready to move the next day so I used the logs for fire wood" (Loving, p. 83).

6. See Letter 9.

7. Jeff's sketch occurs here. It is reproduced about twice the size of the original.

I have done <u>well</u>. I hope I have but I am as ignorant about these
matters as a baby. However I am bound to go through with it
now, sink or tother thing.

Dear brother write me. If you see dear dear Brother George
tell him how fondly we looked for his coming home and assure
him that we were <u>all</u> much, very much disappointed. All send
their love to you and you may be assured you are never absent
from our minds.

Affectionately Jeff

The enclosed letter Mr Lane gave me to send you, wishing me
to say that undoubtedly this Mr Webster[8] could help you and if
he did it would be with the idea that it would help him somehow at some future period, That you must use him (Webster)
if you can. Mr Lane sends his respects to you
At Dinner time to-day Mother told me that Andrew had been
discharged from the yard. Tis too bad but I presume it is on
account of his not being there much of the time. I hardly know
what Nancy[9] is to do with her two children.

Jeff

[13]

Brooklyn, N. Y. March 3rd/63

Dear Walt:

Yesterday I received your letter of Sunday.[1] I was real glad
to hear from you and began to wonder what had happen [to]
you   About the house. I had my plan fixed up as I wanted it
and left it with some three or four carpenters and got bids on it.
much to my astonishment I found that what I supposed would
cost at 11 or $1200 could not be done for less than 20 or

8. On February 12 Moses Lane wrote to E. D. Webster: "Mr W. has been
for a long time connected with the New York Press and is a writer of most
decided ability. His patriotism and loyalty you can rely upon under all circumstances" (Feinberg).

9. Whitman scholars have assumed that Nancy was Andrew Whitman's
common-law wife. However, on September 22, 1852, Hannah wrote to
LVVW: "tell me who Andrew is reported to be married to" (Trent). It seems
more likely that this remark would have been prompted by a legal marriage
than by a common-law marriage.

1. This letter is not extant.

$2100   after thinking the matter over pretty thoroughly I have come to the conclusion that the best thing I could do would be to hold on to the lot and wait for cheaper times. I hardly would be willing to spend that amount of money in a house of that kind and I think it would be much better to wait till the character of the avenue is settled before building. And again, I find (by calculation) that the prospect is that the difference in prices in, say two years, will more than pay rent for that time and then there would be the interest money to pay besides. Dont you think I have acted wisely. I sent word to Blake[2] word this morning that I would remain as I was and he sent back word that he would call and see me this week. That she bitch of Hell, the Brown, is trying her strongest to clear us out and I honestly think Walt that I shall just take and belt old Johny[3] under the eye if he attempts any of his last summers games

To day the bitch could do nothing better than spend an hour or two in getting the lid of the cistern up and has left it in the old dangerous style half on and half of[f] the hole   Mother tells me that Blake is altogether "on their side"   one thing is sure that if he attempts any of his games I shall most certainly clear out. I rather think that Mother would rather that we would move as Brown is continually at her about Mats conduct and keeps her in continued hot water. Everything is going on as usual. I wish you would let me hear from you at least twice a week. I guess that I have received all your letters   Mother got your letter enclosing the $1.00 and is still like Oliver Twist.[4] She has had some 3 letters from you with money in it.

We had received the letter from George (that he spoke of in his letter to you) just before we got yours[5]   Mother wrote to George also Han yesterday. I wish you would tell George that if he cannot possibly get his furlough (if he should make his clothes look awful they might let him home to get a new suit) and will send on his measure we will have them made in

2. Unidentified.

3. Jeff refers to John Brown and his wife, the neighbors downstairs. See Letter 5.

4. Jeff refers to Oliver's famous request for more food: "Please sir, I want some more" (Charles Dickens, *Oliver Twist*, Ch. ii). For another allusion to this quotation, see Letter 21.

5. George wrote to LVVW on February 25, 1863 (Loving, pp. 87–88). WW's letter of about March 1 is not extant.

good style and sent to him. As regards the money in the Bank, there is plenty left for that purpose. Mother had a letter from Han on Saturday she seemed about the same although Heyde wrote in the latter part of the letter that she was not so well the exertion of writing was too much for her[6] Sissy is very well and is growing finely She is great on the mischief, she is just getting at that age where she does it with "malice aforethoughts"

I shall write you oftener hereafter I have been so busy with plans specifications &c &c that I have not been able to write you as ofen as I would like. I think that I have a good bargain in my lot if I can manage to hold on to it. They are now asking $1500 for lots in the immediate neighborhood that are not as well located as the one I have bargained for

How do you get along with your office hunting do you meet with any encouragement. It must be a new life to you. Are you writing for any paper outside of Washington, if so what?[7] You must have pretty good times generally, dont you I should much like to see you for a good talk. Your note book will certainly have a good many strange things in it. What are they going to do to reinforce the army, will they have to enforce the conscript bill[8]

We have not been able to send you any money lately but hope that we shall before long. do you get any from any other source? T will be hard for you to go to the Hospitals if you cant give the poor young heroes something. I think that it would be a good idea for you to write to Mr Lane, tell him that you are

6. Cf. the letter from Charles and Hannah Heyde to LVVW of November 24, 1868 (Trent); after Hannah wrote two pages Charles interrupted, "here I have interfered and compelled Han to break off—She is too weak to continue further." All evidence suggests that the imaginations of both Charles and Hannah tended toward the melodramatic.

7. WW responded on March 18: "Jeff, I wrote a letter to the *Eagle* and sent it yesterday. . . . Look out for it, and buy me 20 of the papers." "The Great Washington Hospital" appeared in the *Brooklyn Daily Eagle* on March 19 (*Correspondence*, I, 79, n. 50). In September WW published another hospital letter in the *Brooklyn Daily Union* (*Correspondence*, I, 95, n. 3).

8. WW's notebooks from this period record the pathetic scenes he witnessed almost daily in the hospitals. But as Jeff guessed these notebooks contain other "strange things," including the poet's meditation on the adjournment of the Thirty-seventh Congress which on March 3 authorized America's first nationwide military draft (Trent).

out, and ask him if he could not get the young men around the office to subscribe 50ᶜᵗˢ a month.⁹ I will, if he puts "the questions" amend that it be made a dollar, and should not wonder that we could send you quite a little sum every month. Of course you wont say I suggested it.

We are all quite well and getting along as well as usual will write you again in a few days. Dear Walt receive love from all and a kiss from Hattie

Jeff.

[14]

Brooklyn, N. Y. March 9th/63

Dear Walt,

Much to our joy and surprise George made his appearance among us on Sunday morning.¹ He arrived home about 11 Oᶜᵏ on Saturday night but we all happened to be abed and he did not wake us up but went to his room and made himself shown at about 8ᵒᶜᵏin the morning   He is well and looking first rate, pretty well played out as regards cloths, but we will fix him up in that respect this afternoon   He wants me to ask you if you can find out if he can get his pay in New York and if so at what office and hour. Please find out what you can about it and answer me at once. He has some $500 coming to him and would like to get it here if he can. Please write me at once will you Walt.

Of course we were all wonderfully glad to see him. I think he looks well. He certainly is well pleased with his position and I think it would be hard to get him to leave it.² He could only get 10 days and that will hardly be time for him to see and

9. For Lane, see Letter 9. WW did not ask Moses Lane and his employees for more money; instead he took a more tactful and indirect approach by instructing his brother thus: "Jeff, you must give my best respects to Mr. and Mrs. Lane, they have enabled me to do a world of good, and I can never forget them" (_Correspondence_, I, 80).

1. George briefly mentions this furlough at home from March 7 to 17 in his Civil War diary (Loving, p. 153).

2. Army life agreed with George. He had held the rank of captain since November 1, 1862, and after the war he attempted unsuccessfully to secure a commission as a captain in the regular standing army (Loving, pp. 6, 26).

shake hands with all his friends. 'Tis a pity it could not have
been for 20 or 30 days, it certainly ought to have been.

We are all in our usual good health. Mother, George says
looks younger than when he went away. I think she looks better than when you left. Mattie, Sis and the rest are all well.

I received a long letter from you Saturday. I like much to
hear from you   you must write often. About your office
hunting[3]   I suppose you will have to wait a long time before it
amounts to anything but patience will bring something
undoubtedly

Hoping to hear from you immediately, I remain

yours affectionately Jeff.

[15]

Brooklyn, N. Y. March 12th/6[3]

Dear Walt,

I wrote you last Monday[1] asking you if you could send me
any information in regard to George's getting his money in
New York. I have not heard from you yet but hope to to-day. I
[want you] now, if you <u>possibly</u> can get them to me by or before
Tuesday morning next to send me those two shirts for George
He wants them very much indeed   Nothing that he can buy
will make him half as comfortable. The thought just strikes me
that perhaps you are using them yourself, if so all right, or if
you want one and can send him one why do so. If you are not
using them I think it would be a "big thing" for George to get
them as they would be very useful both winter and summer. If
you send them direct either to George or myself.[2]

3. Jeff refers to WW's letter of March 6, only part of which is extant
(*Correspondence*, I, 76–77). Earlier, on February 13, WW had described his
efforts to find employment in Washington: "(it is very amusing to hunt for
an office—so the thing seems to me just now—even if one don't get it)—I
have seen Charles Sumner three times—he says every thing here moves as
part of a great machine, and that I must consign myself to the fate of the rest
. . . . Meantime I make about enough to pay my expenses by hacking on the
press here, and copying in the paymasters offices" (*Correspondence*, I, 73).

1. See Letter 14.

2. In a letter of March 18 to Jeff, WW wrote: "I suppose the bundle of
George's shirts, drawers, &c came safe by Adams express. I sent it last Satur-
day [March 14], and it ought to have been delivered Monday in Brooklyn"
(*Correspondence*, I, 79).

We are all well. George is enjoying himself hugely and I shall feel sorry enough when he has to go back. All send love to you.

affectionately Jeff.

Mother wrote you a letter asking you to send on the shirts but when I left home this morning I forgot it so I wrote this one. will send mothers letter this P. M.[3]

[16]

[Brooklyn, March 19, 1863][1]

[Dear Brother Walt,]

I had commenced a letter to you but as it embraced abt what Mammy has said I will not send it just now. I will send the paper[2] &c to day I guess. I am sorry that you omitted to put in Probasco's[3] name in the list of those that sent money, could it be easily corrected. You will hear from me in a day or so.

—Jeff

[17]

Walt Whitman readily acknowledged his admiration for Italian opera and stressed its importance to his poetry, even claiming that the method of "A Child's Reminiscence" (1859; later "Out of the Cradle Endlessly Rocking") was "strictly that of the Italian Opera" (Faner, p. v). Late in his career he again emphasized this influence in "The Dead Tenor" (1884), a memorial tribute to Pasquale Brignoli: "How much from thee! the revelation of the singing voice from thee! / . . . How through those strains distill'd—how the rapt ears, the soul of me, absorbing / Fernando's heart, Manrico's passionate call, Ernani's, sweet Gennaro's."

Jeff and Walt often attended operas together, especially

3. In her letter to WW of March 11, 1863, LVVW asked the poet to send "those flannel shirts" by express because George thought "he could get them better from here than to send them to fortress monroe" (Trent).

1. Jeff wrote this short note at the top of his mother's letter to WW dated March 19 [1863] (Trent).

2. See Letter 13.

3. See Letter 9.

Castle Garden Theatre, or "The Battery," New York. Located at the southwest tip of Manhattan, this popular entertainment house offered opera during the summer months and was a favorite haunt for Walt and Jeff during the early 1850s. Courtesy of the New York Public Library at Lincoln Center, Theatre Collection, Astor, Lenox, and Tilden Foundations.

during the period 1854-62. After the poet left Brooklyn for Washington, Jeff continued, in spite of the war conditions and a shortage of funds, to attend the opera "quite often" on his own. He and Walt shared similar tastes, as those composers, operas, and performers that Jeff mentions—Verdi's Il Trovatore, *Donizetti's* La Favorita, *and the singers Amodio, Francesco Mazzoleni, and Josephine Medori—were ones that Walt praised in essays, notebook jottings, and letters. As Jeff's appreciation for the opera grew, he instructed his former teacher by guiding Walt to the latest arrivals on the New York stage and encouraging him to hear them.*

Brooklyn, N. Y. March 21st 1863

Dear brother Walt,

I have not written to you for the last day or two thinking that I would wait till I could send the prints that you wanted,[1]

1. On March 18, WW had asked Jeff to send "engravings (20 of the large head)" (*Correspondence*, I, 79). This is probably the engraving that served as the frontispiece for the 1860 *Leaves of Grass*.

and I also wanted to send a large picture of George with them. Harrison[2] promised me them to-day and upon calling he told me that he had spoiled the large ones in the printing. However I got a dozen of the kind (I send you a specimen) and I think it's good, dont you   I shall get the large ones by the middle of next week and I will send you one immediately. I wish you could have been home when George was here, 'twas a great pleasure to be with him. I'm sure he enjoyed himself well and I know that we all did. The bundle of shirts &c that you sent to him were first rate and although we had hard work to make him take them all yet I packed them all in his "traps" almost without his knowing it. By the way Walt in regard to those wollen shirts that I sent down to George by you I am real sorry that I did not know that you or he was not using them for I have wanted them pretty bad myself and should have got you to send them to me before. They were all that I had and I had wore them up to the time that you went away. If you do not use them, and you dont think George will want them for the present, (my reason for thinking that George will not want [them] is that we had such hard work to get him to take all that you sent him) I wish you would send them back to me. Understand me Walt, if you do not use them yourself   if you do, why they will do me as much good as if I had them   In regard to moving, I have given up all ideas of building for the present. I had several bids on the plan for a little house that I had made and they wanted 22 & 23. hundred dollars to build it, so I caved. Things go along with me about as usual. Everything in the way of eating and wearing is awful high, but I manage to make enough to keep my head above water yet. I think (am quite confident) that I shall manage to hold on to the lot without trouble and if I do shall be perfectly satisfied. Undoubtedly we shall all live right along just the same as usual, Browns[3] and all.

I have been quite often lately to the <u>Opera</u>   Rather queer and expensive for these hard times aint it? But I take a small dose every time (25 or 50¢ worth)   Walt I wish you could hear a man that is singing here by the name of Bellini.[4] He plays the

2. Gabriel Harrison, a photographer.

3. See Letter 5.

4. Domenico Bellini joined Francesco Mazzoleni and Josephine (or Giuseppina) Medori as new members of Max Maretzek's opera company for the Spring 1863 season. The three opened in *Il Trovatore* on March 6, 1863, at the New York Academy of Music.

same parts that Amodio used to but possesses the (to me) most
wonderful voice, with the single exception of Bertina[5] (of old)
that I ever heard He is in looks and acting almost a likeness
of Bertina [(]the tenor whom we used to admire so much) and
indeed his voice is almost the same, just a little lower, but fully
having all those wonderful qualities of pathos and feeling He
certainly would carry you back to the old Castle Garden and
Bertina singing "Spirit O'Gentil"[6] The tenor (Mazzoleni) is
excedingly good. An immense quantity of rather an unfa[i]ling
voice, with a little overdosing the action, and a constant "trem-
olo" (rather of the hand organ style) but after all good and
following on the heels of Brignoli, who has by not singing
when advertised and cutting the work, and lazy action, he has
made an immense success in New York The woman[7] is just
the same, only a little more so, and they both make an immense point in letting themselves out in all the choruses, more
so than I ever heard before. In Verdi's[8] music it is wonderfully
grand I most particularly hope you will hear Bellini.

Monday Morning—At the same time that I mail this I also
mail the bundle of Engravings and papers directed as usual.[9]
We are all well and jolly as usual. We are having glorious
spring weather and sissy wants to know if I wont write and tell
Uncle Walt to come home and take her out on Fort Green[10] I
took her out yesterday P. M. and after walking around a while

5. Odell's *Annals of the New York Stage* lists no Bertina. This may be a
slip for "Bettini," formerly a popular singer at the Castle Garden and WW's
favorite tenor. See Letter 50.
6. Jeff refers to the period 1845-54, when Castle Garden (or "The Battery Theater") was a leading New York opera house. In June 1851, WW
heard Bettini as Fernando in Donizetti's *La Favorita* sing "Spirto Gentil"
("Spirit of Light"), a sorrowful tune that was among the poet's favorites
(Faner, p. 181).
7. Josephine Medori.
8. The operas of Giuseppe Verdi (1813-1901) were immensely popular.
The 1862/63 season at the Brooklyn Academy of Music featured *Il Trovatore*, *Ernani*, and *La Traviata*. Since *La Traviata* was performed on March 19,
1863, and starred Brignoli, Mazzoleni, and Bellini, this is probably the one
Jeff had just seen.
9. See Letter 16.
10. WW responded with playful formality: "I would like to have the
pleasure of Miss Mannahatta Whitman's company, the first fine forenoon, if
it were possible" (*Correspondence*, I, 87). Fort Greene stood opposite the
Whitmans' Portland Avenue home. WW believed that one of his two finest
achievements as a journalist was "the securing to public use of Washington

took the car and went over to New York, returning she walked from the ferry all the way home. Good for less than a 3 year old wasn't it? Let me hear from you soon. All send their love,

Affectionately Brother Jeff

[18]

Brooklyn, N. Y. April 2nd 1863

Dear brother Walt,

I intended to have written you yesterday but did not have an opportunity. Everything is going along all right with us except Andrew is real sick with his throat.[1] He cannot talk at all and eats but with the greatest agony. He has had some doctor attending him that I think has treated him very badly. I am going to have him have an interview with Dr Ruggles[2] this Eve, and hope he will be able to do something for him at once. Andrew, himself, seems to think that he is a gone case, but I cannot think as badly of him as that. I will write you again tomorrow what Ruggles says.

Mother received your last letter with the shin plasters all right, and in regard to your papers, Mss &c they are all carefully put up, everything, even the smallest scrap is packed up so you will certainly find everything that you left at home all right[3]

About George. We do not hear from him. He wrote mother that he would certainly write her again befor he left

---

Park (Old Fort Greene,) . . . against heavy odds, during an editorship of the Brooklyn _Eagle_" (_Correspondence_, III, 386). For one of WW's editorials on the subject, see _The Gathering of the Forces_, ed. Cleveland Rogers and John Black (New York: G. P. Putnam's Sons, 1920), II, 46–50.

1. For Andrew's illness, see Letter 5.

2. The Brooklyn physician Edward Ruggles (1817?–67) befriended the Whitman family and became especially close to Jeff and Mattie. Late in life, Ruggles lost interest in his practice and devoted himself to painting cabinet pictures called "Ruggles Gems" (_Correspondence_, I, 90, n. 85).

3. On March 31 WW wrote: "Mother, when you or Jeff writes again, tell me if my papers & MSS are all right—I should be very sorry indeed if they got scattered, or used up or any thing—_especially_ the copy of Leaves of Grass covered in blue paper, and the little MS book 'Drum Taps,' & the MS tied up in the square, spotted (stone-paper) loose covers—I want them all carefully kept" (_Correspondence_, I, 85–86).

Newport News and as long as she did not hear from him she
might be sure that he was there. I have an idea that the 51st
were left behind, although it is hard to tell about it. I should
write to George to-day if I <u>knew</u> that he was still down to
Newport News.[4] Walt I should like to have letters from you
much oftener   I am real sorry to hear that the trouble in your
head has again made its appearence. I can tell how you must
feel for I am having something of the same kind myself but in a
much milder form than you are. Dr Ruggles has been quite sick
with the same thing but has recovered. Indeed almost everyone that I know has had a bad time with cold &c in the head. I
hope dear Walt that you will speedily recover. Mother is as
well as usual   Mattie is also quite well. We have not heard
from Han for some little time. I suppose that she is about the
same and I fear that she will be a long time in getting well.[5]
Hattie is as well and interesting as usual. Yesterday she had an
immensely bad fall on the back part of her head. She was sitting in the chair at the sewing machine and reached over to get
a small piece of stuff to stitch, leaned too far and fell striking
the back part of her head pretty hard against the frame of the
Extension table leaves   We bathed her head for a long time
with cold water and this morning although the swelling was
not all gone she appeared abt as well as usual. I was much
frightened though at first I can tell you.

   Walt do you ever have a chance to get hold of any of the
scientific reports that Uncle Sam prints. Would it be possible
for you to obtain a copy of the Pacific R. R. Exploration &c
Reports.[6] I should like much to get hold of anything in that
line, and would be much obliged to you if you could get them

---

   4. As part of General Burnside's Ninth Army, George's regiment, the
Fifty-first New York, left Newport News on March 26 and travelled to Paris, Kentucky, arriving on April 1, 1863 (Loving, p. 90).
   5. Hannah, a hypochondriac, complained for decades of ill health, yet
she outlived her entire immediate family.
   6. Jeff uses the popular name for the series issued by the U.S. War Department and prepared under the supervision of the U.S. Engineer Department, Topographical Bureau, *Reports of Explorations and Surveys, to Ascertain the Most Practicable and Economical Route for a Railroad From the
Mississippi River to the Pacific Ocean,* 12 vols. (Washington, D.C.: A. O. P.
Nicholson, 1855–60). Although an earlier edition of these reports was published in four volumes octavo (1854), Jeff's later references to this work
indicate he means the twelve-volume quarto edition. See Letter 21.

for me. I find them of great use in giving me ideas about my business and they are too cursed costly to buy   Look around you and if you catch anything send it along will you
    I will write you again to-morrow
                                        Yours Affectionately, Jeff

[19]

                                        Brooklyn, N. Y. April 3rd 1863
Dear brother Walt,
    I mailed a letter to you yesterday promising to write you again to-day. Ruggles[1] came up and saw Andrew last eve. and had quite a lengthy interview   He said that the stuff that he was taking was abt as good for him as he could take and to continue but that the thing that would cure him would to be very careful of himself and to breathe nothing but the best and freshest air. Drink none, stay at home nights sleep in a well-ventilated room &c &c and be careful to work out-doors   I walked down with him (Ruggles) afterward and he told me that it was a pretty bad case, that he couldnt take anything that would help him particularly. That the trouble was very low down in his throat and that such cases often ended in consumption. He said that the best thing that he could do would be to get work away from the sea-coast if possible. I hope Andrew will take better care of himself in future. The Dr. will see him again in 6 or 8 days
    The enclosed $5.0 Mr Lane[2] sends you   He wished me to say that he would write you himself but could hardly get time. He told me to tell you that he intended the money for your own especial benefit   That you could not stay there without its costing you something and that you could do this amt of good to the soldiers by telling them good, cheerful things and letting them look at you.[3] The amt of it is I suppose he thinks that as

1. See Letter 18.
2. See Letter 9.
3. WW often prepared "from a couple to four or five hours" for a hospital visit in order to exude "the perfection of physical health" and to present "as cheerful an appearance as possible" (*Prose Works 1892*, I, 52). He wrote, "my profoundest help to these sick & dying men is probably the soothing invigoration I steadily bear in mind, to infuse in them through affection, cheering love . . . . It has saved more than one life" (*Correspondence*, I, 102).

you are giving all your time to the Hospitals that you must want a little money yourself. It is certainly characteristic of the man. I told him I would take it and send it to you and tell you what he said but that you would probably apply it as you had the rest. Anyway you must write him abt it. He told me that the man Crany[4] would send you some more too, or had promised to. I wish you would write Mr Lane.[5]

Mother had a letter from Heyde to-day. He says that Han is not any different. The whole of his letter is taken up with abuse of George for not coming on when he had his furlough. And after a long rigarmarole he winds up with saying that he has no accomodations for anyone. Nice pup aint he. Oh I wish to God he had been in Hell before we ever saw him.[6] Poor Han I hope she will get able to come home. Han had received your letter telling her that George had been home. Mother wrote Han that George was home and that he would come and see her but that his furlough was so short that twould be impossible and received a reply from Heyde that he would not give the letter to her for he was afraid it would excite her too much. We supposed of course, however that she knew that he had been home, but it seems that she did not know it till she received your letter. Mother has written her to-day and I send one of his little pictures.

I believe that Hattie has received no injury from her fall she appears to-day abt the same as usual. She is growing finely and is as smart as a child of her age ought to be. All the rest the same as usual   I am going to try to get Mat to go to the Opera to-morrow to the P. M. performance   I want her to hear this company before they leave.[7] I spoke yesterday abt Public doc. I of course mean scientific ones   those I should be glad to get.[8]

Write me as much and as often as you can   What do you think abt George, & where is he?

Yours affn, Jeff

4. Unidentified.

5. There is no record of WW writing Lane at this time.

6. WW referred to Charles Heyde with similar exasperation, calling him "the bed-buggiest man on the earth"—"almost the only man alive who can make me mad" (Traubel, III, 498).

7. Max Maretzek's new troupe gave a matinee performance of Donizetti's *Linda di Chamounix* at the New York Academy of Music on April 4, 1863. See also Letter 17.

8. See Letter 18.

[20]

[April 6, 1863][1]

[Dear Brother Walt,]

As I was abt putting these in the envelope my eye caught this blank place and I thought that 'twas a pity to let such an opportunity go. It looked like waste.

Walt, how I should like to see you, do you look the same as ever or has the immense number of unfortunate and heart-working cases given you an sobre and melancholy look.[2] I sometimes think, when I get thinking abt you, that it must have that effect upon you. But then the cases that you releive and those dear lives that you save must bring back the old look again. Do you suppose that you will long continue where you are? Do you think Anything will come of your trying to get office?[3] I suppose it is merely a question of time and patience as regards the office. I am in hopes to be able to have a small some of money sent you every week hereafter in this way   I will ask Lane[4] to see how many names of those around in and abt. the W. W.[5] will consent to give $1 per month regularly to be sent to you for Hospital purposes. I have no doubt but that some 25 or 30 names could be had and if we could send you $6 or $7 weekly twould be quite a big thing. We think then that we shall call you "The B. Watr Works soldiers Aid society" with power. Seriously, I think twould be a good thing and that I can come [by] it. I sent you $5 last week, did you get it. Twas from Mr Lane.

Twould make you laugh to see little Hattie brush her hair and teeth. I am almost afraid she will clean them to death. She is tremendious proud of her things that Uncle Walt sent her. Twould please you to see how finely she is growing. Every day I give her a little exercise in singing two or three notes only. I

1. This letter is written on the verso of George's letter of April 2, 1863 (Loving, pp. 90–91). WW's letter to LVVW of April 15 suggests that Jeff wrote this on April 6 (*Correspondence*, I, 87).

2. On April 15, WW assured Jeff that he was "as much of a beauty as ever . . . well, not only as much, but more so—I believe I weigh about 200 and as to my face, (so scarlet,) and my beard and neck, they are terrible to behold . . . like a great wild buffalo, with much hair" (*Correspondence*, I, 89).

3. See Letter 14.

4. See Letter 9.

5. The Brooklyn Water Works.

think she could be made a fine musician and am going to try it.[6] She often asks when you are coming home to take her out on Fort Greene.[7] She often gets one of you[r] pictures and calls it her dear Uncle Walt. She knew Georges picture at once, which I think proves it to be pretty good. Mattie is as well as usual, she has no work and has not had hardly since you went away, and I am glad she has not[8]   Mother is first rate except she works to hard   I wish she wouldnt   she is foolish to clean house so much. Walt do write me a good long letter

Jeff.

The enclosed $10 I got from Van Anden[9]

[21]

Brooklyn, N. Y. April 11th 1863

Dear Walt,

The two books you sent me (also one to Mr Lane)[1] came all right. I am extremely obliged to you for it all and shall, Oliver Twist like, ask for more.[2] I should dearly love to get together a set of the Pacific R. R. Explorations and Reports and intend to do so. I hope you will be able to send me some of the other Vols. I told you that I had written to Boston for a Report on the

---

6. On April 15, in a letter which also provided Andrew with detailed advice on how he should care for his throat, WW instructed Jeff as well: "Jeff must not make his lessons to her in music any ways strong or frequent on any account—two lessons a week, of ten minutes each, is enough—But then I dare say Jeff will think of all these things, just the same as I am saying" (*Correspondence*, I, 89).

7. See Letter 17.

8. Mattie made shirt fronts for New York manufacturers (Waldron, p. 2).

9. Isaac Van Anden, publisher and proprietor of the *Brooklyn Daily Eagle*. WW edited this paper (March 1846–January 1848) until he quarreled with Van Anden over political issues. For more on Van Anden see Raymond A. Schroth, "The *Eagle* and Brooklyn," in *Brooklyn USA: The Fourth Largest City in America*, ed. Rita Seiden Miller (New York: Brooklyn College Press, 1979), pp. 99–119.

1. Presumably two volumes of the Pacific Railroad reports (see Letter 18). For Lane, see Letter 9.

2. See Letter 13.

Hoosac Tunnel,[3] that also has come and I have already found it of great use to me in solving two or three questions that I was not up in. I believe that the best information about Engn'ring is to be got out of reports of this character. I shall, as you suggest keep a sharp lookout for Vol. 12[4] and shall buy it if I come across it. If you, in looking around the second hand book stalls, see any Engnring works please write me what they are and the price. I am very much in want of a copy of "Wisbachs Mechanics"[5] but cannot meet with it in New York. I have been quite disappointed in not getting a letter from you to-day. I certainly thought I should. I sent you a letter on Tuesday last with the $10 from Van Anden[6] and a letter from Han and one from George also a long one from me—6[cts] worth—I hope you received it   The things by Express came all right. George's bundle was 6/ and the last $1.00. Hattie has got entirely over her fall[7] and is as healthy as a child can be, she is growing finely. I am sure twould please you to see her, she is as smart as can be, talks perfectly plain, without the least babyishness. Just below us in the same street there is a young lady from down east, she comes in to see Mat every day or two. she talks in the down east fashion, saying "cant" as if it was made of rrs. the other day she said so before sis. Sissy says "Why dont you say cant, thats no way to talk, carnt" which quite took our young lady aback. And yesterday one of the Hearkness[8] children was in our rooms and they were talking about rolling their hoops. one told sis—4½

3. It is not known which of the many reports on this tunnel Jeff read. He would have been interested in the improved surveying techniques Thomas Doane developed for this project, a 4¾-mile railroad tunnel under Hoosac Mountain in northwestern Massachusetts (1855-76).

4. Volume XII of the Pacific Railroad reports, Isaac I. Stevens, U.S. Topographical Bureau, *Report of Exploration of a Route for the Pacific Railroad Near the 47th and 49th Parallels From St. Paul to Puget Sound* (Washington, D.C.: A. O. P. Nicholson, 1860). This was issued in two parts as a supplement to Volume I.

5. The popular English title for Julius Weisbach's *Lehrbuch der Ingenieur- und Maschinen-Mechanik* (1845). A standard engineering text widely reprinted after 1869, it was available to Jeff as *Principles of Mechanics of Machinery and Engineering*, ed. Walter R. Johnson, 2nd ed., 2 vols. (Philadelphia: Lea & Blanchard, 1858-59).

6. See Letter 20.

7. See Letter 18.

8. Two men named George Harkness—one a bookbinder and the other a carpenter—lived on Portland Avenue near Myrtle. No "Hearkness" appeared in Brooklyn directories at that time.

yrs old—that she had rolled her hoop down the "teet" sis says "I rolled mine down <u>the street</u> thats the way to say it"[9] She often wonders when you are coming home to take her out and show her the ships and steamboats. Mat is first rate and well, she has no work and consequently is living quite like a Christian. we often talk about you and wonder how you are getting along Mat often speaks about how she should have felt if she had gone with you. How much better it was that she did not, wasnt it.[10] Mother is quite well and a little worried about not hearing from you and George I feel quite concerned about Andrew I have had Ruggles[11] see him twice now Ruggles says that he has a bad, very bad throat and about the only thing that will cure him will be his going away from the coast back in the interior somewhere He says that it is hardly possible to give any medicine for such a complaint and the more one takes the worse he is off. However he says if Andrew takes the right care of himself he may recover here.[12] I wish he could get something to do away from here, back in the interior. I have great faith in that for diseases of the kind like his. I will write you every day or two and keep you posted how he is. I should be glad to have you give the Capt Mullen[13] you

9. Although WW "was real amused with sis's remarks," he warned the family that "it is not good to encourage a child to be too sharp" (*Correspondence*, I, 89).

10. When the Whitman family read that George had been wounded, both Mattie and WW planned to go help him. By not going, Mattie avoided the difficulties that WW experienced. See Letter 8.

11. See Letter 18.

12. In his letter instructing Jeff on how to raise Hattie, WW also offered a detailed explanation of how Andrew should care for his throat. Surprisingly, his brothers show no signs of resenting this instruction. WW seems to have been able to combine the roles of the prophetic, all-knowing poet and the dominant, wise family head.

13. Captain John Mullan (1830–1909) had just published for the U.S. Topographical Bureau his *Report on the Construction of a Military Road From Fort Walla-Walla to Fort Benton* (Washington, D.C.: GPO, 1863). Because Jeff and WW were both fascinated by the prospect of a western railroad, they would have admired Mullan's work described in Volume XII of the Pacific Railroad reports (see n. 4 above). On March 31 WW had praised "Capt. Mullin, U.S. Army (engineer), who has been six years out in the Rocky Mt's, making a gov't road, 650 miles from Ft. Benton to Walla Walla—very, very interesting to know such men intimately, and talk freely with them" (*Correspondence*, I, 87). Apparently Jeff wanted WW to write a letter to Mr. Lane concerning Captain Mullan (see also Letter 23).

spoke of a letter to Mr Lane, very glad indeed. I like to become acquainted with such men, It is education to me and I find I am in need of a great quantity of that article. by all means, if he has not left, give him a letter to Mr Lane. Well Walt, I will, after wishing you pleasure and success, bid you good night

affectionately Jeff.

[22]

Brooklyn, N. Y. April 13th/63

Dear Walt,

We hardly know what to think of not hearing from you we certainly expected to have a letter from you this morning. Mother is quite anxious and of course fears that something has happened to you. Walt write to me at once wont you. I have written you two letters, one containing the $10 that Van Anden owed you, and another I mailed you last Sat. eve.[1] Mother gave me a letter to mail you on Monday but I forgot it till to-day. You must not tell mother about it. We are all well and as jolly as usual. Andrew does not seem to get much better. He was at our house to-day to dinner   his voice is [still?] so that you can hardly here him speak.[2]

We had a letter from George yesterday. He was at Mt Sterling Ken.[3] He seems to feel quite well and satisfied. Mother had a letter from Heyde. He says that she must fix up her third story room for Han an him and a lot of stuff. He says that Han must come home. He says that Han wants him to take a house and let her [take?] a man and wife to board. He wants to know what he shall do with his business. How should he get along. All of which I am sure I dont know how Mother can answer him. He is a case. I dont know what to think abt him. Walt I havnt time to write you a long letter, and indeed I havnt anything to write about. I hope to hear from you soon. All send their love, Hattie particulary.

affectionately, Jeff.

1. By the time Jeff's letter reached WW, the poet had already written to acknowledge Letters 20 and 21 (*Correspondence*, I, 87). For Van Anden, see Letter 20.

2. See Letter 5.

3. On April 3 the Ninth Army marched from Paris, Kentucky, to Mount Sterling, Kentucky. For the next two weeks the army camped in this area,

Brooklyn, N. Y. April 20th 1863

Dear Walt,

I was glad to hear—from your letter to mother—that you had received my letters—containing the $10. &c.[1]—Everything is all right with us,—the same as ever. Mary and Louisa[2] are down with us. Came on Friday—will probably stay till Wednesday, down shopping   They are all well. Ancel[3] is down on the coast fishing. George[4] is still on the cars. The rest are all the same.[5] We have quite a joke on Mother which I bring forward almost every time she asks me if I have heard from you, which is everytime she sees me   'tis this. during the time that we were so long without hearing from you Mother really got very much worried about you and when I went home to dinner on the day before we got your letter, she asked me as usual if I had heard and when I told her no she said "well I cannot imagine what is the matter with Walt. I feel very much worried indeed. one thing is sure he is either sick or else he is coming home"   You can readily imagine how mother looked when I poked fun at her and repeated it to her. She says that she didnt say it so it sounded like I say it, &c   Dear Mother, she would be mighty glad to see [you] I know, but I love to plague her   she will then take Hattie and say that sis is the only one of us that has got any sense, and if it wasnt for you and George she should not have much to live for &c, &c   I hope you will be able to get me a copy of Capt. Mullens' report[6] also I hope you will give him a letter to Mr Lane.[7] I like to know

---

although on April 15 it did invade Sharpsburg, Kentucky, only to return to Mount Sterling the same day (Loving, p. 91).

1. See *Correspondence*, I, 87.
2. Born in 1845, Louisa was the third of five children of Jeff's sister Mary Whitman Van Nostrand (Molinoff, p. 4).
3. Ansel Van Nostrand, a shipwright, lived with his wife Mary in the whaling village of Greenport, Long Island.
4. Born in 1841, George was the oldest of the Van Nostrand children. One supposes from Jeff's reference that the young George was a streetcar driver; later he would go into insurance (Molinoff, p. 4, n. 3).
5. The other Van Nostrand children were Fanny (b. 1843) and Minnie (b. 1857). Another child, Ansel (b. 1847), died in infancy (Molinoff, p. 4, n. 3).
6. See Letter 21.
7. For Lane, see Letter 9; for an earlier reference to the letter, see Letter 21.

such men   I can learn from them. I spend quite a good deal of time lately with Dr Ruggles.[8] He comes in the office quite often and I call at his house and see him. There are a good many things about him to like, I think and he seems to like me. I still continue to go to the Opera once in a while. To night is said to be the last night of the season but I hardly think that they will leave.[9] it seems to me to be paying to well. The houses are generally full. We have not heard from Han since I wrote you last. Mother thinks that she will get Mary to go on for her pretty soon. I suppose it is best that Han should come home but I fear for Mother. I fear that she will undertake in her usual way to do too much   I was awful mad at Heydes last letter. If I had been in his neighborhood I should certainly have booted him. He is a damn fool. Hattie is in first rate condition   she reminds me more of a young colt or dog than a child. It seems to be perfect pleasure for her just to get out into the open air. She dont seem to care to go any where, only outdoors. Yesterday Mother locked the front basement door while she went to some other part of the house a moment—to keep Hattie in. Hattie went in the front basement and shoved the window and was out and away leaving her Opandmouth in amazement abt how she got out. But altogether she is as affectionate and good as it seems to me for a human being (and I dont suppose there is anything better) to be.[10] Mattie sends her love.

affectionately Jeff.

[24]

Brooklyn, N. Y. April 25th/63
Dear Walt,

Although I have little to write you about yet I thought I would just "drop you a line" as they say telling you that we all are in our usual style of liberty, health and pursuit of happiness. The latter of course under great difficulties as everything

8. See Letter 18.
9. The New York Academy of Music had announced April 20 as the last night of its opera season but went on to produce at least six more operas with members of Maretzek's troupe, concluding on May 23.
10. LVVW was considerably less charmed by Hattie's antics. Six months later, on Christmas Day 1863, she remarked to WW, "i really think hattie is the worst child i ever had any thing to doo with" (Trent).

is so awful dear that you can hardly get enough to make a happy dinner on for less than 150^{cts} but then we are doing the jolliest we can. How goes things with you. We dont hear from you as often as we used to.[1] I hope you are not so engaged but that you can find time to write home? Do you visit the Hospitals as often as usual?[2] I suppose so. I hope you are enabled to do as much good as formerly

I have had quite a disappointment in a small way   There was a bill introduced in the Leg. to give the Brooklyn Sewer Com. the power to build a large sewer in Kent Av. raise the grade of the streets around there (Kent Av. from Flushing toward Williamsburg) &c quite a large job and we all surely thought it would go through as it is very much needed, and Mr Lane had promised me charge of it. Indeed I had commenced making plans, profiles &c when at the last moment the thing got squelched, but yet I dont know a[s] I am <u>very</u> sorry for we still expect to get the <u>new main</u>, that is to lay a new line of pipe from the Reservoir down to the city, and even if we dont do that why I shall have work enough to keep me along, doing anything and everything that turns up[3]

Andrew is about the same as when I last wrote you   no worse, and I think a little better.[4] I do not see much of him as he comes to the house mostly when I am out. He visits Dr Ruggles[5] now and then. The Dr thinks that he will gradually get over it. Mother had a little attack of her rheumatism yesterday and to-day and I am somewhat afraid that she will have more of it. She has been wonderful foolish in cleaning house as she

1. In his letter of April 28 WW made reference to his letter of April 22 (not extant) which had not reached Jeff by April 25. However, WW did promise to "write oftener especially to Jeff" (*Correspondence*, I, 95–96).

2. WW responded: "Jeff asks me if I go to hospitals as much as ever. If my letters home don't show it, you don't get 'em. I feel sorry sometimes after I have sent them, I have said so much about hospitals, & so mournful" (*Correspondence*, I, 96).

3. Concerned that Jeff might suffer one of his occasional bouts of depression, WW attempted to place his brother's seeming bad fortune in the largest of contexts: "You must not mind the failure of the sewer bills, &c. &c. It don't seem to me it makes so much difference about worldly successes (beyond just enough to eat & drink, and shelter, in the moderatest limits) any more, since the last four months of my life especially, & that merely to *live*, & have one fair meal a day, is *enough*—but then you have a family, & that makes a difference" (*Correspondence*, I, 96).

4. See Letter 5.

5. See Letter 18.

calls it and has overworked herself.[6] I dont think that she ought to do so, and so I tell her but she always answers that it's got to be done and that there is no one but her to do it, &c Mary and Louisa[7] have gone home   They went Thursday last. Mother worked quite hard while they were here which may help account for the rheumatism in a measure. Mat is as jolly and good as ever. I am glad that she has no work from New York as twould be too much for her. Although she often speaks of writing you, yet she takes it out in talking, but she always wants to be remembered to you   Hattie is just the same little Harem-scarem and joyous little thing that she ever is. If she can only get out in the open air 'tis all she wants. It appears to be perfect pleasure to her, she dont seem to care about seeing anybody or going to any place, only get out in the air, that is all. Twould amuse you to see her when I go home, she seems to be glad enough, and always looks at me with an expression "well you've come and you are all right" but otherwise with the utmost indifference, and when I tell her to come and see me she says "what do I want to see you for" or at other times "What are you going to do with me." You would be pleased to see how finely she is growing, seemingly perfect health   We have heard from George but twice since he left home. I wish we could do so oftener. Have not had a letter from Han since I wrote you

Affectionately Jeff.

[25]

Brooklyn, N. Y. May 2nd 1863

Dear Walt,

In your letter to Mother you say that you have written a letter to the Eagle and want me when it is publis[hed] to send you some copies.[1] I have neglected writing you thinking every

6. LVVW overworked herself compulsively. Some years before in one of her own letters to WW she remarked, "i had A pery [*sic*] bad cold and coughf when Jeffy wrote and had been cleaning house and worked very hard but i am well now" (May 3, 1860? [Trent]). See also Letter 47.

7. See Letter 23.

1. WW's letter never appeared in the *Eagle*. Miller thinks it was eventually submitted to the *Brooklyn Daily Union* (*Correspondence*, I, 105, and 95,

day that it would appear and that I would be able to advise you
that I had sent them (Eagles) and the pictures as you wanted. I
now begin to think that it will hardly be printed but still I will
keep a lookout for it and if it does will send them to you at once.
Do you wish me to send the pictures without the papers?

Mr Lane[2] received your letter on Thursday morning and
sent you $5. the same day and to day he sent you $6 more. I
should not wonder if we were able to drop you a few $ every
now and then, right along   I hope so any way. Everything is
going on finely at home. Mother is quite well and Mat is as
usual well and hard at work. Sis is growing like a weed and as
wild as a hawk. To day Mat happened to look out in front and
found her trying by force of arms, to drive a little boy, bigger
than she was however, off the front stoop. They say that she
was wonderfull indignat at being stopped. She seems to remember you and is very anxious that I should always remember to write you that she has been a nice girl

We do not hear much from George. I suppose that he is
farther away from mail communication than he has been here-
tofore. In his last letter he seemed to be glad to get away
from Va.[3] and I dont blame him. Andrew, I think, is getting
better, slowly, I dont think that he takes very good care of
himself even yet. If he would I am sure that he would get better
rapidly   We have not heard from Han since the letter that I
sent you, I suppose she is about the same   Mother speaks of
sending for her &c and then says she hardly knows what to do.
Tis rather a puzzling question I confess. I hope however that
she will come home herself before long. It certainly is a great
relief not to be cursed with letters from Heyde every few days.

I suppose, dear Walt that you will have more to do in the
Hospitals than ever pretty soon. I hardly can see how you can
stand seeing so much of the heart-breaking   I certainly could
not do it. I am sure it would make me sick enough to die. Last

n. 3). In addition to requesting ten copies of the *Eagle*, WW asked Jeff for "5
more of my pictures, (the big ones in last edition 'Leaves'), & a couple of the
photographs carte visites (the smaller ones,)" (*Correspondence*, I, 95).

2. See Letter 9.

3. On April 22 George wrote Jeff, "Kentucky is the most beautiful Country I ever saw,   the people seem much more inteligent, and every way better, than in any other part of the South I have ever been. I like Ky first
rate . . .   there is none of that devilish, Virginia mud to travell through"
(Loving, p. 92).

Thursday I met Bill Hart.[4] He is Major in the 88th N. Y. V. and had been hurt at Kelleys ford. He seemed very glad to see me and said had he known that you were in Washington he certainly should have seen you before this. I gave him your address and he will call on you when he goes through Washington on his return. He looks better than he did when he used to be around Brooklyn. Monday A. M.   Yesterday Andrew was at the house   he, I think, is somewhat better. Everybody else is getting along as usual, and all send their love. Write.

Affectionately Jeff.

[26]

Brooklyn, N. Y. May 9th 1863

Dear Walt

Although I know Mr Lane[1] intends to write you to-day and send you a little money yet I thought I would jot you a note. My main object is to ask you if you can possibly hear anything of Lane's nephew (or boy as he calls him) as he has always been with him and Lane loves him like a son)   He belongs to the 20th Conn. and was in the 12th Army Corps under Gen Birney[2]   The letter of his Company I forget but think it was K. Lane is quite cast down about him, mostly from not hearing from him at all. The boys name is "Horace G. Tarr."[3]

    4. See Letter 8. Recently promoted to major, William G. Hart was granted several leaves of absence from March 24, 1863, through June 1863. He had received a spinal injury at Kelly's Ford, a camp near Falmouth, Virginia.
    1. See Letter 9.
    2. Jeff seems to be in error here. Major General David Bell Birney (1825–64) commanded divisions at Chancellorsville and Gettysburg, both places where the Twentieth Connecticut Volunteers fought, but he never commanded in the Twelfth Army Corps. At this time he commanded the First Division, Third Army Corps, Army of the Potomac, while the Twentieth Connecticut Volunteers was in the Twelfth Army Corps, Second Brigade, First Division, under the command of Colonel Samuel Ross (1820?–80).
    3. Horace G. H. Tarr (1844–?) had just been promoted from private to sergeant major of Company K. His regiment fought at Chancellorsville, Virginia, May 1–5, 1863, but he was not injured. Evidently Tarr became a lifelong friend of Jeff and WW (see Letter 100).

Dear Walt, if you should by any chance or inquiry come across him or any news from him wont you please write Lane for I feel real sorry to see him so cast down. I see by some of the papers that quite a number of the 20th Conn. are at Washington in hospital

I feel thankful indeed that George did not have to go through the dangers of this battle although we know not what is in store for him where he is.[4] I do so hope he will be spared to us and that he will come home without ever being injired.

Everything is moving the same as usual at home of course we all feel pretty well down-hearted at the news but then we try to look on it in the most favorable light. God only knows what will be the next. I had certainly made up my mind that we should meet with partial success certainly, but it seems otherwise[5]

I suppose you are overcrowded with work just now I cannot see Walt how you can stand it. I am sure that I could never get used to all the scenes of pain and horror that you have to witness Tis well though that you can do so, for I know that you are doing a great deal of good.

I suppose you do not have much time to write home We do not hear from you but seldom now. I suppose however that as long as we dont hear, everything is going as usual with you. We have not heard from either Han or George since I last wrote you I am getting along first rate just now, make quite a little money and every thing goes well Mother and Mat and Sis and all are well and send love. Write me Walt

Affectionately Jeff

4. George was encamped near Lexington, Kentucky (Loving, pp. 91-93).

5. Jeff is depressed by the results of the Battle of Chancellorsville, where a Union army of 130,000 men led by General Joseph Hooker was defeated by General Robert E. Lee's 60,000 Confederates. For Northerners, the only encouraging news was that Lee sacrificed 11,000 men—about as many as Hooker lost—and Stonewall Jackson, Lee's superb general, was killed.

[27]

Brooklyn, N. Y. May 12th 1863
Dear Bro. Walt,
Mr. Lane recd. your letter this morning[1] and would have probably answered it to-day but has had to go out in the country (to Jamaica) to make some arrangements for a visit that the Common Council and Water Board intend to make over the works. In his behalf I return thanks for your kindness as regards Horace.[2] Mr Lane however has heard from him He was in the thickest of the fight but was not harmed although he had some pretty narrow escapes He says that some of the rebs took pretty good aim at him

Dear Walt, your letter has given me a great deal of pleasure, so it has Mr Lane in regard to Hooker and his movements.[3] I am so glad to understand that he is going in again. Tis sure that he could not have been badly whipped or he could not have done that, And Lee as you say must have been badly hurt or he would never let Hooker come across the river without molestation I wish you could send me letters oftener. I like to get your ideas of matters and also hear what the people down in Wash'tn think. Twas rather blue here for a few days, almost every one thought that it was another bad defeat.

We are all thriving as usual. Mother is about the same as ever, somewhat lame with the rheumatism but not much the rest are all well. Andrew had a letter yesterday from Jim Cornwell,[4] enclosing him $50 and telling him to come immediately

1. Jeff refers to WW's letter of May 11 (*Correspondence*, I, 98–101). For Lane, see Letter 9.
2. Some casualties from the Twentieth Connecticut Volunteers were in Washington hospitals, and WW had promised "to make immediate inquiry" to determine whether Horace Tarr, the nephew of Moses Lane, was among them (*Correspondence*, I, 99).
3. WW had advised: "You there north must not be so disheartened about Hooker's return to this side of the Rappahannock and supposed failure. The blow struck at Lee & the rebel sway in Virginia, & generally at Richmond & Jeff Davis, . . . is in my judgment the heaviest and most staggering they have yet got from us, & has not only hit them nearer where they live than all Maclellan ever did, but all that has been levelled at Richmond during the war" (*Correspondence*, I, 99).
4. James H. Cornwell was a first lieutenant in the 158th New York Regiment of Infantry. He was the quartermaster in charge of building fortifications at New Bern, North Carolina (Loving, p. 96, n. 5).

to Suffolk,[5] at the bottom was a transportation order from
Frank Spinola.[6] Cornwell said if he did not come to give the
money to his (Cornwells) wife, but to come sure if possible. I
think Andrew very foolish not to go, as Ruggles[7] says he certainly will never get well of his throat here. Andrew was to
come for me and we were going to see the Dr. to-day abt his
going but he did not come and mother thinks that he has concluded not to go. I think it would be much better for him to
go   I think it would be better for his health, dont you? They
must intend to give him a pretty good show or they would not
send "surely come" for him. We do not here from either Han
or George do you? Hattie is the same as ever ever wanting to
be out doors and wonders if Uncle Walt will never come and
take her out on "Ft. Greene."[8] She seems to remember you first
rate and George too. What abt the pictures, shall I send them?
The letter does not come out in the Eagle and probably will not
but to make again sure I will call to-morrow and look over their
file for some weeks back to see if I have possibly overlooked it.
All send their love

Affectionately Jeff

[28]

Brooklyn, N. Y. May 27th 1863
Dear Walt,
    Mother recived your letter of last Tuesday, this morning[1]
We were glad to hear from you   indeed I began to think that
the hospitals had got the better of you, as we had not heard in
so long. I mailed you a letter from Mr Lane[2] to-day containing
some money. I suppose Mr Lane would have written you before but he met with quite a serious accident last Sunday   His

5. As Loving notes, "it remains somewhat of a mystery as to why Andrew was beckoned only as far as Suffolk." Perhaps Andrew was to travel to
Suffolk by boat, at which point Cornwell could have met him and conducted
him to New Bern by land. Andrew never made the trip (Loving, p. 166).
    6. See Letter 6. Spinola, a newly appointed brigadier general, was the
first commander of the 158th New York Regiment of Infantry.
    7. See Letter 18.
    8. See Letter 17.

    1. *Correspondence*, I, 102–04.
    2. See Letter 9.

little boy, abt 5 years old, fell from the balcony down in the area on the stone steps and hurt his head pretty bad. The Dr's hardly know how bad he is hurt, but think he will recover. Dr Ruggles[3] who was called in says that it is hardly possible to say how it will go with him for abt 10 days   It is a great blow to Mr Lane as he was his favorite child. I am in hopes that it is not so serious as we at first supposed. With us every thing is the same as usual. Mother is quite well   Mattie is well yet but how long she will continue so is a question,[4] she is getting along first rate. she has a young girl to help her do the house work and is in the best of spirits   Hattie is getting along finely growing well and has perfect health. She has grown wonderfully since you left. I think you would hardly know her. A few days since she had quite a bad fall, or rather it might have been one but she luckily escaped without doing herself much harm She fell in the yard and hit her forehead on the little curb stones that are set on edge along the sides of the walks. She cut quite a gash in her forehead but it has entirely healed up and indeed hardly leaves any mark now

We had a letter from George written abt the time that yours was[5]   I answered it at once. When you write to George tell him that I write him quite often although he does not seem to get them. Andrew thinks he will go down to Newbern the last of this week. He will go down with Jim Cornwell.[6] Andrew is going to take charge of the building of some fortifications I believe. Andrew's health is not good although I think he is better than he was and I think he would get well easy enough if he took better care of himself and did not drink so much. His family are all well. We or rather Mother had a <u>letter</u> from Heyde the other day reading thus   "Your letter received. Han is better to-day than she has been for months—Charlie" That was all there was in it. Rather short and sweet wasn't it.

We are having what might be called first-class weather here to-day, athoug[h] we have had that same cold, damp North east wind that you spoke of   Everything in the country looks well and I guess that we shall have large crops unless

3. See Letter 18.
4. Mattie was in the last month of her pregnancy at this time.
5. Jeff apparently refers to George's letter of May 15 (Loving, pp. 93–94).
6. See Letter 27.

something unlikely occurs. We are anxiously expecting to hear
from Vicksburg and begin to fear that it is going to turn out
like the Victories of the Army of the Potomac although Grant
aint in the habit of doing such things either.[7] I hope and pray
that he may be successful   I cannot agree with you Walt in
relation to the President. I think that he is not a man for the
times, not big enough   He dont seem to have even force
enough to stop bickerings between his own Cabinet and
Generals nor force enough to do as he thinks best.[8] We begin
also to fear that Hooker did not win a <u>very great victory</u> either
or he would hardly lie idle so long during the best part of the
year.[9] No, A. L.[10] is not the man and I hardly know if we have
one that is equal to the thing. Write me   you have almost
forgotten me. All send their love,

Affectionately Jeff.

[29]

Brooklyn, N. Y. June 13 63

Dear brother Walt,

I received your letter yesterday morning.[1] I am extremely
glad to hear that your health continues so good. Walt I have
thought considerable of the idea that you speak of, that of your

7. The siege of Vicksburg had begun May 22, 1863, and Jeff was apparently afraid that, win or lose, it would be as costly and indecisive a battle as those during the previous nine months at Bull Run, Antietam, Fredericksburg, and Chancellorsville.

8. WW enclosed the preceding three sentences in parentheses. Perhaps in a lost letter WW conveyed to Jeff ideas about President Lincoln similar to those he offered to his friends Nathaniel Bloom and John F. S. Gray in March: "I think well of the President. He has a face like a hoosier Michael Angelo, so awful ugly it becomes beautiful . . . . Mr. Lincoln keeps a fountain of first-class practical telling wisdom. I do not dwell on the supposed failures of his government; he has shown, I sometimes think, an almost supernatural tact in keeping the ship afloat at all" (*Correspondence*, I, 82–83). Despite this and similar remarks, the poet's faith in Lincoln did occasionally waver. See *Correspondence*, I, 174, n. 19.

9. For Jeff and WW's struggle to understand the outcome of the Battle of Chancellorsville, see Letters 26 and 27.

10. Abraham Lincoln.

1. WW's letter of about June 11 is not extant.

giving lectures[2]   I fear that you would not meet with that success that you deserve. Mr Lane[3] and I talked about the matter and both came to the conclusion that it would be much better if you could be appointed dispensing agent, or something of that kind, for some of the numerous aid societies,[4] and he said that he would go and see Storrs[5] and some other of the big guns of those societies in this city and see if it could not be done. What do you think about it. Do you think it could be accomplished.? Everything is going along well with us at home. Mother is not troubled hardly any with her rheumatism and I am in hopes she will get the best of it entirely. Mattie is well and in first-rate spirits, she often speaks of you and says she would like very much to see you. Hattie is growing as nicely as it is possibly for a child to grow. You would love dearly to take a stroll with her now I know   Andrew has not yet gone to Newbern[6] but thinks that they will get off the fore part of the coming week. Jess and Ed are just the same as ever. We were all much pleased with the idea that you would come home to make us a visit, I do so hope that you can carry it out.[7] do try Walt, for me   all want to see you very much

I am glad you wrote Mother about the way in which you board for I have often and often thought how you was doing in

2. In a letter to his mother on June 9 WW wrote: "I think something of commencing a series of lectures & readings &c. through different cities of the north, to supply myself with funds for my Hospital & Soldiers visits—as I do not like to be beholden to the medium of others" (*Correspondence*, I, 109).
3. See Letter 9.
4. On June 22 WW was still firmly committed to this lecturing project. As he wrote Jeff, he hoped it would enable him "to continue my Hospital ministrations, on a more free handed scale—As to the Sanitary Commissions & the like, I am sick of them all, & would not accept any of their berths—you ought to see the way the men as they lie helpless in bed turn away their faces from the sight of these Agents" (*Correspondence*, I, 110–11). Jeff also had questioned the value of the Sanitary Commission (see Letter 10).
5. The Reverend Dr. Richard S. Storrs was a member of Brooklyn's St. Nicholas Society. WW saved a section of the *Brooklyn Eagle*, December 11, 1861, containing a short account of Storrs's lecture to this society on "A Just War—Its Relations to a Nations [*sic*] Highest Development" (Feinberg).
6. See Letter 27.
7. In his letter of June 9 WW indicated that he would try to return home to get "some MSS & books, & the trunk, &c" (*Correspondence*, I, 107). He did not make the trip until November.

that respect and I sometimes thought I ought to do something

in the matter, precisely what or how I never could tell. I am real glad my dear Walt that you are among such good people. I hope it will be in the power of some of our family to return their Kindness some day. I'm sure twould be done with a heartfelt gratitude   Tis pleasant, too, to think, that there are still people of that kind left.[8] You, of course, still continue your hospital "practice" as you might call it. I wish we were able to send you more money than we do but almost everyone you meet is a contributor to some of the aid societies and that is the way in which they are (thinking) doing good

Well, Walt, you and I cannot agree in regard to "Uncle Abe"[9]   I cannot think that he is the man for the place or he would have surrounded himself with men that could do something. He lends himself to the speculators, in all the ways that it can be done. He says "yes" to the last man or "No" as that man wants him to. Everything he does reminds me of an old woman. I hope that the country will last long enough for this damned war to fall through   It seems nothing but an immense bubble, only of a desperate character

We have not heard from Han lately   I wrote you that we had had a letter from George. I fear for George now   I am afraid that they have sent the 51st to Vicksburgh.[10] I do hope that George may escape but I fear not   It seems as if he had been so lucky that it could not continue till the end. If you can learn anything of the 51st write me will you   All send their love, good night dear brother

Yours affectionately Jeff.

8. Because of the generosity of William Douglas O'Connor and his wife, WW had not paid for his meals in Washington (*Correspondence*, I, 108).

9. See Letter 28.

10. On June 4 the Fifty-first New York Regiment, as part of the Ninth Corps, left Stanford, Kentucky, to support the Union forces near Vicksburg. They arrived about June 15 (Loving, p. 97). As late as June 30 WW suspected that George was near Vicksburg, but he had no certain knowledge (*Correspondence*, I, 111).

[30]

Brooklyn, N. Y. July 7th 1863

Dear Walt

    Enclosed please find $10 thus contributed

        $5 from Jas. P. Kirkwood[1]

        $1   "   John D Martin[2]

        $1   "   Chas Botsford[3]

        and $3 from self.

We are awfully pleased and excited at the war news. Feel as if the man[4] had been appointed that was thinking less of political affairs than of licking the rebs. We are just getting news of the surrender of Vicksburgh. Hope to God that it is true. Bully for Meade![5] He has not only licked the rebs but the peace party headed by McClellan.[6] Hope that he will not let them off but will poke it into them   How do you get along? I suppose you hardly have time to write me. I sent you a letter containing $15 last week[7]   did you get it?

    Nothing new at home   I did not have any "time" on the 4th so I send you this money that I <u>might</u> have spent. do the little sums that we send you enable you to do any good.

    Dear brother I am in a tremendious hurry, and you must excuse my letter. Mother sent you a letter a day or two since. Mattie and the babies[8] are first-rate. Mother quite well. rest all right. Will write you again in a few days

affectionately Jeff

  1. See Letter 6.

  2. See Letter 11.

  3. See Letter 9.

  4. Probably Grant. As Jeff explains, he was thinking specifically of the fall of Vicksburg, but he was also encouraged by news concerning the Gettysburg campaign.

  5. Major General George Gordon Meade (1815–72) succeeded Joseph Hooker as commander of the Army of the Potomac in June 1863, and led the army to victory at Gettysburg (July 1–3, 1863).

  6. General George Brinton McClellan was general-in-chief of the army of the United States from November 1861, until July 1862, when he was replaced by General Henry W. Halleck. In 1864, when McClellan ran for the presidency, the Democratic party split between war Democrats and peace Democrats. To satisfy the war Democrats McClellan was nominated; to satisfy the peace Democrats C. L. Vallandigham and his followers were allowed to draft the platform. Jeff evidently considered the entire Democratic party as "the peace party."

  7. This letter is not extant.

  8. Jessie Louisa, hereafter the "Sis" of Jeff's letters, was born June 17.

[Brooklyn, N.Y.] July 8th 1863

Dear Walt,

Mr Lane[1] is again very anxious about his boy, his name is Horace G. Tarr,[2] and is Sergeant Major of the 20th Reg. of Connecticut Vol. If by chance you should hear anything of him will you please write. His Reg. belonged to the 12th army Corps, and I think were in the hottest of the fight. I sent you a letter last week with $15 in it and another yesterday with $10.[3] Did you get them both? We are all well at home. The rejoicing in New York is sincere and almost universal and yet a few, (and yet only a few when compared with the immense city) who try to find some reason why Lee should have been whipped. Copperheads are getting out of circulation being laid up for a future contingency. Hope to hear from you soon. Dont forget me.

Yours truly Jeff

[32]

Shortly after the Union victory at Gettysburg, the Northern cause was damaged by terrible riots in New York (July 13-16, 1863). Approximately 50,000 people, mainly Irish immigrants, battled police over the application of the Conscription Act. The Irish, who made up over half of the foreign-born population of New York and served as the main source of cheap labor, feared competition from the newly emancipated slaves. With justification, the Irish felt that the draft laws favored the rich. Many Irishmen earned no more than $500 per year and so could not raise the $300 necessary to buy their way out of the draft. Even the Whitmans were worried about how they would obtain $300 if Jeff were drafted, although in the

1. See Letter 9.
2. See Letter 26. Although his regiment fought at Gettysburg July 1-3, Tarr was not injured.
3. The letter that contained fifteen dollars is not extant. For the letter containing ten dollars, see Letter 30.

following year the family did manage to raise $400 "to pay for a substitute" for Jeff (Loving, p. 130).

A primary cause of the riots was the foolhardy administration of the draft. The War Department ordered it at a time when the city was nearly stripped of defenses: Governor Horatio Seymour had sent 16,000 soldiers from New York City to check Lee's thrust into Pennsylvania. The draft was held on a Saturday, thus giving citizens a work-free Sunday to build up resentment. Names of those selected were published in the papers, and it was clear enough that the poor were disproportionately represented. Finally, the draft was conducted on a citywide basis. As Jeff realized, it should have been handled district-by-district, which was exactly what orders had suggested U.S. Provost Marshal General James Barnet Fry should do.

The riot caused roughly 500 deaths. Particularly vicious attacks were made against blacks, and one black orphanage was set ablaze. Police were able to protect only the lower half of Manhattan as the mobs attacked banks, newspaper offices, and other symbols of wealth and power. The police, badly outnumbered, were supported by Jeff's friend Julius W. Adams who led the Brooklyn National Guard in defense of the offices of the New York Times and Tribune. Given such violence, Jeff's vindictive comments about the Irish become more understandable.

The political response to the draft was varied. Fernando Wood, a congressman whose support came largely from Irish immigrants, denounced the draft. Governor Seymour, who regarded the draft as unconstitutional, was accused of aiding the rioters. George Opdyke, the mayor, had little sympathy for the rioters and vetoed a $2,500,000 Conscription Exemption Bond Bill which would have provided $300 for each drafted man to buy an exemption.

The riots were stopped only after eleven New York regiments and one from Michigan were rushed to the city at a time when they might have been pursuing Lee. General-in-Chief Henry W. Halleck ordered General George G. Meade to pursue Lee no further than the Rappahannock because more troops might be needed to enforce the draft. After the riots were over, James R. Gilmore of the Tribune urged Lincoln to investigate the causes of the riot, but the president refused, supposedly saying, "One rebellion at a time is about as much as we can conveniently handle."

Dear brother Walt,

We have passed through a wonderful week for our New York. A week that I think will eventually be productive of great good to our country, but had at a fearful cost. From my own personal observations I think that the newspapers would give one the most perverted kind of an idea of the riot. The big type, the general "skeery" look of the articles, was something that did not make its appearance on the public face. I guess the only wonderfully frightened men were Opdike and Seymour, if we perhaps except the Copperhead dem.'s that incited the rioters on and then deserted them.[1] Opdike though was awfully frightened. In the flashy, sensation style the papers were all far from the truth, ahead, but when it comes to the killed, they are fa[r]ther from the truth, behind. Undoubtedly we shall never know the full number but I have it from the very best authority—an eye witness of most of the fights, that there are now more than 400 rioters that have paid their lives for their plunder   The papers are not allowed to publish this[2]   I suppose it is much better not to let it be known, but the lesson was fearful and thorough to these men. Yesterday I saw them taking coffins out of the shanties on 2nd Av. piling them on carts and driving right to the cemetery   I understand they have been doing this ever since Monday night. The police covered themselves with glory. They certainly made a splendid fight. They deserve great credit. God only knows where the city of New York would have been had we had Wood's police.[3] They did well also in Brooklyn. The scoundrels thought to commence operations in Brooklyn, and did set fire to a couple of grain elevators, but the thing has gone no further. I think that rioting in these parts has received its quietus mostly from that Reg of Michigan boys that the War Dept. were kind enough to send us. I hear that they made fearful havoc with the irish ranks. Twas better so—they did not have that "citizen feeling" that our militia would have had. The only feeling I have is that I fear that they did not kill enough of 'em Walt. I'm perfectly

1. WW enclosed this sentence in parentheses. For months the Copperhead press, especially the *Day Book, Express,* and *Freeman's Journal,* had been attacking the draft.
2. WW enclosed the words "there are now . . . this" in parentheses.
3. Fernando Wood was a former mayor of New York City.

rabid on an Irishman   I hate them worse than I thought I could hate anything. Their conduct for the past week has made me do it. The papers say that the draft is to go on in a day or two in New York & Brooklyn   this is right, I think, and will be a victory over a certain portion of the rebel army. I want, if possible to make a suggestion to this man Fry or whoever has char[g]e of this thing, of a manner in which, I think, the draft can be enforced in these larger cities without endangering riots. My idea is this, to take a certain portion of the city, say certain wards that make a district, not too large, and make the draft, carry the thing out complete, get the men in the field and every thing done before drafting in any other part of the same city. The advantages, I think, would be these, you could get along with a much smaller police (military) force as their would be no tendency to mob except in the one district, and when (and this I think would be the great point.) you got all through, the men in the field, the remainder of this whole district would be on the side of the draft and would help enforce it in the next, so that in a short time a majority of the city would want it enforced in the parts where it had not yet been done. The same should be done in Brooklyn   Being the first thing of the kind almost that has ever happened in this country I think a little policy would not come amiss. Another thing I think bad is the publishing of the list of names of the drafted men. This should not be done   I have reasons to suppose that had this not been done in New York they would not have had this organized mob headed by a drafted democratic Alderman[4] and a lot of drafted irishman. Would it be possible for you to do anything in this matter. I mean suggest these ideas to those having the matter in charge. It strikes me Walt that if they could be carried out twould save a great deal of innocent blood   I go in for enforcing the draft at all hasards, and that too without giving in the least to the mob, but if a little politician thing of this kind would help, I think it ought to be done. Won't you try to do something about the matter. Of course all that can be done would be to bring it to the notice of the right parties. Twould defeat the entire thing by giving it publicity. My theory is that before the people found out the thing drafting would be over, and like the fellow that had the tooth out

4. Unidentified.

when he had taken laughing gas they would think it a good joke

Yesterdays Herald stated that the 9th Corps were sent in pursuit of Johnson. To-days Times says that they have arrived back in Kentucky. Tis hard to say which is right, perhaps both—more likely neither.⁵—We want to hear from George much.—Heard from Han 'tother day. She was getting better. heard through Heyde.—Abt. the $300. I'm a little afraid that I shant be able to raise it through Mr Lane as he has been a little unfortunate lately, but still I keep a bold front⁶ I lately got a position where I am getting $90 per month. (through Mr Lane, Tis on the Water Works) This will be permanent (as long as Mr Lane is here, perhaps for years.) and with such a certain prospect of paying it back in a few months, I think that George would lend me the money. I, by sailing very close, think I could pay him in five months. Dont you think he would be willing? Walt will you write me at once I want to hear from you, often. All well at home, first-rate. Hope you will come home soon.

[33]

Brooklyn, N. Y. Tuesday Aug 4th [1863]¹

Dear brother Walt,

It has been a long time since I last wrote you, longer than I meant it should be, but I have been very busy indeed Everything is going about as usual with us at home. We do not hear

5. Shortly after the surrender of Vicksburg on July 4, 1863, the Ninth Corps (including George) engaged in an eleven-day campaign which pushed the army of Confederate General Joseph E. Johnston back through Jackson, Mississippi, which the Union force occupied on July 17, 1863.

6. For Lane, see Letter 9. The $300 Jeff hoped to raise would enable him to buy his way out of the service if he were drafted. WW wrote to his mother on July 15: "if it should so happen that Jeff should be drafted—of course he could not go, without its being the downfall almost of our whole family, as you may say, Mat & his young ones, & a sad blow to you too, mother, & to all—I didn't see any other way than to try to raise the $300, mostly by borrowing if possible of Mr Lane—mother, I have no doubt I shall make a few hundred dollars by the lectures I shall certainly commence soon . . . & I could lend that am't to Jeff to pay it back" (*Correspondence*, I, 117–18).

1. The year is added in another hand, probably WW's.

from George. I feel quite anxious about him and watch the paper quite close for something about the 51st but do not meet with any success.[2] Andrew is not getting any better I fear. I think that he will hardly get well again Walt. The doctor[s] all say that he must go out from the seashore if he wants to get well. I am sure that it would be a good thing for him if he could do so for a while. Do you think of any way that it could be done. As for myself I am over head and heels in debt (borrowed money) which I am striving hard to pay up and hardly know how I can do anything worthy of being called help for him. He is badly off. He can hardly speak, nor eat anything, but worse than all I guess that his home comforts are not much. I dont think Nancy has the faculty of fixing things to eat for a sick man. Andrew still goes to the Navy Yard and thereby gets his pay, but I hardly thinks he does anything. Sometime he is much better than others but as a general thing he is mighty badly off. I wish you would think about the matter Walt, and let us hear what your idea is   Andrew wants to go but dont know where to go or how to leave his family. Mother I see is very much excited about him. Mother is getting along about as usual not quite as well perhaps, the warm,—hot,—wethre has a bad effect upon Mother. I dont think she looks as well as she did a month ago   Mattie is getting along first rate. The baby, as a matter of course, is cross,—cross as thunder—but Mat is patient and hard working and so gets along quite well. Hattie is also showing the effects of a so long continued [term?] of hot days and is cross and fretful. She often wishes that you would come and take her on fort Greene.[3] She seems to think that that is your mission. The baby is growing finely and is getting to look almost like Hattie did at her age. Her hair is getting lighter and I guess will be about the color of mine

The enclosed $2 is sent $1 by John D. Martin[4] and $1 by Henry Carlow.[5] I wish you would write me a Hospital letter. I think I can get some money on it. Any way Walt so long as the

2. As part of the Ninth Corps, George's regiment had fought in Mississippi under William T. Sherman during July and was now returning to Cincinnati where it arrived August 14 (Loving, pp. 97, 100–101).

3. See Letter 17.

4. See Letter 11.

5. See Letter 10.

Spondulix[6] comes. A "Mr Fulton, of the New York Times"[7] came some time since and got your address and again a few days since and wanted me when I wrote you to ask you if you had received a letter from him. He said that he had written you but had not received a reply and [was] afraid you had not received it

Do you have any idea where the 9 Corps is. I guess down in Miss. yet I think not hearing from George hurts Mother about as much as any thing. I too feel pretty anxious

Ruggles[8] thinks that you could make a good thing by writing letters to the Times, better than the lectures.[9] Write me, Walt.

Jeff

[34]

Brooklyn Sept 5 1863[1]

Dear Walt,

Mother gave me the enclosed letter to send you some days since but I forgot to mail it till now. We received your letter [2] last night. The money from George came all safe I sent you another letter from George about last Monday, also sent George a letter with the money in it. Andrew has been away in

6. This slang term, more often spelled "spondulicks," means money or cash. For a similar usage, see Mark Twain, *The Adventures of Huckleberry Finn*, Ch. xiii.

7. Unidentified.

8. See Letter 18.

9. After having contemplated giving lectures for several weeks (see Letters 29 and 32), WW took Ruggles' advice and wrote "Washington in the Hot Season" and "Letter from Washington" for the *New York Times* (*Correspondence*, I, 136, n. 14, and I, 140, n. 27).

1. Dating Letters 34 and 35 is a problem. In Letter 35 Jeff incorrectly says that September 5 is a Wednesday; actually the fifth was a Saturday. One might assume, then, that both letters were written on Wednesday, September 2, if it were not for WW's comment that he received letters from Jeff dated the third (*Correspondence*, I, 143). Perhaps both letters were written on Thursday, September 3.

2. WW to LVVW, September 1, 1863 (*Correspondence*, I, 139–41).

the country but returned yesterday, very much worse.[3] He came in to see me this morning and it has made me feel quite down-spirited. He can neither eat nor drink without the greatest agony. He looks very thin and emaciated. I think that if I had the same sickness that I could get the best of it,[4] but Andrew seems to put his whole faith in thinking that some Dr can give him something that will set him all straight. I am going to see the Dr with him this P.M. and I also want him to consult Ruggles[5] if he will. I fear the worst for Andrew. I wish you was on here. I think that your advice would be a great thing for him. Cant you come. You speak of coming home. I wish you could come just now. Mother is of course much worried about him. Nancy dont seem to amount to much when trouble comes. You would hardly know Andrew. He is thin weak and generally sickly looking   We have heard nothing from Han lately that I know of   Mother and Heyde keep writing letters to one another but what about I know not. At last the great draft has come and gone and I was not one of the elected. I feel thankful   In our ward the screws were put rather tight. out of a little over 3000 names they drew 1056 nearly one in three, while in other wards the proportion was 1 in 6 and 1 in 7 and in the 9th ward 1 in 10. Tom Geere,[6] Tom McEvoy,[7] Pat Hughes[8] two or three in Amermans[9] house, were all hit. It seems to have

3. In her letter to WW of August 31 (?) LVVW wrote: "Andrew has gone to place called freehold . . . he went last monday as far as suffron station" (Trent). Andrew's drinking with Jim Cornwell on this trip apparently worsened his health.

4. Jeff was not merely making an off-hand statement praising his own will and constitution. To judge from scattered references in Hannah's undated letters, Jeff was very sick for a short time in the mid-1850s (Heyde—LC). While it is impossible to determine the exact nature of Jeff's illness, he seems to have suffered from severe depression, loss of appetite, and eventually emaciation. Since this was a period of vocational crisis for Jeff, the symptoms suggest that his illness was psychosomatic.

5. See Letter 18.

6. Tom Geer, a reporter, lived on Myrtle Avenue.

7. Two Thomas McEvoys are listed in the Brooklyn directory: a driver who lived on Navy Street, and a worker in morocco leather who lived on Front Street.

8. Seven people named Patrick Hughes are listed in the 1862/63 Brooklyn directory.

9. Nicholas Amerman was a grocer on Myrtle Avenue. In her letter of May 3 (?), 1860, LVVW noted that she was "in debt to ammerman about 10 dollars" (Trent).

avoided the Water Works, only one or two out of the whole 40 or 50 employed were hit while in Husted & Carls store[10] 7 out of 10 were taken. If this is the last of it I feel thankful but I believe Uncle Abe left off some on account of Seymour,[11] if so I suppose there will be another spurt. However we wont worry till the time comes   The enclosed $5 is from Mr Moses Lane.[12]

We have what remains of [three?] old Reg. on the hills by our house. They are fine looking and well behaved men, and look as if they would do their duty any where. If you was home you could have grand times talking with them   One Reg. is from Min. one from Mich. and one from Ohio. What do you think about coming to Brooklyn   I think you better, for awhile any way. I wish you would write to Andrew. He seems to feel wonderfully cast down   Aint the Administrat[ion] got wit enough to see that now is the hour to end the war by whipping the rebels. Dont they know enough to know that unless it is ended in 6 months they will have a hard time to get men to fill the places of what they have now. I fear not.

Jeff

[35]

Brooklyn Wednesday Eve Sept 5/63[1]

Dear Walt,

I mailed you a letter to-day (also one from Mother) containing $5 from Mr Lane.[2] I write to-night mostly to speak about Andrew. He called at the office this afternoon and I went around with him to see the Dr that he has been doctoring with, a Dr Hull.[3] The Dr went through the usual forms and then went on to tell what ailed him ending with giving him a lot of medicines and telling him if that did not cure him to call again in a day or two. From the moment my eye rested on the Dr I

10. Husted & Carll, a carpet store at 295 Fulton Street.
11. See Letter 32.
12. See Letter 9.

1. See Letter 34.
2. See Letter 9.
3. Dr. A. Cooke Hull had his office on Joralemon Street in Brooklyn.

made up my mind that he was a fool, a regular Doctor. I dont think that Andrew will get any good from him

I had previously made an appointment with Dr Ruggles[4] at our office at 4 o'clk, when we returned the Dr was at the office. He talked a long time with Andrew. He told him that it would be perfectly easy to give him a bushel of medicines but that he could think of no medicine that would be likely to do him any good. That he might use alum on his throat but that what would cure him would be to take heart, go in the country again, and to resolve to get well that there was no medicine that would do him so much good as a cheerful mind. The Dr thinks that what made him so much worse while away was that he went just as we had a very decided change of weather and that he somehow took cold. I had a long talk with Dr Ruggles this eve, and he tells me that he thinks that the only thing that will permanently help or cure Andrew is for him to go up in the North west and live either by working a little at his trade or something like it. I asked mother to-day to let him have one of her rooms upstairs for him to sleep in and I intended to see if he could not be nursed up and fed. Mattie has, I think very kindly, volunteered to cook and take care of him, and I feel that he could, in a short time, be fixed up so that he could carry out the Dr's idea. But Mother, says that she cant let him have the room, because it will bring his whole family here.[5] I tell her to send the whole family back again, but she said, that "she cant let him have it and that's the end of it." I think that that she devil the Brown woman[6] has a great influence over Mother, for she is nothing like she was a few months ago about such things. Perhaps it would not do any good but I think it would save his life   Another thing, Jess is failing very rapidly in-deed,[7] he is a mere shadow of what he ought to be and I have not the least doubt in my own mind that it all comes of his not having anything to eat that he can eat. Somehow or another Mother seems to think that she ought to live without spending

---

4. See Letter 18.
5. LVVW wrote WW on September 10 (?) indicating that despite the generous talk of Jeff and Mattie "they would soon get tired of fixing things" for Andrew (Trent).
6. See Letter 5.
7. For more on Jesse's physical and mental decline, see Letter 43.

any money.[8] Even to day she has 25 or $30 in the house and I will bet that all they have for dinner will be a quart of tomats and a few cucumbers, and then Mother wonders why Jess vomits up his meals   However Mother gets them just as good or better than she has herself[9]

[36]

Brooklyn 22nd Sept. 1863

Dear brother Walt,

The enclosed $25 is from my old friend Joseph P. Davis[1] who is Engineering down in Peru. Although he is far away yet he does not forget home. I have written him in some of my letters what you were doing, with short extracts from your letters.

Well Walt it looks as if we had met rather a bad reverse in the West. If Rosecrans[2] is whipped I should hardly think that the United States was large enough to contain the infernal

8. In her letter of September 10 (?), after noting that Andrew's health was "very bad," LVVW complained because Andrew wanted some roast lamb: "i said get a small peice and have it cooked   i told him to have whatever he wanted but to be saving of what he had but to get anything he could eat but Walt it is no use to talk   they just get the very most expensive things lamb is twenty cents per lb" (Trent). Perhaps one of the reasons for LVVW's extreme frugality was her need to keep money aside in case one of the Whitman family members needed to travel to Burlington, Vermont, to rescue Hannah from her husband (Allen, pp. 292–93).

9. This letter has no signature or customary conclusion and may be a fragment.

1. Joseph Phineas Davis (1837–1917) took a degree in civil engineering at Rensselaer Polytechnic Institute in 1856 and then helped build the Brooklyn Water Works until 1861. He was a topographical engineer in Peru from 1861 to 1865, after which he returned to Brooklyn. A lifelong friend of Jeff's, he became city engineer of Boston (1871–80) and completed his distinguished career as chief engineer of the American Telephone and Telegraph Company (1880–1908). For his work with Jeff in St. Louis, see Letters 60, 68, 69.

2. Major General William Stacke Rosecrans (1819–98) performed admirably in the Chattanooga campaign, but his tactical blunders at Chickamauga (September 1863) were disastrous. He was soon relieved of command on the advice of General Grant and Secretary of War Edwin Stanton.

quacks that administer the military arm of our government. I suppose their is at least 30 000 men <u>nibbling</u> around in Kansas and other parts west. Matters that would tumble of their own weight if the army in front of Rosecrans was thouroughly whipped. Tis awful to think of. I mailed you a letter from George a few days since, did you get it.

Mother is abt the same as usual. I think she fails somewhat. I suppose not more than we must expect however. Mattie and the babies are quite well. Hattie is getting to be quite a girl, and the little one is also getting to be quite a youngster. Jess is abt the same, he is not well. He needs good living more than anything I think. Andrew I suppose Mother wrote you about I think that it is unfortunate that he should be so humbuged by the "Italian Dr."[3] but I suppose he would not otherwise have tried to get well at all The Dr. requirs him to pay $180 in 3 installments in <u>advance.</u> He has paid $46 and is now living his 15 days at the "Foriegn Dr's" as a prepairing course, then he is to take certain baths. The whole thing in my opinion is one of the biggest of humbugs. However if Andrew believs in it I suppose it is best to bolster him up in his beliefs.

I shall write you again [in] a few days sending you some more money. till then good bye

affectionately yours Thomas J. Whitman

[37]

Brooklyn 24th Sept 1863

Dear brother Walt,

The enclosed $25 is from Joseph P. Davis[1] making with the $25 sent you last Tuesday $50 from Jo. Now I will give you a statement of the whole affair Last Monday I received a letter

3. Although Jeff repeatedly complained about this doctor (see Letter 40) George and WW were willing to let Andrew experiment with him. On October 16 George wrote LVVW, "I had a letter from Walt, dated Sept. 28th he said that Andrew was considerable better and was Doctoring with a celabrated Italian Doctor in Court St. I dont have much faith in them new fangled foreign Doctors, but if Andrew is realy so much better, it is good encouragement to keep on and give him a fair trial" (Loving, p. 107). Near the end of October Andrew changed to Dr. John H. Brodie who lived on Myrtle Avenue (LVVW to WW, October 30 [?], 1863 [Trent]).

1. See Letter 36.

from W. S. Davis,[2] Jo's brother [at?] Worcester, Mass. saying
that he had received a letter from Joe directing him to send me
$70. $50 to be sent to you and $20 to be expended in buying a
present for young "Joe Probasco."[3] The $25 I sent you on
Tuesday I borrowed of Mr Lane[4] so that I might send it immediately and to day I received a check for the $70. I have paid Mr
Lane the $25 and according to Jo's direction send you the re-
maind[er] of the $50.

Jo's brother, W. S. Davis, is a lawer, in Worcester,[5] with a
large number of acquaintances and I think liberal. I wrote him
a note acknowledging the recipt of the money and telling him
that you would write him a long letter,[6] detailing the manner,
style, &c &c of your dispensing the money (like those you used
to write us)   ask him to show it to his friends and get them to
give what they can and have him send it to you   He writes me
that he wants you to acknowledge the receipt of the money,
and also that he would much like to hear from you. I consider it
an opportunity for you to make this $50 the father of 100's
without in the least seeming like one asking for it

I certainly think Mother is following a mistaken notion of
ecomony.[7] I think the only decent meals that any of them have
had for three months is what they have eaten with Mat and I.
As regards Mother I am perfectly willing she should live with
us all [the time?] (that is to eat, I mean) but Ed and Jess I cant

2. The lawyer William S. Davis and his brother Joseph were descendants
of a distinguished Massachusetts family (*Correspondence*, I, 152, n. 57).

3. Probably a young son of Samuel R. Probasco, an engineer at the waterworks. See Letter 9.

4. See Letter 9.

5. Someone, probably WW, set off the first half of this sentence with
virgules and underscored "W. S. Davis" and "Worcester."

6. WW wrote to William S. Davis on October 1, 1863 (*Correspondence*,
I, 152–53).

7. There was much ill will in the Whitman household at this time. Jeff
thought that his mother's frugality was endangering the health of his brothers; the mother felt that Jeff and Mattie had themselves been stingy regarding
Andrew. On September 15 (?) LVVW complained that Andrew and his wife
Nancy expected her to pay their rent: "i suppose martha has told nancy i
have got 2 or 3 hundred dollars in the bank   they never gave him one cents
worth when he went away not even a shirt . . . . i said to mat the other day
in a joke if they had another young one they would be so stingey we wouldent
know what to doo but i got the same old retort that it was me that was stingey
with my bank book . . . . i told her the other day becaus i had 2 or 3 hu dolla
if i used it all i might go to the poor house" (letter to WW [Trent]).

stand entirely. Dont understand me that they do eat with us, for they dont as much perhaps as they used to. Mother certainly does not, not as much as we wish her to, for we always call her. I notice however that when Jess does eat with us that he does not throw up his victuals. And Andrew too, his trouble comes as much from his mode of living and sleeping His room for sleeping is without ventilation. the window is coverd with posiness trees. He has no nice little things, [or] all nourishment fixed for him to eat, such as I intended Mat should fix for him. I dont think myself that we have any thing to do with Nancy, she is able enough to make a good living both for herself and the children, if she wasnt so dam'd lazy.

Walt I wish you was home for awhile. I think you would see and think as I do. I have scribbled this to you just as I have thought for a day or two. Ruggles[8] says that Andrew cannot be a well man in this town, to be sure even going away may not help him, but he thinks and is almost certain that it will. I wish if you dont come on you would write me also write Andrew. Oh you dont know how down spirited he is

Jeff.

[38]

Brooklyn Oct 7th/63

My dear Walt,

The enclosed $10 is from Mr James P. Kirkwood[1] for the use of the Hospital soilders   I will mail you another letter with some more money to-morrow

How goes things with you, Walt? What about coming home? I have not written you very lately, I have been so very busy. Mother and the rest are about the same. Andrew does not get better. I fear than Andrew will never get better. He looks very bad rather a painful case. I yesterday wrote you a letter and enclosed some money from myself, after thinking the matter over I destroyed the letter and shall give the money to Andrew, did I not do right

In acknowledging the receipt of money from me please state the amount but not who from as I dont want them to

8. See Letter 18.

1. See Letter 6.

Armory Square Hospital, Ward K, Washington, D.C. Walt made this a frequent stop on his "hospital visits" during 1863. Using money Jeff collected at the Brooklyn Water Works, Walt bought these soldiers writing paper, stamped envelopes, tobacco, fruit, and light reading matter. Courtesy of the Library of Congress, Brady Collection.

know that I dont send any myself but I honestly think when I possibly can give any thing that I ought to give it to Andrew. All the rest of us are the same as usual   Mattie and the babies are very well. the little one is growing finely and is getting to be quite a youngster   Hattie is growing up well   I often wish you was at home   I think you would enjoy her very much and it would be beneficial to her   Jess is about the same. He is not very strong, but does not get worse I think. I should like to have one of the old fashioned letters from you, and cannot you send me the letter to go to Davis[2] before the 12th as the steamer goes out then

Did you write to Wm Davis at Worcester, if not wont you do so,[3] and if you have leasure write to Mr Kirkwood sometime if you will[4]   I will give you his address   Mr Kirkwood is travelling around the eastern states on horseback and is not very well. I think a letter from you would do him good. Let me hear from you. I will write you again to-morrow.

Affectionately Thos. J. Whitman

2. WW probably did not write this letter to Joseph Davis; he makes no reference to it in either his correspondence or his diary.

3. See Letter 37.

4. There is no record of WW writing Kirkwood at this time.

[39]

Brooklyn Oct. 8th/63

Mr dear Walt

I yesterday wrote you[1] enclosing $10 from Mr Kirkwood[2] for the use of the "sogers"   The enclosed $8 is contributed thus

$5 by Moses Lane[3]
$2 " J. D. Martin[4]
"1 " Henry Carlow[5]

In my yesterdays letter I said something about the acknowledgement of the moneys   I fear that I did not express myself so that you could understand me   I do not want to get the credit of sending money that I dont send,—I want to show your letters to those that contribute so that they may see that all the money they give me is duly sent and appropriated and as I proposed this regular contribution I dont like to have them know that I am the first one to back out, but as I said yesterday I think that whatever I possibly can do I ought to do for Andrew, that whatever I can give ought to be given to him. Andrew is in a bad fix, he is hardly able to get around and has no money Mat sends him at least one good meal a day. He generally comes and spends an hour or two at the house. I had quite a talk with Dr Ruggles[6] yesterday about him. The Dr says that had he gone to the interior when he first advised him to in the summer he would have stood a fair chance of getting well, but that now he thinks that it is more than wicked to take his money and make beleive to cure him for in his opinion that is almost impossible   I think that it is about so. It makes one feel rather bad when you think of it dont it   Ruggles says that his lungs are much diseased. I wish that you could come home for a short time and see Andrew   Mother and the rest are quite well. This morning mother is not quite so well,—a bad cold— yesterday Jess was sick all day—there is no doubt Walt in my mind but that Mother is doing injury both to herself and Jess by her economy   they do not have enough <u>good</u> things to eat, and they are both of the age that they require it. I have spoken

1. See Letter 38.
2. See Letter 6.
3. See Letter 9.
4. See Letter 11.
5. See Letter 10.
6. See Letter 18.

of it till I have tired and it dont accomplish any-thing. I wish
you was at home to give a little advice now and then.

Walt I often think of you wonder what you are about and
how you get along. Do you have any employment there. You
must often meet Brooklyn people there   I understand that
they liked your letter at the Times. Twas superior to the Brooklyn one I'm sure.[7]

Walt let me hear from you—a letter that I can show Lane
&c   They like to read your letters   Mattie and the babies are
well and send their love. Ruggles always tells me to remember
him to you. Probasco[8] complains that he has not heard from
you since he sent you some money, fears that it did not reach
you   I will write again soon

Thos J. Whitman

[40]

Brooklyn Oct 15th 1863

Dear Walt,

Mother received a letter from you yesterday[1]   I got one
the day before.[2] Mother did not let me see her letter[3] but Mat
says that she understands that you say that you think about
coming home. I hope dear Walt, that you will come and that
soon   I think if you should come just now you might be able to
do Andrew considerable good   He is in a very bad way and I
really fear, under the present circumstances that he will not
last long. Dear Walt I wish that I could do something more for

7. On October 4, 1863, the *New York Times* printed WW's "Letter from
Washington." This wide-ranging article discussed such matters as the beau-
ties of Washington, the progress on the Capitol Dome, army ambulances,
and the quality of light in the city (*UPP*, II, 29–36). "From Washington"
appeared in the *Brooklyn Daily Union* of September 22, 1863 (*UPP*, II,
26–29).

8. See Letter 9.

1. See *Correspondence*, I, 165–66.

2. WW's letter of October 12 is not extant.

3. On September 10 (?) LVVW had instructed WW to "write on a piece
of paper loose from the letter if you say anything you dont want all to read"
(Trent). It is hard to say why LVVW might have kept WW's letter of October 13 away from Jeff since it was by no means of a sensitive or private
nature.

Andrew, but I have to work all the time, almost day and night and another thing I think he would be guided more by your advice than any one elses   That damed infernal robber the doctor[4] that he has been with (Andrew has paid him $95 and been getting worse all the time) told Andrew yesterday that he must not come there again till he brought him $45 more. Only think of it. The infernal son of a bitch. I would like to hang him for a thousand years, ten times a second. I dont care anything about it for the good that I think that he could do Andrew but that he Andrew thinks that perhaps if he could pay him $45 he could do something for him. The very fact that the scoundrel wants the money in advance is enough   Dear Walt do come home if only for a short time   And unless you come quite soon you certainly will never see Andrew alive.[5] Will you write me at once if you can come.

Mother Mat and Sis are all suffering from bad colds, Mother particularly I think is failing rapidly. I do so wish that I could see you and have a good talk abt family affairs   I am in an awful hurry or would write more. To day I have to go through the whole line of conduit

Jeff

[41]

Brooklyn Oct 22nd 1863

Dear Walt,

This morning I mail with this a letter to you from Mother and also a letter to George from Mother. I suppose Mother has

4. See Letter 36. Jeff seems to be referring to the "Italian Dr" here. But on October 30 (?), 1863, LVVW noted that Andrew "is doctoring with dr Brody." Perhaps Jeff's complaints led to the change.

5. Writing to his mother on October 20, 1863, WW commented: "If I thought it would be any benefit to Andrew I should certainly leave everything else & come back to Brooklyn" (*Correspondence*, I, 166). Nonetheless, despite Jeff's repeated pleas and his assurances that Andrew would listen to WW's advice above that of all others, the poet refused to return home. As Miller comments, WW had "little excuse for delay" (*Correspondence*, I, 165, n. 90). Perhaps the poet was loathe to return to an upsetting and hopeless situation at a time when he was "very happy [in the hospitals]. I never was so beloved." So many men were wounded at this time that he had "to bustle round, to keep from crying." The poet may also have been trying to avoid further strain to his already overcharged emotions. See *Correspondence*, I, 164, 166.

told you fully abt Andrew. My own opinion is that he will not recover, that he cannot last long. However I think that it is owning more to the circumstances that surround him than to his disease. There is no use trying to disguise the matter, Andrew is very unfortunately situated in regard to his home. His wife, I guess is not one of the doing kind, and posessed with rather an ugly high temper.[1] His disease of course makes Andrew fretful and discouraged, and instead of soothing and nursing him Nancy does the reverse. As to his disease I really think that had I the same disease that I could recover from it.[2] However I dont know. I sincerely wish that you would come home for a short time anyway. I think that you could do Andrew a great deal of good In the letter[3] that Mother received yesterday from you, you speak abt my having been reduced in pay. I am sorry Mother wrote you abt it for it only worries you without doing any good, and another thing it is not like you think in regard to cutting down my wages. I was working for the two boards of Commissioners, one at $40 and the other at $50 per month, and I have got all the work for one board finished (the one at $40) [and?] as the Sal. of the office I hold for the Permanent board (that of Map clerk at $50) is put down in their annual appropriation at $50 why of course I have to get along with it for the present. It is not the meanness[4] or anything of that kind of anybody and they would pay me more if they could and will probably in a short time. I shall get some appointment again from the old board I have no doubt, and soon too. As to the worry part, I never think of that A man with a wife like I have got cant worry even if he wanted to. Give yourself no thought abt my worring. Something that I have got entirely past.[5] I have every reason to think that the Commissioners

1. In her letter to WW of October 30 (?), 1863, LVVW condemned Nancy's inactivity more explicitly: "i asked him [Andrew] to day what nancy was dooing if she was dooing any sewing . . . i dont know but i think she is about the laziest and dirtiest woman i ever want to see . . . shes as ugly as she is dirty i dont wonder he used to drink" (Trent).
    2. See Letter 34.
    3. See *Correspondence*, I, 166–69.
    4. WW had referred to the waterworks people as "mean old punkin heads" and "mean low-lived old shoats" for reducing Jeff's pay after "faithful & . . . really valuable" work (*Correspondence*, I, 167–68).
    5. This is one of a number of oblique references in the family correspondence to a period when Jeff's emotional state was less stable. Such references support the idea that Jeff's illness in the mid-1850s may have been psychosomatic. See Letter 34.

(both boards) think well of me, and I know that Mr Lane[6] will ever do everything in his power for me, and I undoubtedly in a short time shall be getting more.

In regard to the Pacific R. R.[7] I am real obliged to you. I learned this morning that our friend J. W. Adams[8] was appointed chief and I've no doubt but I could get a place at once on it, yet I think that in the end I will make more by staying where I am but its rather pleasant to have that to fall back on. I wish you would write me   Ruggles[9] sends his regards.

Jeff

[42]

Jeff and Walt did not correspond in November 1863 because the poet was home for a visit from November 2 until December 1. Knowing that Andrew was near death, Walt attempted to bolster the family before the impending crisis. When Andrew died two days after Walt returned to Washington, new conflicts created even greater tension in the Whitman household.

The worst of these conflicts resulted from the mental disorders of Jesse, the oldest Whitman brother. The genesis of Jesse's illness is not clear. One account is that he injured his head in a fall from a ship's mast, another that he was beaten on the head by thugs using brass knuckles (see Molinoff, pp.

6. See Letter 9.

7. Perhaps WW sent Jeff additional volumes of the Pacific Railroad reports (see Letter 18).

8. A member of the Adams family of Boston, Julius Walker Adams (1812–99) distinguished himself as an engineer working on both railroads and water systems. He designed the Brooklyn sewer system, the first one in America constructed on a general plan according to scientific principles, and is credited with having drawn up the first plans for the Brooklyn Bridge (1866). He also commanded the Fifty-sixth Regiment of the Brooklyn National Guard which defended the *New York Times* and *Tribune* offices during the draft riots of July 1863. He wrote several standard textbooks on engineering and served as chief engineer of Brooklyn from 1869 to 1877 and president of the American Society of Civil Engineers from 1873 to 1875. There is no evidence that he worked for any of the Pacific Railroad companies.

9. See Letter 18.

19-22). Jeff, however, suggests that Jesse suffered from syphilis. For much of 1863 Jesse enjoyed good relations with the Jefferson Whitman family: he played amicably with Hattie and rocked Jessie in her cradle (Loving, p. 91; LVVW to WW, August 31, 1863 [Trent]). But on December 4, in reaction to Andrew's death, Jesse exhibited a vicious outburst of temper that convinced Jeff that his eldest brother should be committed. Mother Whitman persuaded Walt that she could still care for Jesse, so no immediate action was taken (LVVW to WW, December 25, 1863 [Trent]). Jesse's condition must have deteriorated, however, for Walt committed him to King's County Lunatic Asylum on December 5, 1864, where he remained until his death on March 21, 1870.

Brooklyn, N. Y. December 3rd 1863

Dear brother Walt

I have just telegraphed to you that Andrew was dead.[1] Poor boy he died much eaiser than one would have supposed. I do hope to God you will come on. I have been with him, Mary, Mother Mat and I, almost all the time since you left. Mary and I watched last night. He has been dying ever since Wednesday morning—full 24 hours—Poor Nancy, she takes it woful hard   Mary has acted like the best of women   It is very affecting to see Nancy and the children   Mattie did everything that she possibly could[2]   She watched with us till near 3oclk this morning   Andrew was very desirous of having us all around him when he died. The poor boy seemed to think that that would take nearly all the horror of it away. If you will come on I will try and give you the passage money. Mother and the rest take it very hard. I hope to get an answer by telegraph.

Jeff

1. This telegram is not extant.
2. According to LVVW, Mattie remained at Andrew's side the day before he died "nearly all day [and] only came home to nurse the baby . . . martha was there till late   then she came home and mary and Jeffy staid all night . . . they had to fan him all night and bathe him in brandy . . . when she [Nancy] came out in the morning she brought such a smell that Jeffy got sick" letter to WW, December 4, 1863 [Trent].

Springfield Mass Dec 15th 1863

Dear Walt,

I came up here to make some surveys and run some levels for a Mr Worthen[1] who has been appointed to make an examination and report on supplying the city with water. I came up just a week ago to-day, went home on Sat. and returned again on Monday—yesterday. I shall probably get through this week   I found all home about as usual execpt Mat—she has not been very well since Andrew's death   The next day after Andrew's death—Friday the 6th[2]—an affair occured at home which has given me a great deal of anxiety—twas this   Hatty was down stairs—and Mat with the baby—Mother and Jess in front of the stove was a chair upon which Mat had hung a diaper. Hattie commenced shoving the chair slowly toward the stove. Jess told her to stop—she kept on—he all at once jumped up and swore out at her, and said he would break her damn'd neck.—Mat, of course was bound to defend her child and—although trembling like a leaf with fright—she as bold as she could—told Jess to set down and let Hattie be—not to dare to lay his hand on her. Jess then turned from the child to Mat and swore that he would kill her.—said that she had been at him for a long time and now he would finish her   Mat thinking—a mistaken idea it proved—that by putting on a un-frightened and daring manner that she could ca[l]m him down she dared him to touch her or the child either. Jess essayed twice to get at her. Swore he would beat her brains out. Called her a damed old bitch—in the same breath added—"not you Mother, not you"   Mother managed to keep Jess away till Mat

---

1. William Ezra Worthen (1819-97) graduated from Harvard in 1838 and soon became a leading civil and hydraulic engineer. He designed and built many dams and mills in New England, some of which still operate. Originally from Massachusetts, he settled in New York in 1849 and served as sanitary engineer of the Metropolitan Board of Health of New York City, 1866-69. He became noted for designing and testing pumping engines, including some for James P. Kirkwood during the early stages of the new St. Louis Water Works, and developed a major reputation as a consultant. He published several books on engineering and served as president of the American Society of Civil Engineers in 1887.

2. Jeff is in error; Friday was the fourth.

got out of the room. Mat was over <u>one hour</u> in getting from the basement up to her rooms. She had an awful attack of the old complaint in her back and had to set down every few step[s]. When I got home she was not able to set up—there she was with her two children frightened almost to death but very lucky I came home quite early and still luckier we had an Irish girl to work that day so that Mat did not have any work to do. You may imagine when I got home and understood the condition of things I felt pretty [w]rathey. I went down stairs and Mother met me at the door and begged and prayed that I would say nothing to Jess—Andrews body laid just above us.—for her sake and hers alone I said but little.—Jess said that he didnt care a damn—&c. I at first thought that I would at once go out and get rooms and remove Mat and the babies away—but Mother said that it would kill her to part with Mat[3]—that she couldnt stand it and begged me not. Since that we dont allow Jess to come in our rooms,—or rather we only allow him to come when he has some errand for Mother. He seems to have qu[i]eted down,—but still I fear to trust him.—he is a treacherous cuss any way. Probably had I been home he would not have done anything of the kind but if he had, so help me God I would have shot him dead on the spot—And I must confess I felt considerably like it as it was. I love Mat as I love my life—dearer by far—and to have this infernal pup—a perfect helldrag to his Mother—treat her so—threaten to brain her—call her all the vile things that he could think of—is a little more than I will stand   He says he dont know any better   he lies—he does know better. I wish to God he was ready to put along side of Andrew   There would be but few tears shed on my part I can tell you. All this occurred some 10 or 12 days ago and you see how I feel about the matter now. I hav'nt written you before because I was afraid to think about it. To think that the wretch should go off and live with an irish whore, get in the condition he is by her act and then come and be a source of shortening his mothers life by years   As long as we keep him out of our rooms, I dont suppose that one need fear—at least immediately—of his doing any one any harm, there   but I feel a constant fear for Mother—she says that he has these kind of things quite often with her   calls her everything—and even

3. Despite some complaints about Mattie, LVVW's letters generally show a deep affection for Jeff's wife. See Waldron, pp. 17–21.

swears that he will keel her over &c. Just at the time of this affair with Mattie, he had been unduly—I think—burdened with the babies Mat having her time engaged with Andrew till his death and then in fixing for the funeral—and with Andrew because up to the time of his death Andrew could not have the child about him—and after[ward] Nancy had [to] be out getting things to appear at the funeral. But no excuse can be given to going to such extreme measures as to frighten poor Mat so that she has not got over it yet—Now Walt aint there some way in which we can take this immense load from the life of Mother   It certainly is telling on her every hour—she is I think failing rapidly—and I am quite sure unless something is done [will] not live but a few years.—There are three of us, You George and I—and it seems as if we ought to be able to relieve Mother in a measure of this thing—if Jess is sick why we ought to put him in some hospital or place where he would be doctored   There certainly must be plenty of such places and it could'nt cost much. Suppose Mother dies   a place then will have to be found for both Ed and Jess and it seems to me as if it—so far at least as Jess is concerned [could] be done a little sooner, and I think thereby prolong Mothers life some years. As to Mother herself I should be perfectly willing—if she were so situated that it could be done—to take her and provide and do for her as long as she lives[4]—I think she has had trouble and care enough—Mat and I both would dearly love to do it. And I know it would be relief and pleasure to Mother. But now she seems to think that she must deny herself everything and devote her live to those two poor wretches.—Ed I dont mind so much because he could'nt help being what he is.—but Jess did to himself and made himself what he is—and I think is answerable for it. If things are left the same as now I think I shall get other rooms and move Mat and the Children, for I honestly fear to leave them in the same house with Jess—no more than I fear for Mother and willingly would I take her too.—If such a thing were possible. It will be a sad thing to leave her with them but I can't think I am doing my duty to my wife if I leave her in a place of such constant fear as her home is now.

4. Jeff's unsympathetic attitude toward Edward and Jesse made it impossible for LVVW to consider becoming dependent on Jeff and Mattie.

I suppose Mother wrote you an account of the affair.[5] I hope she did. I wish you would write me as soon as you can and let me have your ideas about the matter

Jeff

[44]

Copake, Columbia County, N. Y.
December 28th/63

Dear brother Walt,

My last letter to you was dated from Springfield Mass. I went home on Sat. and had an opportunity to come up here and make some surveys for an Iron Company. I shall probably be kept here all this week and possibly part of next   About the Eagle that had the little squib in about you.[1] I have not had much of an opportunity to try to get one to send you. I have not been able to get to the Eagle office, but tried at a number of the paper stores and could not get it. As soon as I get home I will go to the office and get one if I can, if not I will copy from their file the piece and send you. Walt there is no disposition not to get it, to send you or any unwillingness to take some trouble in the matter, but I have been so very busy the little time that I have been in Brooklyn that I really could not have time to go down to their office. Of course I have had to keep my work up in Brooklyn just the same as if I had not been away,—had to work day and night sundays and all, hardly had time to go home to see Mat. and the babies   The fact of the matter is that I am a

5. LVVW's version of Jesse's outburst differs little from either that of Jeff or Mattie (see Waldron, pp. 32–36); however, Mother Whitman attributed Jesse's behavior to "seeing his brothers corps" and thought Jeff overreacted: "of course Jeff had to hear it all in the strongest light" (LVVW to WW, December 4, 1863 [Trent]).

1. The squib Jeff refers to was a short "Personal" item in the *Brooklyn Daily Eagle* of December 3, which praised WW's work with the soldiers and read in part: "Who is there in Brooklyn who doesn't know Walt Whitman? Rough and ready, kind and considerate, generous and good, he was ever a friend in need." Jeff and his mother believed Dr. Ruggles to be the author of the *Eagle* item, but WW thought it was written by Joseph Howard, Jr. (see *Correspondence*, I, 190 and 190, n. 76).

little overdoing the thing and if it was going to continue long should stop it but as I had this opportunity to make a little extra I felt as if I must tax myself a little. For instance I got to Brooklyn at 12ock Thursday night, went to the office early on Friday morning and I hardly left it till abt. 10ck on Sunday night. I tell you last night I felt the thing pretty bad.—In the early part of this month Mr Kirkwood[2] sent me $5 to send you but I have been pretty hard up and had to use it. I will get some money as soon as I get back to Brooklyn again and will send it to you then.—When I wrote you last I was in rather a high state of excitement in regard to Jess and probably wrote rather strong—but I felt very angry and bad I can tell you. Mat has even hardly yet got over the trouble in her back, and altogether it was a mean dirty thing for Jess to do, for I know he knows better. You wrote Mother abt getting Jess in the Asylum—It does not seem to meet with her wishes.[3] When I wrote you my idea was that by each of us paying—say a $ a week—you and I and George   that we could keep him in some one of the Hospitals around New York—I think it would be best yet. Can you, from your intimacy with the doctors around Washington, get any information in regard to the matter. I have had several talks with Ruggles[4] abt the thing and [he] says that there might be such a thing as it curing him.—helping him any-way   but I feel as if it was our duty to relieve Mother of him— I still feel very nervous abt leaving him with them at home, with Mother, Mat and the babies, for I think he would be guilty of anything when the fits of passion and devilment are on him—he is certainly not to be trusted.—I have made several enquires and am told that he could be put in Hospital and have things all done for him at at $15 per month. I am sure that it would not be much and it would add many years to Mother's life I know. Mother seems to me to act foolish abt the thing—

2. See Letter 6.
3. WW's letter is not extant. Apparently the poet agreed with Jeff that their brother Jesse needed to be institutionalized. Mother Whitman, how-ever, defended her firstborn: "Jessy is a very great trouble to me to be sure and dont appreceate what i doo for him but he is no more deranged than he has been for the last 3 years   I think it would be very bad for him to be put in the lunatic assiliym . . . i could not find it in my heart to put him there withou i see something that would make it unsafe for me to have him" (December 25, 1863 [Trent]).
4. See Letter 18.

for instance she won't come up in our rooms because she cant bring Jess along—<u>I will not allow him to come there</u> consequently it amounts to keeping Mother out. I feel mightly unpleasant abt it I can tell you—downhearted—dispirited—and matters dont go quite so pleasant at home as they used to. Mother thinks that we are foolish—I think I am right Dont understand me that either I or Mat have any enmity against Jess—for its not so. Mat speaks and acts towards him as she always has done, better I think than any other person on earth would after the affair of that Friday—Walt let us try and see if we cant get him in some place that Mother and Mat wont feel so bad about as they would if he was sent to the Asylum. I think it is a duty to our Mother for her comfort and indeed for her safty and of course I have another stake in my wife and children. For the safty of all of them I want that we should do it. Dont you think it could be done

Well Walt here I am abt 110 miles from New York, up in the Harlem and New York R. R. just on the edge of the state of Mass. among a mass of high mountains and deep valleys. The night is one of the wildest that I ever remember, the wind is blowing a gale, the snow and sleet and rain by turns come plashing against the windows. I am boarding at an old fashioned country house (I learn from a book on the table that it is the "Hon. Peter Kissenbrack" of the state Legislature of /62 [)]⁵ as comfortable quarters as I ever enjoyed—good living good fire—good rooms and good bed—clever old dutch-fashioned American people. I've just been drinking some good cider and eating some fine apples. Everything thing is as comfortable and country like. Did you hear of the death of James Ward,⁶ Jennie [DeBevoise's?]⁷ husband, a most singular case and very sudden. I suppose that Mother has written you abt. it.

5. Peter G. Kisselbrack (1825–?), a local politician, was elected to the New York State Assembly from Columbia County in 1862 and served one term, through 1863.

6. James Ward died December 14 (*Brooklyn Daily Eagle*, December 14, 1863).

7. Although Jeff appears to have written "DeBenor's" or "DeBevor's," neither name is listed in the city directories. However, Jeff had maintained a long friendship with the DeBevoise family of Brooklyn, and perhaps this is the name he intended. Jeff would then be referring to a sister of his old friend William DeBevoise, which would explain Jeff's use of the maiden name. See Letter 11.

Walt Whitman in Washington, D.C., as photographed by Alexander Gardner in 1863. At this time the poet made frequent visits to the army hospitals. Courtesy of the Library of Congress, Feinberg Collection.

That iron-clad that sunk at Charleston drownded one of my intimate friends H. W. Merian[8] as splendid a young man as ever lived. Do you remember I introduced you to him at Pfaffs[9] a long time ago. He had a large circle of friends in Brooklyn, was the only son and almost worshipped by his family. He was

8. Henry W. Merian (1840–63), third assistant engineer, USN, perished with twenty-six others when the monitor *Weehawken* sank in a storm off Charleston on December 16, 1865.

9. From roughly 1854 to 1862 WW moved in a circle of literary and theatrical people that met at Charles Pfaff's restaurant on Broadway near Bleecker Street. Here he met such writers as William Dean Howells, Richard Henry Stoddard, Thomas Bailey Aldrich, and Edmund Clarence Stedman.

in my party on the line and was my room-mate for a year. I felt pretty bad when I heard he was dead. Probasco[10] I see every few days, that is when I am in Brooklyn   The other evening he came in the office, asked me how Andrew left his widow. I told him almost destitute. he handed me $10 and told me to give her that. I thought it wonderful generous for one who hardly had ever seen Andrew. He said $5 of it was from Tom Tweedy,[11] the Gent we saw at his store the one that gave you the hat. Abt a week ago one of the men in the department that Andrew was in in the navy yard came and gave Nancy $30 saying that they had raffled off Andrews chest of tools at that price, so as she had considerable money I did not yet give her the $10 (indeed I have had to use some of it) but will give it to her the first of next week—Nancy is abt the same as ever—she seems to have no idea of getting along—she says she would work if she had it—but no idea of getting it. Mat has been trying to get her some and I think will succeed in a few days

Matters and things around the office are the same as usual. Mr Lane[12] is as kind as anyone could well be—the Dr comes in every day for a short time, and things looked jolly enough around there the few days I was home. There is some talk that Sam. Powell[13] will be made Water Com. I hope so. I should consider it a good thing for me   About my coming to Washington, do you think you could get the pass. if so I will surely come on. try for it wont you.—Kingsley[14] is very sick. Ruggles is tending him. Kingsley also has a little girl just lying at the point of death—a very painful affair—

Otherwise that I have spoken of things are all quite well at home. When I was at Springfield Mother had a very hard time,

10. See Letter 9.
11. "Tom" is probably the nickname of either Edward or John Tweedy. The Tweedys lived in Brooklyn and worked in a dry goods store in New York.
12. See Letter 9.
13. The new mayor of Brooklyn, Colonel Alfred M. Wood, nominated Samuel S. Powell for water commissioner on February 1, 1864, but the Board of Aldermen refused to confirm him. On March 1, Wood nominated W. A. Fowler who was confirmed.
14. William C. Kingsley (1833–85) was one of the first contractors for the Brooklyn Water Works (1857). For his role in building the Brooklyn Bridge, see Letter 98.

but almost recovered from it. Mother works too hard   I hope we can arrange it so that she wont have to always.

Let me hear from you   I shall be at home, I think the first of next week—

affectionately Jeff

[45]

Brooklyn, Jan 8th 1864

Dear Walt,

The enclosed $5 is from Mr James P. Kirkwood[1] and is the money spoken of in my letter from Copake.[2] The other $1 is from John D. Martin.[3]

I mailed you some 3 or 4 Unions[4] to-day directed to the care of major Hapgood[5] as usual

At home everything is going along abt as usual, all abt the same.

A few days ago there came to the house for you the proof sheets of a small book which the author (no name given) wants you to read and give an opinion on   the Circular you find within. The stuff itself is disgusting, the whole of it going to prove that the nigger is better than the white which the fool says over and over again[6]—do you want it sent on to you.

affectionately Jeff.

1. See Letter 6.
2. See Letter 44.
3. See Letter 11.
4. Copies of the *Brooklyn Daily Union*.
5. Major Lyman S. Hapgood, the paymaster of the army volunteers, employed WW as a copyist from December 1862 to January 1865. Charles W. Eldridge, co-publisher of the 1860 *Leaves of Grass* and later a clerk in Hapgood's office, helped the poet gain this employment (*Correspondence*, I, 11 and 162, n. 83).
6. No record indicates the poet read this book, but he probably would not have been sympathetic with its thesis. WW also rejected arguments for white superiority: he marked an article on "The Slavonians and Eastern Europe," *North British Review*, American edition, 11 (August 1849), 283, which argued that there are "three varieties of human beings" and that "up to the present moment, the destinies of the species appear to have been carried forward almost exclusively by its Caucasian variety." The poet responded in the margin: "? yes of late centuries, but how about those 5, or 10, or twenty thousand years ago?" (Trent).

Brooklyn March 11th 1864

Dear Walt,

The enclosed $5 is contributed for the wounded men by Moses Lane[1]

I am at a stand to know whether to beg pardon for not writing you before or to scold you for not writing to me.[2] I have been away for nearly three weeks, down in Conn. making surveys for an "Iron Co." and only returned last Monday night. since then I have been very much engaged in getting my work up so that I have not, lately, really had an opportunity to write you   We have had, and are having, considerable excitement in relation to moving and the house. Just so soon as I had got away in the country, the next day, Mrs Brown[3] informed Mother that they had hired the house and that she could remain by paying $8 per month ($3 a month increase) but that our rooms they should rent to other parties, would not allow us to have them anyhow &c—This came rather hard on Mat and Mother, for we thought sure that things would go on as they had the last year, only with a slight increase of rent. On my return Mat told me all about it. On Tuesday, the next day some masons &c came with their tools to make repairs to the rooms and house. I told Mat, (she was going to take up her stair carpet oil cloths—clear out closets &c) to not touch a thing, informed the men that I paid rent for the rooms that they were abt fixing that I didn't want them fixed and should charge the landlord with all damage done. In the afternoon I went to New York to see Travis[4] (the new landlord) to give him legal notice about it. After talking with him awhile I found that the Browns had lied to us and lied to him.—that they had not hired it, but merely talked of it—that they had offered to get a tenant in our place that Travis had told them that the rent of the house would be $400 and that if it returned that to him they might have it if they wanted it and if I was not going to stay &c. In the mean

1. See Letter 9.

2. On March 31, April 5, and April 26 WW promised to write Jeff a long letter. The poet remarked that "the devil is in it . . . . I have laid out so many weeks to write you a good long letter, & something has shoved it off each time" (*Correspondence*, I, 213).

3. See Letter 5.

4. Unidentified.

time the Browns were trying to let our room to Jim Jourdan's wife.[5] Mr Travis said that he would just as soon have us stay as they. Travis sent them a note not to let the house till they saw him. They both went over in the evening to see Travis and lied again by telling him that they had rented it but as they had not passed any papers he would not let them have it.—The increase of rent is $52—$36 of this they were going to fasten on Mother—I offered Travis that I would pay $18 a month for the rooms that Mother and I had—that would leave them to pay 15 1/3 a month increasing our rent $3 and theirs $1 1/3 or if they would not agree to that, that I would take the whole of it at $400.—He is to decide this week which—if either—he will do   in the mean time they are moving everything to get Mat and I out.—I think the chances are about even whether they succeed or not. Rents are very high in Brooklyn   for that floor over Browers[6] (cor of Cumberland st. and Myrtle) they ask $350 for one floor and 275 for the third story.—There is a story around that Travis bought the house we live in for $3000, but I can hardly think it. If so I wish I had known it   I would have tried to get it myself

Mr Crany's[7] address would be best "care of Moses Lane Box 192 Brooklyn P. O." I wish you would write me a letter to show Mr W. E. Worthen[8] of New York   I think I could raise you some $20 or $25 per month out of him   He is the man I went down to Springfield to work for.—he spoke of it himself—said that he thought he could do something out of his friends,—although poor himself

We suppose that George is at Camp Nelson[9] again but we have not heard from himself since he went away. Sims[10] is here yet, got a recruiting office.

5. Probably the wife of James Jordan, a laborer.
6. James C. Brower owned a hardware and house-furnishings store located at the corner of Cumberland and Myrtle.
7. Unidentified.
8. See Letter 43.
9. George had written a letter to Jeff from this encampment near Hickman's Bridge, Kentucky, on September 22, 1863. He had returned to Brooklyn for a thirty-day leave in January 1864, reenlisted, and rejoined his regiment on February 25. On March 6 he wrote LVVW that he was in Nashville and would soon be in Knoxville; apparently the family had not yet received this letter (Loving, pp. 105, 111).
10. See Letter 11.

Mother is not well. I think she has the worst cold that I ever knew of I wish she could be made to think that she must not wash scrub and clean house.—I had quite a time with her this morning about it after exhusting every excuse she said she "could not afford to hire it done"—She is foolishly worrying herself about George—thinking that he does not want her to use so much of his money She says that when he went away he did not say as usual "Mammy dont want for anything" If he didn't God knows he meant it. To me his whole life and actions home seemed to say so. But Mother seems to feel quite bad about it. Several days after he first went away she was either crying or planning how to take "boarders" and make her own living. Poor Mother, how foolish her dear old heart gets sometimes. Mat has been quite sick but is well again. the little one is quite well and Hattie too. Matters are going on about as usual. I wish you could find time to write me a good long letter. also one to Lane, and the Dr[11] too you said you would write.

I will write again soon

Yours affectionately Jeff.

[47]

Brooklyn March 19th/64

Dear Walt,

The enclosed letter from George[1] I should have sent you before but have been so busy that I have neglected it There is nothing particularly new at home with the exception that Mother is not well. She has been very unwell for the last few days. She has a very steady and severe pain, she thinks a gathering or enlargement, in the right side of her chest. For a day or two she was almost helpless. Night before last Mat made her a poultice of elm and it seems to have done her good. I can not get her to allow herself to be taken care of or to take care of herself. She has been very foolish in house cleaning, she has done more work—whitewashing and cleaning—than any man

11. For Dr. Ruggles, see Letter 18.

1. Jeff's letter was written on the verso of George's letter to his mother, March 6, 1864 (see Loving, p. 111).

ought to have done. Yet all the talking that Mat and I could do was no avail. I am really fearful that she has permanently hurt herself. If she does not get better by tomorrow I shall have the doctor to see her   Its very provoking to have Mother kill herself so persistently. She is much worse I think than she used to be. She has an idea that she cannot afford to have anything hired. Im in hopes that you will make and carry out the idea of coming to New York.[2] I cannot imagine what it is that ails mother. I hope nothing serious

In regard to the house I belive its settled that we all stay as we are. I sent for Brown[3] to come up and see me the other evening. He said that if he had to pay more rent he would have to move. That he should like to stay but that he would move rather than pay more   I thought the matter all over—I did not want to take the whole house—I did not want to move—it would not make but a difference of abt a $ per month so I told Brown he could stay and I would bear the increased rent. As it now stands it is as follows   Mother pays $85 per year, I pay $147 per year and Brown $168 per year. I took out an agreement for Mothers and my names at $19 33 per month

Did you get my letter enclosing $5 from Mr Lane.[4] Why do you not write me? is there any reason? I was in hopes that I would hear from you sometime ago.

I wrote you to write me a letter to show Mr Worthen[5] of New York. I think we could get some money through him.

Mattie and the babies are quite well. The children are both growing finely   If Mother does not get better in a few days I will write you again

Yours truly Thos J. Whitman

2. In his letter to LVVW of March 2, WW indicated that he wanted to return to New York to see the family and to bring out his new book of poems, *Drum-Taps* (*Correspondence*, I, 201).

3. See Letter 5.

4. For Lane, see Letter 9.

5. See Letters 43 and 46. Worthen sent twenty dollars to WW on May 23, 1864, and expressed his hope "to send more from time to time" (*Correspondence*, I, 228, n. 90). WW replied on May 24 (?) and wrote Worthen again two years later on December 20, 1866; both of these letters are lost (*Correspondence*, I, 368, 369).

After suffering from dizzy spells, Walt left Washington on June 22, 1864, for an extended period of recuperation at home. While the poet was in Brooklyn, his brother George was captured on September 30, 1864, at Poplar Grove, Virginia, sent to prisons in Salisbury, North Carolina, and Richmond, and eventually placed in a Confederate military prison at Danville, Virginia, about October 22 (Loving, p. 18). Letters 48–51, written after Walt's return to Washington on January 23, 1865, reveal how Jeff and Walt coordinated their efforts in sending food and clothing to George and attempting to secure his release.

This was a period of great fear, anxiety, and frustration for the Whitman family. Daily they read lurid newspaper accounts of the barbarous conditions in Confederate prisons and hospitals, including several articles by an escaped prisoner of war, Albert D. Richardson. In public testimony before a congressional committee, Richardson charged "that the rebel authorities are murdering our soldiers at Salisbury by cold and hunger, while they might easily supply them with ample food and fuel" (Brooklyn Daily Union, *January 31, 1865). He accused the Confederates of deliberate and systematic atrocities and estimated that prisoners "were dying at the average rate of twenty-eight per day, or thirteen per cent per month"* (Evening Post, *January 31, 1865). Such harrowing stories must have moved the Whitmans to despair of recovering George.*

At the same time, the likelihood of a general prisoner exchange seemed ever more remote. Exchanges had seldom worked well in this war and had long been a subject of controversy among Union leaders. Grant had ordered all exchanges halted until the Confederates improved their treatment of black prisoners and released enough Union men to offset those Confederates who had been exchanged but had illegally returned to arms. Richardson's articles and former Brigadier General Benjamin Franklin Butler's speech of January 28, 1865, confirmed Jeff's fears that Grant did not want to exchange "good men for poor ones," and he somewhat pathetically asked Walt how Grant could be "willing to let the men starve and die without result" (see Letter 49). But Richardson claimed that such was the "cold-blooded" policy of Secretary of

War Edwin Stanton and that it had already cost the lives of ten thousand Union soldiers; and Butler, who had long advocated a more liberal exchange program, exculpated himself and placed responsibility squarely upon Grant.

While modern historians have rejected the notion that conditions in Confederate prison camps resulted from a willful and systematic policy, they have confirmed that Grant did halt prisoner exchanges in order to deprive the South of needed reinforcements. Only in late January 1865, when he realized the war was coming to an end, did Grant agree to a policy of even exchange. The uncertainties and tensions of these two weeks intensified Jeff's fears for George's health and safety and gave added cause for his skepticism of public officials.

Brooklyn, N. Y., Jan 26th 1865

Dear Brother Walt,

Mother received your letter[1] to-night—we were all very glad to hear that you arrived so nicely and were so well established—The enclosed two letters came to-day[2]—I sent the box to dear brother George yesterday at noon directed just as you left word—I got some hoop iron and straped the box up strong—I dont suppose there can be anything wrong in sending it straped in that way—do you suppose there is? I had in it a ham piece of smoked beef can of milk (condensed) coffee can of peaches—crackers—potatoes—salt—and the clothes that he sent for—I think I will send him another next week or week after—We were all elated upon seeing the letters published yesterday about the exchange of prisoners.[3] O I so hope they will make an exchange—can you not write something that will keep up the talk about the matter, sometimes little weights when the[y] fall at the right moment turn the scale and accomplish great results   Seems as if twould be worth almost a

1. WW's letter of about January 25 is not extant. This letter is not listed among the poet's lost letters (*Correspondence*, I, 368).

2. Unidentified.

3. On January 24, 1865, the *Evening Post* published on the front page Grant's letter of January 21 to Secretary of War Edwin Stanton stating that a limited exchange of prisoners was under way at Richmond and that a general exchange should soon follow. Grant added that supplies were being distributed to prisoners by Union agents. The *Post* also reprinted Stanton's letter to the House of Representatives which indicated that Grant had had authority to make such an exchange since October 15, 1864, and that now the exchange appeared likely.

life time to help along such a thing as the general exchange of prisoners—

so you have assumed the duties and honors of an officer of the government[4] Mother was wondering at tea to-night what you would have to do—I told her that undoubtedly the first thing would be to calculate just exactly how many little indians John Brown[5] did have—as that was the first thing the clerks had to do in the Indian dept.—What the devil is the Indian dept.—? It is suggestive of scalps, war and paint—whiskey and laziness However I suppose you have not yet had time to tell what the business is about but anyhow if it is only a comfortable berth without too much hard work, it will come in good[6]—I hope you will have good health—I would suggest that you should not go it too strong in the Hospital way, for a while—I would draw it mild for a month or so—How does it seem to you to go back—I suppose it looks quite natural—I hope to be able to come and make you a visit soon—probably some time next mont[h]—Write to me Walt—I like to hear from you often—Write to George tell him we sent his box and will send more

Yours affectionately Jeff

Mother, Mat and the babies send their love   the baby calls <u>Walt</u>—and asks if he is gone—Hat wants to be remembere[d] to Uncle Walt—

[49]

Brooklyn, N. Y., Jan 31st 1865

Dear Brother Walt,

I received your letter[1] to day   glad to hear that you was getting along so nicely and feeling so well—I hope you will

---

4. WW was a first-class (lowest grade) clerk in the Indian Bureau, a branch of the Department of the Interior.

5. Of course Jeff refers not to his neighbor John Brown but to the abolitionist leader who had seized the U.S. arsenal at Harpers Ferry and been memorialized in a popular song, "John Brown had a little Indian."

6. WW responded on January 30: "It is easy enough—I take things very easy—the rule is to come at 9 and go at 4—but I don't come at 9, and only stay till 4 when I want" (*Correspondence*, I, 250). The job was perfect for it allowed WW time for both his hospital visits and his literary pursuits.

1. For WW's letter of January 30, see *Correspondence*, I, 249-51.

write me often   I feel very sad and downhearted to-night—I have just been reading about the prisoners as detailed before the committee on the conduct of the war[2]   is'nt it perfectly awful—have just read also Butler's speech[3]—I begin to think that after all that it is quite likely that Gen Grant is the one that does not want to give an exchange—do you think that it is so—can it be that he is willing to let the men starve and die without result. I have almost come to the conclusion that it is hardly possible that the things that we send to George can reach him (yet I propose to keep sending, hoping that a proportion may do so.)[4] and have for the last few days been trying to think of some other way in which he might be relieved—I see by the papers of to-day that a certain "Gen Haynes["] and a another a first Lieut in a Michigan Reg had arrived at Richmond from Danville to be specially exchanged[5]—I have heard that they are making such special exchanges every now and then when the right "axe to grind" influence can be brought to bear—Now Walt if you will remember among the first men

2. This joint congressional committee, dominated by Radical Republicans, had been investigating the conduct of the war since December 20, 1861. Both the *Brooklyn Daily Union* and the *New York Evening Post* of January 31 carried Albert D. Richardson's testimony before this committee about conditions in Southern prisons.

3. Brigadier General Benjamin Franklin Butler (1818–93), a controversial and outspoken Radical Republican, was dismissed from command by Grant's special order on January 7, 1865. He was the last civilian commander in the Union army. On January 28 in Lowell, Massachusetts, he addressed four thousand people in a speech defending his war record and attacking the policies of his former superiors. Two days later the *New York Times* printed the entire speech, devoting almost the whole front page to it. Butler explained that in March 1864 he had successfully conducted numerous prisoner exchanges but that Grant had ordered him to cease in the following terse telegram: "Do not give the rebels a single able-bodied man." Butler explicitly placed "the responsibility of stopping exchanges of prisoners . . . upon [Grant,] the Lieutenant-General commanding." The next day the *Times* characterized this speech as "exceedingly able, defiant, and mischievous" and "thoroughly insubordinate" in temper.

4. On February 3, Richardson would write in the *New York Tribune* that it took twenty-five to forty days for packages to reach prisoners and that only one of every six or ten reached its destination. Confederate officers, he charged, confiscated the rest.

5. In a brief note entitled "Arrivals at Libby Prison" the *New York Tribune* reported on this day that Brigadier General James Hayes and Lieutenant J. W. Lucas would leave military prison in Danville (where George Whitman was also held) to be "sent North by flag of truce."

that blowed for Grant and wrote him up, so to speak was our friend John Swinton,[6]—When Grant visited New York the Dr[7] says he sent for Swinton or expressed a desire to see him and Swinton called on him and they had a long interview— Swinton I believe passed quite a length of time with him on his Vicksburgh campaign &c—Now I am positive that a letter could be got from Swinton to Grant signed as Editor of the Times asking that a special exchange might be made in George's case[8]—and I believe it would have effect—If Grant has charge of the matter and it could be made to look as if this great man—for I suppose of course he looks so to Grant— whatever may be the fact this editor of the administration paper of the City of New York desired the release of a certain man in fair exchange that it would be done—or at least they would be quite apt to do it.—Now Walt dont say that it would have no effect till you have thought the matter all over—the circumstances that are now surrounding the whole question— Gen Grant is just now in the position when a few words of censure in a print like the Times would do him great injury—I know he is in no danger of getting it from the Times yet he would—I should think like to make it sure by doing a supposed favor to its editor. Then it would be such a small thing for him to do. I fear that it is true that Grant has had charge of the matter for a long time and if so why then certainly he does not mean to exchange[9] fearing that they will get good men for poor ones—Think the matter well over dear Walt—you can think of it in more bearings than I can—remember it would be but a small thing for us to attempt—If you would send me a note to Swinton asking him to do it for your sake I would will-

6. John Swinton (1829–1901) was the managing editor of the *New York Times* and a strong supporter of WW and *Leaves of Grass*. As a candidate of the Industrial Political party, Swinton ran for mayor of New York in 1874. After leaving the *Times*, he worked for the *New York Sun* from 1875 to 1883 and for the following four years edited *John Swinton's Paper*, a weekly labor journal.

7. For Dr. Ruggles, see Letter 18.

8. WW took Jeff's advice and wrote to Swinton on February 3 (*Correspondence*, I, 252–53). On February 5 Swinton replied, enclosing a letter for the poet to send to Grant (see Traubel, II, 426–27).

9. In his letter to WW of February 5, John Swinton noted that his letter to Grant (dated February 6) might not be "worth mailing. Since your letter was written, the statement has been published . . . that Grant has made the arrangements for a general exchange" (Traubel, II, 426).

ingly take it to him and plead for a trial—I could, I think—get Ruggles to ask him to do it—Poor mother reads about the treatment of prison[er]s and will set with her head in her hand for an hour afterward—she seems to feel it much more for the last few days than s[h]e did I feel as if we ought to do something—even if it looks flimsy and of no success on purpose to cheer Mother up—I am glad you wrote to Mason[10] yet I hardly think he will send anything—he is a good enough fellow but of course would have very little interest in this matter—Do write me Walt at once what you think of the matter—If the matter is in Grants hands I am confident twould be a success. Swinton told Dr Ruggles that he would like to send George something in the way of provis[ions]   the Dr also said he wou[l]d send something in the next box—

Mother is quite well—but downhearted Mattie and the children are very well and the young ones grow like everything—Last night Morris Roberts[11]—a friend of George's and Andrew's died of spotted fever—you of course remember him—he was suprnt of the poor—he caught it somehow connected with his business I understand that there is a great deal of it in the city some 9 cases in Johnson street near Navy—

No news to tell—write me   all send love—

Affectionately Jeff

[50]

Brooklyn, N. Y., Feb 3rd 1865

Dear Brother Walt,

As I was at the office and nothing particular to do this evening I thought I would have a little talk with you

Did you see the Tribune of to-day—It had a long letter from Mr Richardson about the exchange of prisoners[1]—I

10. See Letter 11.

11. Morris H. Roberts (1828–65), a local baker and superintendent for the poor of the Western District of Brooklyn, died not of spotted fever as first reported, but of typhoid fever (*Brooklyn Daily Union*, January 31 and February 1, 1865).

1. On February 3, the *New York Tribune* devoted two and a half columns to Albert D. Richardson's "Our Prisoners in the South." Richardson had been imprisoned at Salisbury, North Carolina, from February 3, 1864, to

thought strongly and well written—to-night's Evening Post extracts quite a long passage from it.[2] How horrible the whole thing is. It does seem as if the Government could hardly dare to turn a deaf ear to the call for an exchange—I wish you could write upon the same subject and keep it before the reading public—I intend to send another box to George this week if I can—oh if he could only get them—What do you think about it—is it Grant's policy, after all, that prevents a general exchange—do you learn anything about the matter—I wrote you a few days ago about trying to get a special exchange of George through a letter from John Swinton[3]—what do you think of it—I have thought a great deal about it and think it perhaps might work

There is nothing new with us—yesterday the landlord sent over word that he should want more rent for the house—he did not say how much more   I told Mat and Mother that we would tell him to set the price on the part we occupy and if we did not wish to pay it we would move—I suppose it will be some weeks yet before we know how much he wants—but one thing is certain I am not going to make and have such a time as we all did last year[4]   Mother is quite well—I think to-day [she] is [or] seems in better spirits than usual—Mat has been over to New York "looking for work" as usual to-day with partial success I believe—and as a matter of course bought a new carpet and some other things. The children are getting along first-rate

Somehow I dont see as much of the Dr[5] as I used to   the

December 18, 1864, when he escaped. Richardson not only argued that the Confederates were "deliberately killing" Union men, but he also attacked the inactivity of "well-fed and well-clothed Senators in their warm chamber . . . [and] cushioned chairs . . . . I wish they would look into those foul pens at Salisbury, which by a perversion of the English tongue are called hospitals; . . . I wish they could look on the dead cart with its rigid forms, piled upon each other like logs—the stark swaying arms—the white, ghostly faces, with their dropped jaws and their staring, stony eyes— . . . I think a few hours in the stillness of that garrison . . . would change their view of the matter."

2. Under the headline "The Peace Question" the *Evening Post* for February 3 quoted three paragraphs from Richardson's letter, including his comments on the high mortality rates.

3. See Letter 49.

4. See Letter 47.

5. For Dr. Ruggles, see Letter 18.

last time I saw him he asked how you was getting along and how you felt—He exp[r]esses a desire to learn in regard to your health—So you like your place—I am glad of that—for it makes it much more pleasant to have a steady income per month if one can only not dislike the duties that are to be performed for it—I hope to be able to come and see you some time this month

I have been quite exercised lately about trying to build a little "extension of a house" on the lot in Flatbush Av.—but have about come to the conclusion that I had better wait— material is so very high just now and I should have to borrow the money which would cost me say on a $1000. $100 for the coming year—well the rent for the year will not be much more than that and dont you think that things must be cheaper before another year—What is your idea of this peace business⁶— is there anything in it. It seems to me as if there is   I think if they once get to talking in earnest that it must come without much more fighting

I wish you would write me quite often Walt   somehow since you went away this time I have felt lonely—I suppose its because I dwell so much on the thought that something ought to be done to see if we can't do something to help George. Oh if we only could it seems to me it would be worth almost a life time—Jess I have not heard from since you went away   I suppose I ought to go see him but they are taking such quantities of small pox patients out to that hospital (even out in the cars they take them) that I am almost afraid to   We are having an immense quantity sick with that disease—and the excitement is quite intense

Just now in looking over the Evening Post I saw among the musical gossip a notice that our old friend Bettini was winning great success in Warsaw⁷—tis the first time I have seen his name in 10 or 12 years—I've no doubt the mention of his

6. Newspapers of the day were filled with rumors of an impending meeting between Union and Confederate leaders at Fortress Monroe, Virginia. See Letter 51.

7. "Bettini and his wife Trebelti have been winning successes in various Italian operas in Warsaw" (*New York Tribune*, February 3, 1865). Although Allesandro Bettini performed in New York for only a year (December 5, 1850, to about February 1852), he was WW's favorite tenor (Faner, pp. 59–61; see also Letter 17).

name will call to you many pleasant thoughts—those were very pleasant times Walt.

Of course any information in relation to George—or about the exchange—or treatment of prisoners—or what not that relates to keeping up a fellows courage you will write me at once

All send their love

Affectionately Your brother Jeff

[51]

Brooklyn, N. Y., Feb 7th 1865

Dear brother Walt—

Yours received[1]—We are all very joyful over what you wrote in regard to George—It seemed to put new life in mother—I went to see the Dr[2] to-day—He said immediately that he would go and see Swinton[3] and talk with him about the matter and urge him to write to Gen Grant   The Dr. thinks that Swinton will do it and that Grant will grant the request— He seemed to feel very sanguine about it—Oh I so hope that we will prove successful in getting George exchanged

I was glad to see that Mason[4] made a response to your asking him to send supplies to George—I intend to send a box this week if I can

The enclosed letter[5] came to the house for you   Mother opened it—I thought I would send it to you and you could tell me if any more of the same style came whether to send them to you or not—

We are now having quite a snow storm—it looks as if it would be quite deep—I am rather sorry to see it for it looks hard for the soilders   I feel disappointed in regard to the

---

1. WW's letter of about February 6 is not extant.
2. For Dr. Ruggles, see Letter 18.
3. Swinton had already written a letter to Grant on February 6. See Letter 49.
4. See Letter 11. By February 10 Julius W. Mason, a lieutenant colonel in the Fifth Cavalry, had sent a box to George and had promised WW that the poet's letter to his imprisoned brother would be sent by the first flag of truce (*Correspondence*, I, 250÷51, n. 19).
5. Unidentified.

peace talks.[6] I was in hopes that we had had war enough   It seems almost impossible that the south can keep up the fight much longer—however I think the president showed a great deal of cuteness in going down to see them and if he only told them that the Union was all he asked [he showed] more states-manship than I ever gave him credit for   I see that a great many here have not yet given up the idea but what there is something more to come—the desire for a peace on the basis of the Union alone seems so far as I can see meets with universal applause

Well Walt so you have gone to keeping house[7] have you   You must be car[e]ful or you will get sick again—I fear you do not live well—I think the great cause of good health is good eating—Keep up the supply of good things—Do you have about the same experience in the Hospitals as you used to—were the men glad to see you back—were any remaining that you used to visit   if so I know they were glad to see you—and it must seem like old times for you to go among them—Do you see many of the friends that you used to know then—I suppose you visit the Hospitals once a day—are there as many in them as there used to be—I hope not—tis so long since we have had any very large battles that I should suppose the Hospita[l]s were not full[8]

What is it about the Exchange of prisoners—do you know it looks to me as if they were trying to delay the exchange and yet talk about it as if they were going to do it and wished to do it all the time—I was very glad to have you write that Hichcock

6. On February 3, 1865, Lincoln and his Secretary of State William H. Seward met with Vice-President of the Confederacy Alexander H. Stephens on the Union transport _River Queen_ lying in Hampton Roads. All through 1864 Lincoln had insisted that he would consider any peace plan that included restoration of the Union _and_ the emancipation of all slaves; he now also demanded a complete end to the war, refusing to consider a temporary cessation of hostilities. Lincoln's last requirement frustrated the South-erners' desire for an armistice, which would, they hoped, allow for a cooling of passions before the beginning of negotiations. The meeting ended with no agreement reached.

7. In his letter of January 30, WW briefly described the comfortable room he rented from "a very friendly old secesh landlady whose husband & son are off in the Southern army" (_Correspondence_, I, 250).

8. The hospitals were fairly full because, as WW noted, some soldiers remained with "bad old lingering wounds" while others were moved to Washington as field hospitals were dismantled (_Correspondence_, I, 253).

said Butler lied[9]—I thought as much but did not dare to believe it either I do hope that Grant will make an exchange—The people seem almost to demand it—Do talk it up—Walt—write it up if you have a chance—One thing I think I see and that is that whoever does delay it that they are pretty well frightened about it and want to humbug the people with the idea that they are going to exchange at once—I was almost overjoyed a few nights since to see a dispatch that the President had ordered a complete and general exchange—but alas it turned out to be nothing

Mother is quite well—Mat and the babies are well and all send their love—the baby often calls "Walt" to come   Write me

Mar. 16, 1865

[52]

Brooklyn, N. Y., March 16th 1865[1]
Mr. W. D. O'Connor[2]
Dr. Sir,

I received this morning yours of March 14th[3]—I am deeply sensible of the interest you have taken for me and return my sincere and heartfelt thanks for it. The position—although very desirable in all respects is one that I am not in the least qualified to fill—it is an entirely different branch of the pro-

9. Major General Ethan Allen Hitchcock (1798–1870), military advisor to Lincoln and U.S. commissioner for the exchange of prisoners, had long feuded with Butler (see Letter 49) over the question of exchanging prisoners. He may have pointed out to WW that Grant was not solely responsible for the exchange policy because Stanton and Lincoln shaped it also.

1. This note may have arrived with a letter that has not been found. It is enclosed in an envelope inscribed by WW, "Note from Jeff enclosed to me for Mr. O'Connor, March 17, 1865."

2. Journalist, author, and civil servant, William Douglas O'Connor (1832–89) gained lasting fame as the champion of WW. O'Connor's panegyric *The Good Gray Poet* (1866) helped define a new role for WW, a role which seems to have shaped in subtle but far-reaching ways the closing decades of the poet's career. See Jerome Loving, *Walt Whitman's Champion: William Douglas O'Connor* (College Station: Texas A&M Univ. Press, 1978).

3. O'Connor's letter of March 14 is not extant.

fession from that in which I have been engaged—My Engineering education and <u>entire experience</u> has been in the <u>con-
struction</u> of work[s], such as laying out masonry, location and
the general superintendance of building a piece of work—As a
draughtsman I am totally deficient—my efforts in that direc-
tion being limited entirely to a rough pencil sketch to convey
the idea of what is wanted to the workman—Therefore I am
certain that I am not qualified and could not justify your generous recommendation of me for the appointment

Hoping sir, that I may some time personally thank you for
the trouble you have taken and kindness shown me I am very
respectfully

Yours Cdially Thos J. Whitman

[53]

Brooklyn, N. Y., May 4th 1865

Dear Walt,

We received your letter[1] and [were] glad to get it too—We
had all begun to feel a little worried about George—glad to
hear that you are getting along so nicely—The Expressman
did not come for your trunk yesterday as he promised so I
called last night and [a]gain left the order—to-day at noon
they came and got it giving a receipt for it   Enclosed I send
the Key. I like to get letters from you   Matters are going about
as usual with us. Mother is pretty well Mattie and the Children
very well—I hope you will enjoy your cake that they put in the
trunk—It looked nice when I put it in   I packed it Tuesday
night and had it already Wednesday, but they did not come for
it   I hope to be able to make you a visit this summer yet—
How would it do to come when the review of the Army
happens[2]—could I see it or would it be like our New York

1. WW's letter of about May 3 is not extant.
2. The Grand Review of the Union armies took place in Washington,
D.C., on May 23 and 24, 1865. Jeff was unable to attend, but WW wrote him
about it in a letter to LVVW (Allen, pp. 336-37, and _Correspondence_, I,
260-63).

shows—how long do you suppose George will remain around Washington?[3] I should like to come before he goes away— Write

Jeff

[54]

Brooklyn, N. Y., May 14th 1865

Dear brother Walt

I received your letter[1] in due time. I am indeed glad to hear that you are so well and get along so nicely—We are all well as usual—and time slides along as usual—a day or two ago I to[ok] Mat and Hattie out on the line for a ride—very pleasant—and Mother said the little one was as good as she could be—indeed I think Mother rather likes to have her all to herself—When you come on again we must certainly take a ride or two out—The country looks splendid—everything is growing as finely as can be

We had a letter from George a few days ago—Mother tells me that George is wanting to get a position as Captain in the regular Army—I have though[t] considerably about it and have made up my mind if we all go to work it could be done quite easy[2]—Jule Mason[3] was at my house yesterday and I had a long talk with him about it—he said that just now there was no way—as the regulations only admitted officers that had graduated at some military school—but said that undoubtedly that in a very short time that objection would be removed—he said that he could help us in the matter a good deal and would do all in his power with pleasure—he said he (George) ought to go about it at once by getting a good first class endorsement from the officers he had served under—all that he could—and then

3. On February 22, 1865, George gained his freedom as part of a general prisoner exchange. He was soon granted a thirty-day furlough, which was extended, because of his poor health, until about April 24. On his return to military duty he was assigned command of a military prison in Alexandria, Virginia, where he remained until July 27, 1865 (Loving, pp. 134–36).

1. WW's letter of about May 13 is not extant.

2. In his final months in the army George attempted, without success, to become a career officer (Loving, p. 136).

3. See Letter 11.

bring what ever other influence he could on the Sec of War and Gen Grant—He said in his duties he was brought sometimes (quite often) in such intercourse with Gen Grant that he could (and it would come in good too—not far-fetched) speak a recommendation for George   I spoke with Mr Lane[4] and he said that he knew very intimately the new senator from California (Bidwell)[5] and that he was certain he could get him to give his influence to the thing and would willingly do anything in his power—And then there is John Swinton[6] I am sure he would help—perhaps by writing a letter to Stanton[7]—and we ourselves could get Congress man Bergen[8] to aid the matter— thinking it all over I am sure that if the restriction prescribing those not educated in a military school is removed George can get the same position in the regular army that he now has— but for God-sake dont let him think of enlisting in the army with the expectation of being promoted   that is too dangerous—Will you give the matter some attention and see how the matter stands—Mason is stationed in Washingt[on]   hunt him up and talk the matter over—he can and will help us if we will only make the effort

I am going to try all in my power to come on to Washington at the time of the review[9]—if I can possibly leave I shall come—I want very much to see something that will make me remember the war—

4. See Letter 9.

5. John Bidwell (1819–1900), a representative from California, was elected as a Unionist to the Thirty-ninth Congress (March 4, 1865–March 3, 1867). Earlier in his extraordinary life Bidwell had crossed the Rockies and Sierras with the first overland expedition (1841). In California he became the first man to discover gold in the Feather River, the most noted agriculturalist in the state, one of the early regents of the university, and an unsuccessful candidate for governor. In 1890, he was the Prohibition party candidate for president of the United States. Moses Lane and Jeff might have been especially interested in Bidwell because he was one of the early proponents of a transcontinental railroad.

6. See Letter 49.

7. Edwin McMasters Stanton (1814–69), secretary of war from 1862 to 1868.

8. In the *Brooklyn Daily Advertiser*, June 1, 1850, WW had applauded Tunis G. Bergen for various services in the New York legislature and for being "a very Cerberus in his watch over the Treasury" (*Correspondence*, I, 37, n. 1). Jeff worked with the congressman's son, Van Brunt Bergen, at the Brooklyn Water Works (see Letter 59).

9. The Grand Review of the Union armies. See Letter 53.

Mother received a letter from you Friday[10]—I heard that
Worthen[11] had sent a letter to you containing $25. did you get
it? When you see George give my love to him—talk over the
matter that I have written abt. and see what he thinks of it. All
send their love

                    Affectionately Jeff

[55]

                    Brooklyn, N. Y., June 4th 1865
Dear Walt,
     Mother sent you a letter yesterday[1]—and a few moments
afterward received one from you—Mother is getting quite
around again—although I think she fails considerably—she is
always quite bad mornings—it takes her some time before she
can get around much   When I got home last night Mat told
me that during the afternoon Mother came up stairs crying as
if her heart would break all on account of that lazy baggage
Ed—Mother cant do anything with him—he wont wait on
himself hardly and wont do the least thing for her—I think he
is the most infernal lazy and the most ugly human being I ever
met—unless something can be done he certainly will shorten
Mothers life by years—I cant express the amount of work that
he causes her—and the excitement and worriment he causes
her every moment of her life
     I told Mother last night that if he could be boarded, some-
where that I would take her, that she should have a good room
to herself and that Mat and I would do and provide for her in
all respects as long as she lived and that she need not do
another thing in the way of work, except for her amusement
besides I would pay part of Ed's board   She seemed to feel that
if it could be done she would like it much—I sincerely wish that
some arrangement could be made—for I greatly fear that
Mother will not live long if she has to go on in this way—Walt
wont you think over the matter and write me what you think
could be done in the matter—

10. WW's letter of about May 11 is not extant.
11. See Letter 43.

1. In her letter of June 3, 1865, LVVW complained of suffering "considerable distress" from headaches (Trent).

If it wouldnt be too much trouble I wish you would write a letter to the young ones that sent you the money through Lane[2]—they are all awfully disappointed—they are all little girls of 8 and 12 years old (some even younger) and have been speculating what they should do with the letter—which one it would be directed to &c—at last they settled it by agreeing that each one should have the letter for a week at a time in regular order—they have called to see Mr Lane several times to see if it had been received—They of course are too young to know that the great point was to give it and of course look for the praise that is usually bestowed. Did Lane explain to you that they were the children of the people that sent you money last winter a year ago—Durkee's, Crany, Lanes &c &c[3] they remembered hearing your letters read to their fathers and mothers, and heard a great deal of talk about the great good you could do with even a few dollars   This fair they got up entirely among themselves and resolved in solumn conclave (after voting down resolutions to give to the Sanitary Com. Christian Com, &c &c) to send the money to you to be spent &c   Mattie and the children are very well—I am writing this at the office with Hattie at my side—she wants to send a kiss to Uncle Walt

We do not hear from George   I wonder why he don't write—I wish he would—Mother gets very down hearted— and a letter cheers her up wonderfully—you must write her as often as you can too—

all send their love

affectionately Jeff

2. See Letter 9.

3. As Jeff indicates, this was not the first time some of these children had contributed to WW's hospital work. On January 26, 1863, Moses Lane sent WW $15.20, including five cents from Willie Durkee and fifteen cents from Miss Kate Lane. Moses Lane commented that these contributors were the only ones "thus far that will have to deny themselves anything" on account of their gifts (Feinberg). Crany may have sent WW money in 1863 and 1864 (see Letters 19 and 46); Durkee is unidentified.

[56]

Brooklyn, N. Y., July 16th 1865

My dear brother

We duly received your letter[1]—We of course all felt very indignant at the way you had been treated—but[2] when I came to the statement that Harlan was a parson[3] of course his conduct was to be expected   From that class you can never get anything but lying and meanness—I hope you do not allow it to have any effect on you   you must not—The poor mean-minded man—If Christ came to earth again and did'nt behave different from what he did when he was here he would have a mighty poor show with Harlan would'nt he—

The most outrageous thing was published in the Eagle[4]   If you have any curiosity abt it I will send it to you   It was perfectly in keeping with the paper and I'v no doubt was considered a very good thing by little Van[5]—

1. WW's letter of about July 15 is not extant.

2. WW enclosed in parentheses everything after "but" to the end of the paragraph.

3. James Harlan (1820–99), secretary of the interior from 1865 to 1866, dismissed WW from his second-class clerkship on June 30, 1865. Harlan apparently took offense at the copy of the 1860 *Leaves of Grass* which WW was revising and which he kept at his desk. With the help of William Douglas O'Connor and Assistant Attorney General J. Hubley Ashton, WW secured a position in the attorney general's office. The Harlan episode led directly to O'Connor's pamphlet "The Good Gray Poet." Although Harlan was a Methodist, he was not a parson. WW may have sarcastically applied this term to Harlan because on May 30 Harlan had issued an official directive asking for the names of employees who disregarded "in their conduct, habits and associations the rules of decorum & propriety prescribed by a Christian Civilization" (Loving, *Walt Whitman's Champion*, p. 57).

4. On July 12 the *Brooklyn Daily Eagle* published "Morality in Washington," which noted that "Walt Whitman has lost his position in the Interior Department at Washington under the general order discharging immoral persons, his 'Leaves of Grass' being produced as evidence of his immorality. . . . Walt is personally a good-hearted fellow, with some ability, but he was bitten with the mania of transcendentalism, which broke out in New England some years ago." Perhaps Jeff's outrage resulted from the charge that WW "wrote of things no right minded person is supposed ever to think of, and used language shocking to ears polite. . . . He now occupies a desk in the Attorney General's office, where we suppose they are not so particular about morals."

5. Isaac Van Anden. See Letter 20.

I see by the papers that the 51st will probably be mustered out in a few days[6]   How does George feel about it[7] I wonder—I still think if he wishes he could get in the regular army—Mother had yesterday a letter from Heyde—10 pages—of the most disgusting trash[8]—the vilest and meanest things that he could get together   He says he shall leave Han, and go out west[9]—I wish he was in Hell—Mother of course is considerably exercised about it—and thinks she will go on there and bring Han home—thinks she will go next week   Of course it is foolish for Mother to attempt any thing of the kind and I dont mean to let her go—I am in hopes that George will get home next week and then he could go—I am sure that Mother would never live to get there and back let alone bringing Han—I read Heyds letter through and it is plain to me that they have had a quarrel abt some women that Heyde had in his room—they had a big row and Heyde has written to mother while the thing was fresh in his cussed head[10]—I suppose mother will get another letter soon rather taking the edge of[f] of this one—I've no doubt that Han has a most outrageous existance—and that she had better leave Heyde but I certainly dont think that Mother—old as she is can think of going there—she can hardly move in the morning till she gets

6. On July 25, 1865, the Fifty-first Regiment of New York Volunteers was discharged from military service.
7. In her letter to WW of August 8, 1865, LVVW wrote: "I gess they are all sorry   i dont know as they are sorry the war is over but i gess they would much rather staid in camp . . . [George] is very restless" (Trent).
8. Jeff may be thinking of this passage from Heyde's letter of June 1865: Hannah "will not dress herself decently, but in place of this when I come home to dinner . . . she manages to quarrell me out of it—so that I leave it half eaten—she begins by questioning me about my women [Heyde's art students], . . . and goes so far as to intimate that I have sexual intercourse with my pupils, at my room
This is damned mean—reckless characterless, common, and disgusting" (Trent).
9. Heyde intended to separate from Hannah and "go West." He planned no return: "I would rather go to Patagonia" (Trent).
10. Jeff is inaccurate here. Heyde's letter is clearly dated "June 1865," and while he may have written in a fit of passion he had restraint enough not to send the letter immediately. As Heyde himself explained: "This letter has been written for a long time. I have concluded to send it to you. Realy my experience robs my heart of all charity—Han has a plausible superficiality, but under that she is she devil, to men" (Trent).

some coffee with Mat—You must write her that she had better
not go till George comes home and he can go with her—or
something of that kind—dont fail to write mother—

Everything is going as usual with me—all keep about the
same   Mattie and the children are well   the baby is a little
down just now—but I guess she will be all right again in a few
days—My friend Davis[11] has got back from Peru—he spent 3
or 4 days with me last week—

Write to me

Jeff

[57]

Brooklyn, N. Y., Sept. 11th 1865

Dear brother Walt—

I received your letter last Friday[1]—I should have sent the
bundle before but Mother told me that you said you was coming home[2] and we have been expecting to see you all the last
week   Mother left last Monday—we had a letter from her the
next Wednesday—she arrived all right—found Han better
than she expected she says[3]   I have been suffering since Friday with a "run-around" on my middle finger   I have been
unable to do anything for the last three days—and seems to me
I never suffered so much pain before in so short a time—I send
the bundle this morning by Wescotts express—you must for-
give me for not attending to it before—I should have done so
had not Mother told me you was coming home   And Walt
why dont you come home   we would be glad to see you and I
think you would enjoy a visit home just now—come and make

11. See Letter 36.

1. WW's letter of about September 8 is not extant.

2. WW took roughly "a month's furlough" in Brooklyn from early October to November 7, 1865 (*Correspondence*, I, 267, n. 57).

3. On September 4 LVVW travelled to Burlington, Vermont, to visit
Hannah and Charles Heyde. Mother Whitman was pleased to see that Hannah was in good health and had plenty to eat, but she found it "the greatest
hardship . . . to be pleasant" to Charles (LVVW to WW, September 11,
1865 [Trent]).

us a visit—George has started in his building business[4]—he is in hopes of getting a pretty large job in New York—will know to-day—Mr Lane[5] offered him a first rate berth—he thought at first he would take it but afterwards declined—perhaps he did better in going on with his venture—

Everything is going the same all rosey—we hope you will come on and see us—I am in a great hurry this morning—or would write longer

affectionately Jeff

[58]

Brooklyn, N. Y., Sept. 29th 1865

Dear brother Walt

We hav'nt heard from you for some time[1]—you say the bundle was not the right one—I read the label and thought it read the same as you described in your letter—would you like me to send the other or right one if I can find it—Mother told me she knew the one you meant and that she would put it on the table for me[2]—that is the one I sent

We had a letter from Mother to-day—she seems pretty well—talks a little of coming home but does not say when—I have just written her this eve—We are all as well as usual—the baby has a bad boil on its forehead but I suppose it will get well in a day or two and then she will be all right again—it looks just now though about as bad as anything of the kind I ever saw   by-the-way it was me that had the "run around" on the

---

4. After the war George entered the speculative building business with a man named Smith. In September 1865 George hoped to construct an office building in New York City but lost the contract because, as he explained to his mother, "the architect was in favor of the new york bosses" (Loving, pp. 27–28).

5. See Letter 9.

1. WW's most recent letter to the family had been written on about September 20 (*Correspondence*, I, 369)

2. In her letter to WW of September 5 LVVW seemed confident that she knew which bundle the poet wanted: "if you want Jeff to send that package of papers you must write to him" (Trent). It is not clear what material WW was seeking.

finger[3]—and I have just got well of it—and a cussed bad time I
had of it too—it accounts for my not writing you before—

George is getting along first rate I guess—He dont say any
more about getting a position in the Custom House—I hope
he wont try but I am quite sure that if he can keep devoted to
his present undertaking he will make a handsome fortune in 8
or ten years[4]—he certainly has the prospect of it—there is an
immense amount of building in the city this season—though
material is wonderful high—brick $12 per thousand—should
be abt 5 or 6—I have given up all thought of building this
fall—at one time I thought I would sure   perhaps next spring
will be better

Matters about Brooklyn are much the same—with me just
the same—Mr Kirkwood[5] has been on a visit to Brooklyn and
just gone back to St. Louis—I think it more than likely that he
will build the water works of that city—if so it will be as large a
job as the Brooklyn works

The Doctor[6] returned from the country last week—he
looks first rate—says he had a wonderfully good time—he was
spending the summer up in Vermont near Burlington—
speaks of it as being a splendid place to live—

In her letter to-day Mother says she wants either you or
George to come on and come home with her[7]—so I suppose
she begins to think of coming home

Mattie and the children desire to send their love to you—
the child[ren] are growing first rate—

I wish you would write me   I want to know how things are
going with you

affectionately Jeff

    3. Jeff's failure to include a period after "says" in Letter 57 created ambi-
guity. The poet must have understood Jeff's letter to mean that LVVW had
the "run around" on her finger.
    4. Jeff was right in thinking that George would eventually prosper. At
his death in 1901 George left an estate valued at $59,348.14. No one has
discovered how he accumulated so much money (Loving, p. 33).
    5. See Letter 6. Kirkwood had been appointed chief engineer of the pro-
posed new St. Louis Water Works on April 22, 1865.
    6. For Dr. Ruggles, see Letter 18. While near Burlington, he may have
visited Charles and Hannah Heyde.
    7. LVVW was especially interested in having WW come to get her be-
cause she and Hannah hoped he would buy a place in Birmingham near
Burlington, Vermont (Allen, pp. 352-53).

[[59]]

Brooklyn Dec 21st/66

Dear Walt,

Sent letter to Worthen[1]—as soon as received   Mother received letter and book—by the way can I get one of the books to present to Ruggles[2]   The $31 was made up as follows   Moses Lane $5. Davis $5.[3] self $5. McNamee,[4] Brower,[5] Story,[6] Bergen,[7] Ward,[8] Lewis,[9] Clapp[10] and Van Buren[11] (all young men employed in our office) each $2. Hope you wont be disappointed in the smallness of the amount—but Davis had to go away and did'nt have time to see if he could collect any at his office.

Mother Mat and the children are all quite well—but have rather a hard time to keep warm[12]—wish when you write Mother you would always say something abt Hattie's learning to read and play &c   it sets her ahead wonderfully—you know

1. See Letter 43. WW's letter of December 20, 1866, is not extant.

2. Jeff probably wanted to give Edward Ruggles a copy of _Drum-Taps_ or _The Good Gray Poet_.

3. For Lane, see Letter 9; for Davis, see Letter 36.

4. Probably either John or Robert McNamee, both of whom were engineers.

5. Probably David Brower, an engineer who worked for the city.

6. Probably William H. Story, a surveyor.

7. The son of Congressman Tunis G. Bergen (see Letter 54), Van Brunt Bergen (1841–1917) graduated from Rensselaer Polytechnic Institute in 1863 with a degree in civil engineering. He was employed on the Brooklyn Water Works from 1864 to 1895 and wrote a short history of the department which was printed in Henry R. Stiles, ed., _The Civil, Political, Professional, and Ecclesiastical History . . . of the County of Kings and the City of Brooklyn, N.Y. from 1683 to 1884_ (New York: W. W. Munsell & Co., 1884), pp. 584–94.

8. In Brooklyn at this time there were three engineers by the name of Ward: James, John, and Timothy.

9. Probably David J. Lewis, an engineer.

10. Unidentified.

11. Robert Van Buren (1843–?) graduated from Rensselaer Polytechnic Institute in 1864 and joined the Brooklyn Water Works in 1865 as an assistant engineer. He was promoted to chief engineer in 1877, resigned in 1879, and was then reappointed in 1880 and held the post until 1893.

12. The family had moved to 840 Pacific Street on May 1, 1866. Located on top of a hill, this house was difficult to heat, but as LVVW noted, "Jeffy makes my fire when it is very cold" (LVVW to WW, January 17, 1867 [Trent]).

how such things please children—should like to have you
write me that long letter—I hope also to be able to pay you a
short visit this winter—soon after the Holidays—everything
is going abt as usual with us at home

affectionately yours Jeff

[60]

*In his previous letter to Walt, Jeff indicated that every-
thing was "going abt as usual," an innocuous phrase which hid
the frustrations of his life. His career had stagnated, money
was short, and he was still living at home. His mother thought
he looked "bad" and needed "a month of leave from all cares
and anxieties"; she noted, too, that he suffered "nervous spells
sometimes and is quite moody" (LVVW to WW, June 7, 1866,
and January 17, 1867 [Trent]). Jeff's depression must have
worsened on March 15, 1867, when he attended the funeral of
his good friend Dr. Edward Ruggles, whose absence he would
long lament (see Letter 63).*

*In the month following this low point, Jeff's life changed
abruptly. On March 26, James P. Kirkwood, his former boss in
Brooklyn, recommended that Jeff replace him as chief engineer of the new St. Louis Water Works, a system Kirkwood
had designed for the state Board of Water Commissioners and
the city council. By April an offer had been made and Jeff discussed it with William Douglas O'Connor. O'Connor quickly
relayed this information to Walt who urged his brother "to
accept the offer, & go, by all means" (Correspondence, I, 326).*

*Jeff reported for work in St. Louis on May 7, 1867. He was
initially uncertain whether this would be a permanent move:
he left Mattie and the children in the East and asked Walt to
visit only "if I stay here long." But he liked the energetic young
city, the companionship of prominent men like Henry Flad,
the excitement of a large project, and the improved salary—in
Brooklyn he made two hundred dollars per month, in St. Louis
three hundred and thirty. Quickly he assumed the responsibilities that would dominate the next twenty years of his life, the
task of building and supervising a waterworks as extensive as
that in Brooklyn.*

The plans called for drawing muddy water from the Mis-

sissippi, allowing it to settle in reservoirs, and then pumping it into a sprawling distribution system. Partly because the city council had rejected Kirkwood's original location for the works and insisted on a less expensive site nearer the city, Jeff was plagued with such problems as poor soil for foundations and periodic flooding from the river. By drawing freely on the expertise of his old friend Joseph P. Davis and the government publications sent him by William Douglas O'Connor, he overcame these obstacles and completed the job on schedule in 1871.

St. Louis, May 23rd 1867

Dear Brother Walt

Yours I received yesterday   I also had a lettr from Mat to-day[1]   As you can imagine I am very glad to get news from home—I was glad you sent me Mothers letter—

In regard to the house I think too that it is far better to do as you propose and build on George's lot—twill be a home and a good one too I think for Mother[2]—I see from Matts letter that they are going to be turned out from their place there—that Olmstead[3] and all the rest are a mean set of cusses as ever lived—there is no need of their wanting the house

I hav'nt written to Kingsly[4] yet—am thinking of perhaps some other way of raising the money—anyway I am pretty sure—indeed <u>am</u> sure that it can be had—how soon will you want it? write me about it—

I am glad you went home[5]   I guess it did Mother and all of them a great deal of good—Mat writes that she is going out to hire rooms as soon as she can   It seems to me d—m mean that they manage to want the whole of that big house   It looks more like being a little ugly than anything else—I wish Mattie would be a little stiff with them—the Bullards[6] I mean the

1. WW's letter of about May 21 and Mattie's letter of about May 22 are not extant.
2. Once Jeff left Brooklyn LVVW's domestic arrangements became a matter of concern. The long-range plan was for George to build her a home.
3. Unidentified.
4. See Letter 44.
5. WW returned home on May 4 mainly, it appears, to calm LVVW who was alarmed over George's health (a case of malignant erysipelas) and Mattie's impulsive decision to sell furniture and spend the money on clothes (*Correspondence*, I, 328).
6. Unidentified.

Henry Flad and Jeff Whitman in a St. Louis biergarten about 1870. Flad was an important local engineer with whom Jeff developed a lasting friendship. The postwar success of both men is implicit in their attitude and surroundings. Stereopticon slide, courtesy of the Missouri Historical Society.

people that are going to move in—the d—m cusses shant have my water pipe unless the[y] behave decent—yet I suppose the Park people are mean enough to prevent my taking it up—

Matters are beginning to get into shape with me—I am in need of Davis[7] very much—I have been urging him to come as soon as possible but received a letter to-day saying that he could not possibly get here before the 15th June if then—I hope however that he will certainly get here by that time.

Mr Kirkwood[8] left me this morning—he has been here since Saturday—The Board of Commis[sio]ners I like very much—they do just whatever I ask—at once—indeed almost

7. See Letter 36.
8. See Letter 6.

too much so.[9] I begin to feel as if I should get along if I have decent luck—Yet it is hard to say what will turn up—

I manage to get the N. York papers pretty regularly now. I had the Times of Friday while eating my Breakfast on Sunday—that is pretty well isnt it. The weather is quite cool—but nevertheless vegetation is getting forward fast—and just out side the city—where we are to build part of our new works, matters look perfectly beautiful. I hope you will be able to come on here and make me a visit if I stay here long—I begin to like the city better—Yet it dont come up to B[rooklyn] by a long chalk—

Give my regards to Mr and Mrs O'Conner[10]—write me as often as you can

Affectionately Jeff

[61]

St. Louis, Aug 2nd 1867

Dear Walt

Yours duly received[1]   I have had so many things to attend to lately that I have not been able to get time to answer and can only do so now so that you may know that I hav'nt forgotten you

We are still at work getting out specifications for the settling Reservoirs[2]—a job of about $700 000—and of course we feel mighty anxious to cover all points so that we wont be upset by any sharp practice

On the street to-day I saw a very interesting yet somewhat painful sight—twas that of a family moving in from the plains—An old woman—I shoud judge all of eighty—another woman of about 35—a young man and his wife abt 25 a boy of 12 two children 8 and 6 and a little babe—all but the young man and his wife were in the wagon drawn by 4 oxen—the wagon covered with dirty white canvass—The boy had leading

9. On May 17 Jeff had urged the Board of Water Commissioners to construct a temporary reservoir on Gamble Street to store water while sediment was removed from the main reservoir on Benton Street. This plan was immediately adopted.

10. See Letter 52.

1. WW's letter of about August 1 is not extant.

2. Located at Bissell's Point, three and a half miles north of city hall.

with a rope a fine old cow—a young cow and calf were alongside—under the wagon was a large white dog and inside by the old woman was a small black terrier—They had met with an accident in the way of b[r]eaking one of the hind wheels and were therefore hard up—The faces of all were a study—but particularly of the young man and his wife— neither of them was at all handsome but yet I shall remember their faces for a long time—The old woman had that peculiar look of crazy stupidity that you can hardly tell whether they are really stupid or thinking of by-gone life   The talk of the crowd was that they had been driven in by the Indians—but I doubt that part of the story—

There is a report in town to-day that some of the "bloody injuns" were stealing cows &c just outside the town—about where we propose to set our pumping engines—Of course I suppose its all humbug—but yet cannot see what such a detailed statement as is in the paper this morning is printed for—[3]

I had a letter from Mother a few days ago—she appears to be getting along middling well yet I wish she could get a better place to live—[4]

From a letter received from Mat to-day she is having a first rate time yet—I wish you would write her—address care of G. F. Mason,[5] Towanda, Give my regards to Mr & Mrs O'Conner[6] and friends that I met in Washington—

I hope you may be able to carry out your idea and come out to see us—

good by for the present   write me as often as you can

Jeff

3. The first reports of this incident were, as Jeff says, "humbug." Forty Winnebago Indians returning by steamboat to their tribal lands in Wisconsin had stopped for a few days in St. Louis and temporarily encamped near the Bissell's Point works (*Missouri Republican*, August 2 and 3, 1867).

4. After Jeff's family left Brooklyn, LVVW gave up the house at 840 Pacific Street and in July moved to a new house at 1194 Atlantic Avenue. She complained of the small rooms and the "bad smells" from the sewer (LVVW to WW, August 1, 1867 [Trent]).

5. Gordon F. Mason, father of Jeff's old friend Julius Mason from the Brooklyn Water Works (see Letter 11 and Waldron, p. 37). Mattie and the children lived with the Masons in Towanda, Pennsylvania, until mid-September 1867, when she and the girls returned to Brooklyn.

6. For William Douglas O'Connor, see Letter 52. Jeff had visited WW and the O'Connors in February 1867 (Allen, p. 379).

[62]

Pittsburgh, [January 17, 1868][1]
Friday Night

Dear Mother

We all arrived safely at Pittsburgh abt 2 oclk to-day—Mattie and the children stood the journey first-rate—and Mat seems to feel fully as well as in Brooklyn   I find I shall probably have to stay here longer than I anticipated—possibly shall not get away tomorrow but hope to—

We had quite a pleasant time in coming on—Mrs Rice[2]—(with child and nurse) met us at the Depot—I succeeded in getting a state room in the sleeping car—and was particularly fortunate in doing so—as many were left out or rather had to get along without sleep

I write this merely to tell you that we got through so far all right—and also to send you this [t?][3]—Mat has worried about my not giving it to you ever since we came away—you must thank her for it not me—for to tell you the truth, dear old Mamma I have so much to think about that I do not remember you as often as I ought to.

Mattie sends love to you and all—I ditto—and the young ones likewise, will write again from St Louis as soon as we get there

affectionately Jeff

1. Jeff returned for a Christmas visit to Brooklyn on December 18, 1867, and by early January 1868 had convinced Mattie to move the entire family west. Mattie's earliest letter to LVVW from St. Louis (February 1, 1868) implies that the family had been there for over a week (Waldron, pp. 44–46); it therefore seems likely that Jeff wrote this letter en route on the third Friday of January.

2. Mr. and Mrs. Rice lived in St. Louis at this time, but they seem to have been old acquaintances of the Jefferson Whitmans from the East (Waldron, p. 45).

3. Probably a gift of ten dollars. For a similar present from Mattie, see Letter 66.

[63]

St. Louis, July 12th 1868

Dear Walt,

Tis a long time since I have written to you[1]—not since I wrote a short note from Pittsburgh   I received a few days ago a paper (Boston) containing a notice of you[2]—I was much pleased upon reading it—

We are all pretty well all <u>very</u> well except Mat   she has a bad cough[3]—and she has had it so long that I begin to feel quite anxious that she should be rid of it   I have had a doctor examine her lungs two or three times but he says they are not as yet to any extent affected   I miss the advice and counsel of Dr. Ruggles[4] in all such cases much—Mat caught a bad cold when we first moved to the house[5] we are living in and she has not been entirely free from it since although she has been better once or twice—I am in great hopes however that in a few weeks she will get the better of it. How are matters progressing with you—I suppose as usual—is the hot weather in Washington pretty bad   We have had a visit from Grant[6] but he is

1. Jeff was so busy at this time that it would be wrong to suggest he was neglecting WW. After receiving a letter from Jeff, LVVW remarked to WW on March 11, 1868: "i thought when i read it he must have written it running for i could hardly make it out   he is very busy" (Trent).
2. The only such notice in a Boston paper for this month was Ferdinand Freiligrath's "Walt Whitman" in the *Boston Commonwealth*, July 4, 1868. Freiligrath claimed that "For his admirers, Whitman is the only American poet, derived from the soil, expressing his age . . . . He makes ordinary verse-making seem childish." Surprisingly, Jeff noted Freiligrath's admiration of *Leaves of Grass* before WW himself, who first mentions it on September 27, 1868 (*Correspondence*, II, 48).
3. Jeff first noted Mattie's chronic sore throat on February 10, 1863 (see Letter 11), but it was only in 1868 that he began to express deep fears about her condition. For an account of the progress of Mattie's disease, see Waldron, pp. 2–4.
4. Edward Ruggles (see Letter 18) had died the previous year.
5. On March 1 the Jefferson Whitmans began renting a seven-room house on Olive Street for sixty-five dollars a month (Waldron, p. 50, and LVVW to WW, February 12, 1868 [Trent]).
6. Now the Republican nominee for president, Grant arrived in St. Louis on July 7 to visit his wife's parents, the Dents, who lived on a farm outside town. He deliberately avoided public appearances, shrewdly preferring to play the role of the simple soldier while the Democrats politicked in New York.

coming and going like any other "man" and I guess it is a good thing people dont get excited [during] this hot weather

What do you think of the selection of candidates by the New York Convention[7]—rather a lame affair isnt it—but of all the poor devils old Chase[8] must feel the worse   I can not conceive of a more general "cave in" than Mr Chas[e] made—and our friend A. J.[9] cannot be over jovial at the result.

Do you ever see anything of Mason[10]—if so how does he look and what will he do when Grant is elected Prest.

We are progressing slowly with the work[11]—not so fast as I hoped or expected—Yet I guess 'twill come out all right   We have most of the work under contract—one will be let to-morrow and but one or two more after that   I am kept pretty busy   the little questions of all kinds coming up require nearly all my time—we have a pretty large Engnring force—larger than they usually employ on work in the west—still none to many to keep every thing straight

Walt cant you get some tickets on the next great Pacific Rail Road spree[12] and come out and see us and if you or I can get the tickets Mat and I will join you and go to the end of the road—would[n't] it be a jolly good time—I suppose they will have a trip or two of that kind this fall

I went a few weeks ago on a little sail up and down the river with the party that were "doing" the "Editors Assotn"[13]   I was much amused by the style of a large number of them—

7. After numerous ballots, the Democrats surprised the nation by nominating Horatio Seymour for president and Francis P. Blair, Jr., for vice-president.

8. Chief Justice Salmon P. Chase (1808–73) had aspired to be president for many years, and in 1868, though known as a prominent Republican, he made a bid to become the nominee of the Democratic party but failed.

9. Andrew Johnson received sixty-five votes on the first ballot; however, after Seymour was nominated, Johnson supported the ticket.

10. See Letter 11.

11. By this time Jeff had completed the settling reservoirs at Bissell's Point but still had to construct the pump houses and water intake towers.

12. As part of their promotional schemes to encourage western settlement, railroads such as the Missouri Pacific offered free passes to writers and journalists who agreed to take one of the special excursions over the newest routes.

13. On June 25, 1868, the mayor and city council of St. Louis entertained a group of newspaper editors from Wisconsin and Minnesota by giving them a one-day champagne cruise on the Mississippi steamboat *Belle of Alton.* Jeff mingled with local politicians, judges, and journalists, including

particularly of the young style—like young Noah[14] used to be—fellows that thought that they had to <u>look</u> the newspaper as well as report for one   The speeches were sickening—and the "eat" jolly—the sail splendid   I wish you could have been along—not so much that you might have seen the "eds" but that you might have enjoyed the sail—yet it was'nt the sail to Cony Island by a long ways.

What will be the result so far as you are concerned should Mr Evarts[15] be made Atty Gen—will it make your place any less secure? Are your friends in Washington all right as regards their "sits" O'Conner[16] and the rest—I suppose the political boiling is really more heard than felt in regard to office holding—I know lost [*sic*] of fellows in Brook[lyn] (and it is the same with Engineers) that always think they are going to be deprived of office and "<u>clout.</u>"

Well Walt I have to stop and go home to dinner—you would be very welcome to go if you only could I can tell you— Mat and the Children would almost love you to-death   The children are growing nicely—Hattie has got so she can read a letter—Jess is still the baby and therefore dont learn or anything else but play—they both grow though quite fast—and will I think go through the hot season without much trouble—

I wish you would write me when you can—a letter way off here is quite an event and highly prized

Give our love to Mother when you write and the same to yourself

Affectionately your Brother Jeff

Carl Schurz of the *St. Louis Democrat*, and he listened to numerous speeches proclaiming the virtues of the city and its illustrious guests (*Missouri Republican*, June 26, 1868).

14. Probably the son of Mordecai M. ("Major") Noah (1785–1851), a prominent New York editor. WW wrote two articles about New Orleans which appeared in the April 2 and May 21, 1848, issues of Noah's *Sunday Times* (Rubin, p. 373).

15. William M. Evarts (1818–1901), Andrew Johnson's brilliant defense attorney in the impeachment proceedings, was rewarded with the appointment to attorney general in 1868.

16. See Letter 52.

[64]

St. Louis, August 20th 1868

Dear Brother George

I must beg pardon for my seeming delay abt sending the enclosed draft. But I have had so much bad luck lately in one thing and another that I could not do it sooner

I have made the draft for $510[1]—I wish you would give the $10 to Mother as a present from Mattie

Mat is pretty bad yet[2]—can just get around a little—very lame—but I think 'twill get away in a week or two if we have no more of the same sort—It pains me very much to see her try to walk—but she stands it like a good fellow—dont grumble a bit   I hope you have been occasioned no inconvenience by my failure to send you this on the 1st of the month   I meant to have done it but could not get matters into shape to do it till to-day—please write in regard to [receipt?] of this draft so that I may know that it came to hand safely   I believe I wrote to you or mother that Mr Lane[3] would take the draft after you endorsed it and put it in his bank and draw the money for you—twill save you some trouble probably—

We are quite anxious to hear from Mother and the rest of you—Mat has tried to write once or twice but does not succeed—she will make an effort to-day I believe—

We are having the most delight[ful] weather here just now except that it is very dry indeed—yet we are having a little shower this morning. I hope it will be a good one for we need rain—we have great troub[le]s in carrying on our work the dirt is so dry—bad weather for building Reservoirs[4]—

How do matters go with you—is the 48 inch pipe all laid yet[5]—I wish you would write me occasionly and I often wonder

1. George was building houses on speculation at this time and needed substantial amounts of cash. By June 23, 1869, he had borrowed $3,400 from Jeff (LVVW to WW [Trent]).

2. When Mattie was thrown from a buggy on July 30, she suffered a badly bruised hip; only Jeff's quick thinking prevented a more serious accident. For a full account of this event, see Waldron, pp. 56-57.

3. See Letter 9.

4. At this time Jeff was constructing the large storage reservoir within the city on Compton Hill.

5. George had a part-time job supervising the laying of water mains for the city of Brooklyn (Allen, p. 396).

why Mr Lane or McNamee[6] does not write me—certainly they are in my debt for letters—I shall give em fits if I ever get on east again—

The first time you are at Mr Lanes Office I wish you would ask Johny [M. McMear?][7] if he will see what taxes &c are due on that lot of mine on Flatbush Av and write me and I will send him a draft if he will pay it for me—or if he will give you the statement you can write me and I will send it to you

I should judge from Mothers letter that she thought you would move—do you really think that you will abandon old 1194[8]—You must keep me posted—Do you ever hear from Walt—I wish he would write me occasionaly—Love to Mother and all—affectionately your

Brother Jeff

No of Draft 966 on Jay Cook & Co of N[ew] York[9]

[65]

St. Louis, August 23rd 1868

My dear Mother,

Having a half hour to spare I thought I could not better employ it than in writing you—We are getting along pretty well—Mattie has gained a great deal in the last week—although to-day she is not as well as she was a day or two ago yet she can go around without a cane—and without limping much—Hattie and Jessie are well as can be—Jessie is getting fat again—and Hattie looks remarkably well—indeed I think St Louis agrees with her if it dont with the rest of us[1]—

Mat has got a pretty good girl now[2]—not the best—but

6. See Letter 59.
7. Unidentified.
8. LVVW moved from 1194 Atlantic Avenue to more spacious quarters in September 1868 (*Correspondence*, II, 46 and 48).
9. Jay Cooke & Co. was a large bank at the corner of Wall and Nassau streets, New York City.

1. Interestingly, the water of St. Louis bothered the Jefferson Whitmans. LVVW reported to WW that "the water dont agree with them in the morning when they first get up they often all vomit at once" (February 12, 1868 [Trent]).
2. Mattie had already informed LVVW on August 4 that she had to discharge her "darkey": "she got so lazy she was worse then nobody. last thursday I got another girl (a white one this time)" (Waldron, p. 56).

good as they run—as soon as she can get around though and see to things herself I suppose matters will go better

Do you see or read anything about a toy called "Planchett" There is an article in "Lippencotts" Mag for August on it[3]— Davis[4] bought one a few days ago and we tried it but it woul'd[nt] go for us at all—Yesterday a little daughter of a neighbor came in and Mattie and she tried it and it commenced to write answers to all questions like the devil—The thing is a little piece of black walnut abt 7" by 8"—heart shaped and abt ¼" thick ⟨ with two little wheels and a hole in front in which you stick a pencil. ┼══—you lay a sheet of paper on a table and set this thing on it and then sit down and put the tips of your fingers on the top of the wood—in a few minutes the wheels begin to roll and the pencil to mark on the paper—then you ask questions and the "toy" will write answers I went home last evening and found that they were all in a high state of excitement from the fact that they (Mat and this little girl) had got it going and lots of questions answered—Mat asked it if you would come out and see us this fall and it wrote "Doubtful" (it makes a flourish like this at the end of every sentence)[5] To a question of who would be next President it wrote "Grant"—then they asked it why Grant would be President and it wrote "Because"—lots of other questions were answered in the same way—you would laugh to see the excitement and expectancy when an answer's abt half written

I had a letter from McNamee[6] a few days ago—he told me that George had been sent down to Florence[7] for a short time—has he returned yet—I was glad that the draft came all right—and by the way is that car stable yet on the lots opposite my lot in Flatbush avenue—tell George to look when he goes in that neighborhood If they should clear that out I dont

3. "My Acquaintance with Planchette," *Lippincott's Magazine*, 1 (1868), 217–18. Jeff accurately describes the appearance and operation of this early psychic instrument, which was invented about 1855 and later used without a pencil as the pointer on the Ouija board. Jeff's two sketches are reproduced about full-size.

4. See Letter 36.

5. Jeff's transcriptions of the planchette's writing all end with a terminal line encircling the entire word.

6. See Letter 59.

7. Florence, New Jersey, where George went to inspect iron pipes at the R. D. Woods foundry. In November 1868 he became pipe inspector at a foundry in Camden, New Jersey (Allen, p. 404).

know but what it would be a good idea to build on that lot one of these days

Mat will write you soon—everything is going abt the same as usual with us—I dont ever hear from Walt—I suppose he is well however—has he been home lately—Love to George Ed and all—write when you can—affectionately

Jeff

[66]

St. Louis, Sept. 6th 1868

Dear brother George

Enclosed I send you draft on New York no. 5104, for five hundred and ten dollars[1]—the ten you will please give to Mother as a present from Mattie

We are getting along abt the same as usual. Mat still has a bad cough—yet I hardly think it as bad as it was a few weeks ago. I should'nt wonder if she and Jessie made you a visit in the course of a month or so[2]   The doctor told Mat yesterday that he thought a visit east would do her cough more good than anything else—and if that is the case I am anxious that she should go. Tell Mammy not to commence to worry about it yet though for perhaps she may not be afflicted.

How are you getting along with your new house[3]—well I hope   Is there much building in B[rooklyn] this year—in St. Louis there are more houses going up this year than ever before—some 2500 dwelling houses are reported in process of construction.

What is the news about the water works office—I find every body there as tight as a bottle in the way of writing   I sup-

1. See Letter 64.
2. When her doctors suggested a change of air, Mattie went to Brooklyn with her two daughters on October 14 and lived with LVVW until mid-December. Jeff joined his family around November 20 (Waldron, p. 60). Despite her poor health, Mattie did little to ease the strain on her throat. LVVW informed WW on November 11 that the doctor had "performed two moderate operations on her throat   but O dear if you could hear her talk   it would make me hoarse to talk a steady stream as she does when any one comes in to see her" (Trent).
3. For a discussion of George's difficulties in building this three-story house for his mother and brother Edward, see Loving, pp. 28–29. Located at 107 N. Portland Avenue, this was LVVW's last home in Brooklyn.

pose they must take their cue from Mr Lane[4]—I wish you would drop me a line telling me what news there is—did you go to Phillipsburgh[5]—and if so what did you see

I see by the papers that you have had some pretty bad rain storms in Brooklyn—we have lately had two storms that has put us back on the work very much indeed—the contractors were not prepared for them and so were damaged a good deal We have had a pretty severe storm this morning—but nothing like the others.

I understand you were down to Woods at Florence[6] did you see our 36″ pipe and if so what did you think of them—

Do you think you will continue to live in Atlantic street this winter—or do you think you will "move" as mother has been talking about for the last year or two—and by the way when do you expect Walt home—

How are political matters about Brooklyn—Seymour[7] I suppose will be ahead just in and about New York City but will he carry the state do you think—The only thing that will save this state to Grant—if it is saved—will be the "iron clad oath"[8] The rebs are, I judge, in the majority here—but they dont allow many of them to register and when they do do it they have to do some pretty tall swearing. I took the oath 'tother day—as I want to vote for Grant—all the other questions though I think I shall leave out[9] Write me and tell me all the news in and about Brooklyn—Love to Mother and all—

affec Thos. J Whitman

4. See Letter 9.
5. In New Jersey, about forty-five miles north of Camden.
6. The R. D. Woods foundry at Florence, New Jersey, was a major supplier of iron pipe for the St. Louis Water Works (*Proceedings of the City Council*, St. Louis, June 23, 1868).
7. See Letter 63. As the Democratic candidate for president, Horatio Seymour carried New York state by a bare ten thousand votes.
8. The Missouri state constitution of 1865 required that all citizens take a stringent loyalty oath before they could register to vote, thus effectively disfranchising many ex-Confederates and their sympathizers. This controversial oath, one of the strictest in the nation, was repealed in 1870. Despite Jeff's fears, Grant carried Missouri by a wide margin.
9. One of these "questions" was a proposal to enfranchise black citizens. The measure, which had lost the year before in Kansas, Michigan, Minnesota, and Ohio, was rejected three to two.

St. Louis, Sept. 8th 1868

Dear George

I mailed you yesterday draft on Jay Cooke & Co. for $510[1]—which I presume has come to hand

How soon will your house be done—Do you intend Mother shall move there and live for awhile?[2]—[these] are the two questions that are in my mind just now—

Mattie has a bad cough and I have had several first class physicians to see her and they all unite in saying that a trip east for a few months would cure her[3]—I have been very unfortunate in the selection of a house—and unfortunately have a lease of two years on it under very stringent papers too—It occurred to me that if Mother was not going to move I would try and get a furnished room in your neighborhood and send Mat and Jess on and if your new house was in the neighborhood of completion and you proposed to move in it I thought perhaps you could hire Mat a room in that.

The house is damp and I cannot seem to bettr it. I have spent abt $125 on it trying to fix it. I'm in a pretty tight place and will have to "wiggle" out of it—I am looking just now for some sort of a boarding school to send Hat for a few months till I can see how the matter is going to turn out—. The doctors all unite in declaring that Mat has no disease of the lungs[4]—it is all in the bronchial tubes of the throat—of course it is going to be hard for us to break up just now—but I do not think it worth while to risk everything in trying to "stick" it out in a bad bargain—

Give my love to Mother—tell her Mat has a letter written

1. See Letter 66; for Jay Cooke, see Letter 64.
2. George did not finish the house on Portland Avenue until May 1869, at which time LVVW did move into it (Loving, p. 29).
3. See Letter 66.
4. Six weeks later, after consulting with Dr. A. D. Wilson, WW wrote Jeff a detailed report of Mattie's health which indicated that the disease *had* reached one of the lungs. Nonetheless, WW remarked, the doctor "thinks there is no imminent danger at all—thinks that the physician in St. Louis who advised a change from there here, couldn't have had any knowledge of Brooklyn climate . . . nevertheless thinks that the journey & a temporary change will be very salutary" (*Correspondence*, II, 68).

to her[5] that I will mail in the morning—and write me in regard to questions asked

affectionately Jeff

[68]

St. Louis, Jan 21st 1869

My dear Walt,

Tis a long, long time since I have written you, and I am somewhat ashamed of it I assure you—but somehow I cannot seem to get time—and so day after day passes without writing. When I was at home I expected to be able to come to Washington to see you but matters turned out so—combined with Mats poor health at the time, that I could'nt make it out.

You have learned, of course, through Mother of our safe arrival in St. Louis   We at first put up at Barnums Hotel[1] but the place was inconvenient and price very high so I have hired a large room (abt. 25' × 20' by 16 high)   we have a large stove in it, two beds and have our meals served from the Restaurant in the basement—the room is directly opposite the office[2] and altogether quite pleasant—yet of course we should prefer to keep house—and shall do so if Mattie gets well enough—I think Mat is getting better fast. Her cough is very much less—she is gaining in flesh and is much stronger—she goes out with me on the work almost every day that it is pleasant and enjoys it hugely. The children go to school—quite away off too—so that they take the cars that run past the door and within a block or so of the school. They are both very healthy and when night comes are just as tired as they can be what with their ride in the car—their studies and play   Both of them grow fast—Hattie inde[e]d is quite a large girl.

The works are going along pretty well although just at this moment we are in ill-luck consequent upon the river having

5. See Waldron, pp. 58–60.

1. Erected in 1854, Barnum's Hotel at Second and Walnut was still among the finest in St. Louis. In 1866 Fay and McCarty purchased the hotel from the original owners, Theron Barnum and Josiah Fogg. Jeff had apparently broken his lease on the Olive Street house (see Letter 67).

2. This room was in the Hotel Garni, Billiard Hall, and Restaurant, owned by George Wolbrecht and located at the northeast corner of Fourth and Elm streets. Mattie described this room in detail to LVVW and complained of the high rent—twenty dollars per month (Waldron, p. 63).

risen and overflowed our cofferdam and thereby stopped progress on the river work.[3] I have just come down from there and found the water slowly falling and I hope in a few days—by Sunday next—to commence again—this is the part of the works that we expected would be difficult and we have got along with them better than we had a right to expect. For the last three weeks the river has been just on the verge of overflowing us—the consequence was that we worked hard to crowd the work and fight the water to keep it out of the dam— the foundations are from 25 to 30 feet under the surface of the water in the river and I felt it would make bad work to be drowned out   It would (the river) go up to within just a few inches of the top of the dam some days and then fall a few inchs—this style of worry and excitement has had rather a bad effect on me as I have for some two weeks had a pretty bad diarrhea—but since the matter is settled I am getting better of it—and shall undoubtedly be all right in a few days now.

I had a letter from Davis[4] to day who is now in Brooklyn— he says he took dinner on Sunday with Mother and George— that they were well and that George was getting along quite fast with his Portland Avenue house   Davis thinks of coming back to St. Louis _via_ Washington—if he does you will see him and he will give you an idea of what we are attempting to do here—I wish, dear Walt, that you could come out and see for yourself tho   'twould do us lots of good—cant you ring in on one of the R. Road examinat[ion] excursions[5] and come as far as St Louis   I think it would do you lots of good to come west for awhile just to see how big 'tis getting

How goes things with you Walt? Will you be able to retain your sit under the new come ins?[6] Do you write anything for publications now adays.[7] Tis so long since I have heard from

3. On January 17 the Mississippi River rose twenty inches above the cofferdam that protected the construction site. Just before this, Jeff had been "jubilant" about the progress on the works (LVVW to WW, January 19, 1869 [Trent]).
    4. See Letter 36.
    5. See Letter 63.
    6. Since Grant had not yet announced an appointee to attorney general, WW did not know who his next employer would be (Allen, p. 407).
    7. WW's essays "Democracy" and "Personalism" were published in the _Galaxy_ in December 1867 and May 1868. The poet also planned to publish a third essay, "Literature," in this journal, but the piece was rejected. These three essays were later combined in "Democratic Vistas" (1871).

you directly that I suppose you have had quite a good dea[l] published that I have not seen.

Mattie and the children send love—when you can, scribble us a line—tis a good day when we get a letter from any of you Do you hear much about Han,   poor girl I think of her often if I say but little. she has a hard lot of it.[8] Give my love to all mutual friends in Washington—particularly the O'Connors.[9]

Affectionately your brother Jeff

[69]

St. Louis, March 25th 1869

Dear Walt,

We have just had a letter from Mother telling us abt George's troubles in getting money for the house and how you stepped in and helped him out.[1] I am mighty glad that you was able to do it for I feared that George might have the blues and Mother get downhearted

Mat and I and the cubs have had a high old time for the last week or two. I wrote you when we left the hotel to go to a sort of hotel where they sent meals to the room "Hotel Garni"[2] they called it   we lived quite comfortably for awhile but it got rather dirty—and Mat concluded that she would leave—so she got a place in a boarding house in Pine street—I had'nt been there more than an hour before I saw we were awfully taken in—and told Mat to give the week's notice that we agreed to give before leaving—our week was up last Tuesday so we told the woman to give us our bill   she wanted pay for a month first then concluded she would take two weeks and last got down to within abt $6 of right—but even this Mat would'nt

8. Hannah's left thumb became so infected that she had to have it amputated in December 1868 (*Faint Clews*, p. 225).

9. See Letter 52.

1. In exchange for a mortgage, Jeff was paying George $3,000 in installments of $200 per month. George needed $600 immediately, however, to pay for a last coat of plaster on his own new house. Jeff's letter is the only evidence that WW sent the money George required. See *Correspondence*, II, 79, n. 11, and LVVW to WW, March 15, 1869 (Trent).

2. See Letter 68.

consent to pay—so we had some high old talk and concluded to leave the shantie at once   This was abt 8o̲c̲l̲k̲ on Monday evening—we moved next door and have (seemingly) a very excellent place—Yankee people, and clean—we are looking for a house and hope to find one to suit us soon

Matters are going abt as usual with me—Lately I have been taken up in time a good deal by the attacks of a lot of Dutch Enginers[3] here who have assailed our works—say they are failing &c particularly in regard to the foundations of the settling Res and by the way there is a report published by the Light House Board called "Memoirs on Foundations in Compressible Soils by Rich. Delafild"[4] that would be of great use to me in this connection   Can you get O'Conner[5] to send me a couple of copies (one for Davis)[6]   I enclose a letter[7] to him to ask him to send them to me with any other reports that he may have—out here these reports, particularly those made by U.S. Engineers are just of the greatest use and I do wish Walt when you ever have an opportunity to send or get any of such things you would do so. Send two when you can as Davis is as anxious to collect them as I am   They are really of a great deal more worth to us than the expensive publications, for they tell of what has really been done and how it was done   Dont fail Walt to give this note to O'Conner and if he can get him to send 'em

Mattie is about the same   To-day has been a miserable day for her and she is not as well as usual on account of it. The children are first rate with the exception of a little cold. they go

3. Probably Jeff's derogatory name for the journalists who claimed that the works were being constructed on unstable soil and would soon collapse (*Proceedings of the City Council*, March 16, 1869, pp. 373–75). Jeff may also be including the state committee which investigated the works on March 20 and noted several deficiencies in construction, including walls with cracks that had been plastered over (*Missouri Republican*, March 21, 1869).

4. Rich'd. Delafield, comp., The Light-House Board, *Memoir on Foundations in Compressible Soils, with Experimental Tests of Pile-Driving and Formula for Resistance Deduced Therefrom* (Washington, D.C.: GPO, 1868). This thirty-seven page pamphlet surveys the difficulties engineers encountered in building foundations on wet, sandy soils. It recommends that wooden piles be driven as deep as fifty feet before any foundation is begun, an expensive practice not followed at the Bissell's Point works.

5. See Letter 52.

6. See Letter 36.

7. See Letter 70.

to school and are learning quite well not very fast but steadily

We hav'nt commenced active work yet on our works—but I hope to be able to in a few weeks—we shall be pretty busy this summer—twill mostly be out-door work tho and not so tasking as last seasons work. I wish you might get an opportunity to come out and see us and see what we have done and are doing, cant you?

How do you get along under the new administration[8]   Will you remain fixed in your old place as usual   I suppose there is to be or has been considerable change as to employers. I hope that you will be able to hold on to the bite you have 'till better comes   I suppose Gra[n]t has found out before this that the country dont astonish worth a cuss and that he had better settle down and be like other Presidents.[9]

I often wonder how you are getting along and think I will write you oftener, but to tell the truth something is coming up all the time that keeps me busy—I was nearly a whole week in writing a report[10] to the City Council in answer to a Resolution passed at the instance of them same d—md Dutch engineers— but I think I gave them a full 20″ gun—anyway I hav'nt heard from them since—still I dont know where they will come at me next

When have you heard from Han—sometimes Mother

8. WW's relationship with the new attorney general, Ebenezer Rockwood Hoar, remains somewhat mysterious. On April 7 WW wrote Abby Price that Mr. Hoar "treats me very kindly." But earlier, on February 17, his mother had asked: "walt what is it you alluded to that was disagreeable in the office" (Trent). According to John Burroughs the poet had been subjected to "dastardly official insolence" from a person equal in rank to Harlan. See *Correspondence*, II, 80, n. 12.

9. Jeff's meaning here is difficult to ascertain, but he is probably concerned with Grant's Indian policy. In his inaugural address on March 4, 1869, Grant called for the "civilization and ultimate citizenship" of the "original occupants of this land," thereby implying that Indians had a proprietary claim on the land and rejecting the widely held notion that Indians were savages incapable of civilization. Given Jeff's racial attitudes in general, it is possible that he felt Grant's policies were misguided.

10. In response to the allegations printed in the local press, the city council on March 12 requested the Board of Water Commissioners to determine whether the waterworks were defective. Jeff was asked to report, and on March 15, 1869, he sent a firm reply that concluded, "there is no good ground for any statement or rumor that the foundations of any of the work . . . at Bissell's Point . . . in any way endanger the stability or permanency of the structures" (*Proceedings of the City Council*, March 16, 1869, p. 375).

speaks of having heard from Heyde—but she hardly ever says
anything abt Hannah—I wish she was happier in her situation
in life—tis a shame that her whole life should be made miserable by that puppy

Cant you come [on] that Pacific R. R. excursion dodge,[11]
and get out here to see us—try it if you have a chance

Walt, dont fail to look around for any report by U.S. Engineers on works and if you can get them send them on—I get
great aid from them—Love to all friends and as ever affectionately yours

Jeff

[70]

St. Louis, March 28th 1869

Wm O'Connor[1]
My dear friend

I am anxious to obtain through you whatever copies of Engineering reports that you can send me without too much trouble.
Particularly would I like to get the "Memoir on Foundations in
Compressible soils by Rich Delafield"[2] lately publish[ed] by
the Light House Bd.

Such reports are of great use as they show what has been
done, and particularly would any report on such a subject be
useful to me just now   Mr Davis[3] is associated with me here,
and when you can duplicate the copies we would both be
thankful

I must beg pardon for my wholesale style of asking for
these things—but being away from all advising engineers and
when books on the subject cannot well be had (not worth much
when had) I am forced to secure as best I can the records of the
experience of others

Please give my best regards to your wife—hoping that you
are all well and again asking pardon for the trouble I may give
you I remain

Yours very truly Thos J Whitman

11. See Letter 63.

1. See Letter 52.
2. See Letter 69.
3. See Letter 36.

St. Louis, April 5th 1869

Dear brother Walt

A few days since I received from Mr O'Connor[1] six of the little pamphlets[2] that I wrote to you about   They came in just right and have enabled me to make some very important changes in our work—I also received a letter from him yesterday saying that he would visit the U.S. Engineers office and pick up what he could for me—I do so hope he will—for they are just the books that do me the most good—and books that you cannot buy   Matters are about the same with us. Mattie is not so well for a week or so back—but I think it is the weather and then we are not so happily situated as we were before we left our room over the beer house[3]—nor do we live so well—I am trying to get a house and must succeed in a week or so then if Mattie dont get better I shall try and send her and the children up to Min. or Wis.[4] for some four or five months. I hope and feel pretty sure that when we get to housekeeping and Mat has a better time and better food she will get all right again—she is not near as bad as she was in Brooklyn but she is not as well as she was when she had been here a few weeks. The children are well and are learning to read and write and all that sort of thing—they behave well and get along nicely—yet they are not as comfortably situated [as] I hope to have them after awhile.

We hav'nt heard from home in a long time   I suppose matters are going as usual there however. I shall try and send George some money to-day[5]—I hope he will succeed and get his houses done before the 1st of May[6] so that Mother can get into one of them. I see that they are having some sort of a turn about in regard to the political offices in Brooklyn[7]—I hope

1. See Letter 52.
2. See Letter 69.
3. The Hotel Garni. See Letter 69.
4. See Letter 74.
5. See Letter 64.
6. May 1 was moving day in Brooklyn, a time when leases were given up or renewed.
7. On April 4 and 5, 1869, the *Missouri Republican* reported on "A Political Muddle in Brooklyn" in which Radical Republican state legislators threatened to abolish the Democratic Common Council. In what may have been a related action, a new independent water board was created on April 2,

that they wont reach Lane[8] both for his own sake and for George's—It would be too bad to have any change in the Water Dept—The city would suffer more than could be calculated.

There is a series of papers called "Papers on Practical Engineering, published by the Engineer Dept."[9] that I would like very much to get—I have seen no 5 and no 7 of them—they are of some 30 to 40 pages each, unbound—but give what of all things is the best for me—how certain works were constructed and the difficulties that they had to overcome. If Mr O'Connor or you can send me some of them I hope you will do so. Anyway the one he sent ("Memoir &c") gave me information so that I changed some portions of our work and I guess got me out of what might have turned out to be a bad fix—on the question of foundations. I shall write Mr O'Connor to-morrow—in the meantime please thank him for me—

How does the new administration affect you[10]—I hope that it will not be to your detriment. Are you still living the same as when I was at Washington[11] and do you get along well.

By the way, in my last I forgot to tell you abt the "bitters" and to thank you for them—Mat likes them first rate and I think they do her good. I would like to get a gallon or two of them if I could—Will you ask the party making them if they can be kept in a jug and if so write me how much it will cost to get a one or two gallon demijohn and fill it and I will send you the money. Mattie takes them regularly and her appetite is kept up thereby

All send love to you—and hope to hear from you soon

Affectionately yours Jeff

Or can I buy the bitters here   if so, and you can learn where, it will do as well

---

1869, which was no longer responsible to the Board of Aldermen. Shortly thereafter, Moses Lane resigned the position he had held for seven years and was succeeded by Colonel Julius W. Adams. George evidently continued to work part time in Brooklyn until the end of the year.

8. See Letter 9.

9. The series "Papers on Practical Engineering," published by the Engineer Department, was intended for use by the United States Corps of Engineers. Brevet Lieutenant Colonel James L. Mason wrote Paper Five, "An Analytical Investigation of the Resistance of Piles to Superincumbent Pressure" (1850); Captain D. P. Woodbury wrote Paper Seven, "Treatise on the Various Elements of Stability in the Well-Proportioned Arch" (1858).

10. See Letter 69.

11. See Letter 61.

[72]

St. Louis, April 18th 1869

Wm O'Connor Esq[1]

My dear friend

The package of "Reports"[2] and afterwards your letter were received—I intended before this to write you and return thanks for the same—but like many other of my "good intentions," I failed in it. I am under great obligations to you for the Reports—they furnished me with just the information I needed and you will please receive my most sincere thanks

In your letter you spoke of trying to get me some other reports of a like nature   I am very greedy to get these things and shall probably show it in my letters. Anything you can send me in the Report line will be of great use and a great favor to me

Matters are going about as usual with me—the works are progressing slowly—but we are doing pretty good work   I wish you might be able to pay us a visit—I would take great pleasure in showing you what we are doing, and telling what we intend to do.

I hav'nt heard from Walt for a long time, although I have written him several times. I hope he is well and that the change of "government" will not hurt either you or him

I remember with a great deal of pleasure my visit to Washington[3] and hope that during the coming season I shall be enabled to see you all again—if I get East during the summer I certainly shall manage to get around to see you all

I have again commenced keeping house—my wife was not so well boarding as when we are keeping house. I think I have a good dry house this time[4]—and quite convenient too—for a St. Louis house

My wife is better than she was in Brooklyn but not as well as when we first came back from the east. I hope she will get

1. See Letter 52.
2. Presumably six copies of the Delafield pamphlet. See Letter 69.
3. See Letter 61.
4. The Jefferson Whitmans had evidently moved into 934 Hickory, where they lived until 1873. Joseph P. Davis boarded with them until he left around March 1870 to build the waterworks in Lowell, Massachusetts (Waldron, p. 68).

better now that she is so fixed that she can have better food
than when boarding   The children are as well as ever—
Please remember me to your wife and family—I hope they
are well—and when you see Walt tell him we are all as usual—
I remain yours very truly

Thos. J Whitman

[73]

St. Louis, Mar 18th 1870

My Dear Mother

Mattie arrived all right on Wednesday abt 3ocl[1]—in the
afternoon—We were all glad enough to see her I assur you—
The weather had been very bad ever since she left Brooklyn—
but she got along very comfortably—and looked very well
when she got in—I should have written you yesterday—but I
understoo[d] Mat to say that she either would or had done so

Mat had a fine visit home and I think it has done her lots of
good—also I am very glad to hear that there is a prospect of
getting you and Walt out here[2]—hope you will come sure—

Please excuse this letter as I have just time to say that Mat
arrived safely—the children are well and happy as can be—

affectionately Jeff

[74]

In the spring of 1872, after consulting with numerous doc-
tors in St. Louis and the East, Mattie learned that she had
cancer. Jeff's letters from this period provide a detailed account
of her struggle with and death from the disease. Jeff hoped that
Mother Whitman and Walt would visit, partly to ease the
emotional strain and partly because he knew they had little
time to see Mattie. Illness, however, prevented such visits, and

---

1. Leaving her daughters with a housekeeper and Jeff's colleague Davis,
Mattie travelled to Brooklyn in mid-February 1870. Jeff accompanied her as
far as Pittsburgh where he stopped for business before joining her in Brooklyn. After a few days Jeff returned to St. Louis but Mattie remained in Brooklyn until mid-March (Waldron, p. 68).
2. These plans were not acted upon (Waldron, p. 70).

Cabinet photograph of Thomas Jefferson Whitman, about 1872. Courtesy of the Missouri Historical Society.

Jeff and the girls were left alone to cope with the death. As Hattie wrote Walt two days after her mother's funeral, "Every body is very kind out here but if one of you could only be here it would be so pleasant for Papa. Dear Papa feels so badly" (February 24, 1873 [WW Papers]).

St. Louis, Oct 5th 1872

My dear Mother

Mattie has returned from St. Paul[1] but I am sorry to say is hardly as well as when she went away   Up to yesterday she was very sick but seemed to be quite a good deal better this morning—A few days since when the doctor came to see her he told her that he thought he would have her go to Philadelphia again to see Dr Gross[2] and also to New York to see Dr

1. Mattie and her daughters had been to St. Paul and Wyoming, Minnesota, in hopes of improving Mattie's health (Waldron, p. 81, n.1).

2. Dr. Gross (or Grosse, as Mattie spells the name) was probably the Philadelphia physician who diagnosed Mattie's disease as cancer (Waldron, p. 77).

Cabinet photograph of Martha Mitchell Whitman, about 1872. Courtesy of the Missouri Historical Society.

Clark[3]—Of course if she comes I will write George—if she continues to gain she will not come yet awhile

I heard her tell Hattie this morning that she would certainly write you a letter to-day—

Enclosed I send draft for $25. and I want it expended thusly $10. of it George must take and go over to that place in the city that I found out they had good liquors and buy some good wine[4]—California Port and Muscatel Sautern and "sich"— The tother $15 you can do what you please with—but dont go back on me about the wine—

How is George and Loo[5]—and Ed—I suppose Ed has hunted up an "organ" before this[6]—

3. Unidentified.

4. In August 1872 LVVW and Edward reluctantly moved into George's home in Camden, New Jersey.

5. Louisa Orr Haslam Whitman, who had married George in April 1872.

6. While in Brooklyn, Edward Whitman seems to have spent most of his time running errands for his mother and attending his favorite church. Jeff imagines that Edward has found a new church and suggests that it was the church music that engaged the limited mental powers of his brother.

Matters go middling well with me—have been very busy—had no time to do anything—could'nt even go a fishing

Love to all—tell Walt that I wish he would come and see us—shall leave it to Mat to persuade you and Loo and George out here—Hat and Jess are as well as can be   I sometimes think they are "weller"

Good bye—Keep up your temper and dont get tight

Affectionately Jeff

George can get your draft cashed at Starr's—[7]

[75]

St. Louis, Nov 10th 1872

Dear Walt,

Your letter to Mat received[1]   We were very glad to hear that you were with Mother—Mattie and I both feared that Mother was having a bad time with her swollen hand—I suppose you have ere this received Mats letter to you at Washington.[2]

Now about Mats going to Camden and Mothers return with her—our situation here is just this   we have a nice house—and good servants   Mat has nothing to do in the housekeeping way—nor is it needed—the children—one or tother—attends to the marketing—so that there is nothing to attend to—now our idea was that the great change of air, diet and scene that coming west would be to Mother might do her great good—I have a good horse and buggy that she could ride often (every day if she wished)   she could thus see all the city without trouble—Our good weather is now, the fall and early winter—As to her traveling I do not think she would have any trouble—she would take a car in Philadelphia that comes to within abt a mile and a half of my house   here she would take the R. R. stage and be brought to the door—no change but that—and her ticket in Philadelphia brings her and her trunks and puts them both in the house (is not that an improvement over old times)   The run from Philadelphia is about 38 to 40

7. Starr & Co., evidently a pipe foundry in Camden, New Jersey (Loving, p. 161).

1. WW's letter of about November 9 is not extant.

2. Probably Mattie's letter of October 28 (Waldron, pp. 83–85).

hours (say a day and two nights) good beds (taking a section)
and [I] do not believe hardly Mother would know she was traveling. Unless Mat thinks Mother would come back with her I
hardly think Mat will go East just now—her chest and lungs
both seem better now and if by care I can get her in the way of
taking some little food I have hopes she will get along yet

Not much news with me   am still pegging away—write
us what you think of Mothers coming—I would like to write
more but am called away by a notice that a pipe is "busted"
affectionately Jeff

[76]

St. Louis Dec 8th 1872

Dear Mother

Your various letters were received. I was up to Chicago[1]
when they arrived and thus Mattie did not get [them] for a few
days after they came to the office. Mattie is pretty sick   she
has had a great deal of trouble with her right arm and hand—
a[nd] is not able to use it to write just now—for the last few
days she has suffered the torments of Hell in being blistered—
she had four large strong blisters on her at once and this morning I had to thake them off or I feared she would go crazy—she
is some easier now—yet suffers much from the terrible places
places left by these blisters   It seems to have helped her arm
and hand some and perhaps her lungs a little yet she coughs a
grat deal   Since the receipt of your letter saying that you
would not come out here Mat has about given up her idea of
going East—at any rate just now she is altogether too sick to
think of such a thing. She has had quite a sleep this (Sunday)
morning the first since Wednesday last. As soon as the places
heal up a little I hope she will be comfortable—yet my dear
Mother it is no use to try and think she is getting better—she is
failing all the time—yet by care and attention and all that I
hope she will get through the winter and if she does I shall try
and get her to go out towards California or into the Rocky

1. Jeff may have been consulting, especially since his old boss Moses
Lane had recently worked with E. S. Chesbrough, the chief engineer of the
Chicago Sewerage Commission.

Mountains[2] As good luck would have it we have been more than fortunate in regard to help—Mat had two girls, sisters, one a good cook and the other [a] house girl some fellow came out from Jersey City and married the house girl and the cook thought she would leave but as she had another sister also a cook Mat made an arrangement by which the second cook came to us as cook and our old one took the place of the married one so you see we are in good condition for eating—they do splendidly and Mat has not the least care of either house or house keeping

The children are perfectly well and go to school regularly Jess has just begun to take lessons in music and they both go to dancing school[3]—so all this—with the marketing and going to the stores—occupies all their time—indeed they seem to work as hard as anyone

I have just had to stop and go over to the bed and dress these blister sores with sweet oil—Mat is suffering very much—you may know how much when I tell you that for the first time she cannot restrain groaning—I do not know whether the Dr will like my taking off the blisters or not—but I do know that Mat could not have stood it many hours longer

We have just commenced with the horse sickness here[4] and it is quite an interesting thing to see how quickly people in a big city will adapt themselves to circumstances—only a few days ago and all the affairs and business that the horse entered into were progressing the same as usual—to-day not one hundretth of the horses are out—oxen quite plenty—last night quite a fire broke out—the fire engines were on the spot pretty near as soon as usual—but drawn in the old fashioned way by men.

My own horse is sick but not very bad—yet bad enough to make me feel mighty sorry for him—I hav'nt had him out

2. As early as March 1872 Mattie made reference to a proposed trip west for her health (Waldron, p. 76).

3. According to Mattie's letter to LVVW of October 28, 1872, both Hattie and Jessie were taking dancing and music lessons. Their music teacher was a Mr. Bowman (Waldron, p. 59); their dancing teacher was probably either Carl Emilie or Julius Blemner, both of whom had "Dancing Academies" at this time.

4. The nationwide epidemic of horse disease swept over St. Louis in December 1872, disabling nearly all of the horses and mules. Businesses requiring the use of these animals were suspended, and the fire department had to hire 350 additional men to pull equipment to fires.

since last Tuesday—I hope he will not be out of use more than a week

I was up to Chicago last week   Mr Lane[5] came down from Milwaukee to see me, we had a few hours of good old fashioned talk and I was extremely glad to see him—he looks first rate, certainly coming west was a good move for Lane

We noted what you said about receiving a letter from Jo Barkeloo[6]—and nothing would give Mat more pleasure than to make them a visit—but she cannot think of such a thing now—I hope she may be able to accept the invitation next season

I am well, have a good deal to do but still manage to get along well enough—the works progress well and we have just worked through a pretty bad season—but we got through without much trouble after all

How do you do, dear Mammy   How goes it with you? What sort of wine did you get and how do you like it?[7] How is George and Loo and Ed—how I would like to see you all—does George still have plenty of work—What do you hear from Han—I suppose Walt comes to see you now and then—Has Ed found a church in Camden to his liking—it must be quite a draw back to the Bedford Av affair, Ed's leaving   have they had to shut up the shop on account of Ed's moving away from Brooklyn

Do you ever get over to Philadelphia, and if so how do you like it? and a thousand other things I would like to ask you if I could see you

Do you ever hear from Brooklyn? I suppose George does tell him to drop me a line and tell me how things go there since the new dispensation[8]

5. See Letter 9. Lane was appointed chief engineer in charge of constructing the Milwaukee waterworks in 1871.

6. LVVW received letters from Josephine Barkeloo dated October 17, November 3, and December 16, 1872 (WW Papers). Like Helen Price, "Joe" seems to have been deeply attached to LVVW, and she was also fond of the Jefferson Whitmans. The first of her letters closes in an unusually intimate way: "it is my bed hour. Good night, you are in your dreams, and I am kissing you in imagination   you half awaken and say 'Is that you—Walter?' but you are mistaken   it was—Yours truly, Joe."

7. See Letter 74.

8. On April 28, 1872, Brooklyn again reorganized the administration of the waterworks by creating a Board of City Works, which in 1873 was renamed the Department of City Works. Jeff's old friend Colonel Julius W. Adams remained chief engineer despite the changes.

Well dear Mammy I guess I will consider this a dose for this time—you must write whenever you can—all send love—Mat and I and the children too are much very much, disappointed that you do not think well of coming out and staying the winter with us—did you know how easy the travel is you would not mind that part of it

All send love to Loo and George and Ed—I will try and write a little more frequently

affectionately Jeff

[77]

St Louis Dec 25th /72

Dear Mother—

A Merry Christmas to you all—and many of them—We to-day, have been experiencing about as cold weather as one can stand   For the last four or five days it has been terrible cold—but yesterday it was a little too much for anything   10, 12 and down to 20 below Zero has been our experience—what do you think of that?

Mattie received your letter all right—Mat is feeling about the same—no better, nor do I see that she fails much more—she keeps her bed about half her time—she has no appetite—has not eaten anything for two months—except her raw eggs and whiskey[1]—this seems to be about the only food that agrees with her—

We have had this horse disease here[2]—but not as bad as you have had it East I guess—my horse has been very sick—I thought at one time I would lose him but he is getting well again now   I hav'nt used him for abt three weeks—nor shall I be able to unless the weather changes, for a long while to come.

Nothing new—I was up to Chicago a couple of weeks or so ago—saw Mr Lane[3] up there—he seems to like it west—he looks first-rate and has plenty to do—I judge from what he says all his people like it at Milwaukee

I was sorry to hear that George had been discharged from

1. In October 1868, WW discussed Mattie's case with Dr. A. D. Wilson of Brooklyn who recommended a diet she apparently adopted: "whiskey, wine, condensed milk, &c" (_Correspondence_, II, 68).
2. See Letter 76.
3. See Letters 9 and 76.

the Brooklyn payroll—I suppose however that when they have pipes to make he will get the work again—will he not[4]—I do not hear from Brooklyn any more—have not heard for a long time—I had a letter from Joe Barkeloo[5] yesterday telling me that she was about to start for Europe—I suppose she has gone ere this—did you hear from her

Mattie speaks of you all very often—she would like above all things to see you and have a talk—but she is altogether too sick to undertake the journey just now. I was sorry, very sorry, that you made up your mind that you would not come this way—as I thought, and still believe, that it would have done you both good—but as the season now stands of course it would be impossible on account of the weather

I suppose you have quite quiet times—as of course you do not go out much—and I hardly expect you make many acquantances—how do you like Camden—I cannot tell how 'tis in the winter—but I remember it last summer as being very pleasant and quiet—How does Ed get along without a church to attend—or has he obtained a "situation"

The children are well as can be and have been fixing up their christmas all day   They all send love—Mat and all—I hope dear Mother that your arm is not so bad as it was. We think that Mattie is getting better of her lameness—at one time she could not use her arm at all

All send love to Loo & George and hope you will write when you can—

affectionately Jeff

[78]

[St. Louis,] Jan 14th—1873

Dear Mother

Mat has been at me for a long time to write you but I have not been able to get at it—Mat's hand and arm is so lame that she is not able to write herself and so I promise each day that I

4. Soon after this, George took a job as a pipe inspector for the Metropolitan Water Board of New York City, although he continued to live in Camden (Loving, p. 30). Jeff's powerful friends in New York and Brooklyn, William E. Worthen and Julius W. Adams, may have helped George obtain this position. See Letter 78.

5. See Letter 76.

will do it as soon as I get to the office—but day after day gets away and I do not do it   Last night Hattie had a letter from Walt and to-day one has come from you—but as Hat has gone to school we shall not know what is in it till she gets home Mat also had a letter from Walt[1] a day or two since and some weeks ago one from Loo—she would answer them all if she could write—at times her arm gets a little better but the instant she attempts to use it it pains her so that she can hardly live—Her chest pains her some but not like it did—her great trouble is her lungs—and I fear she is failing not fast but surely in this.—lately even the eggs and whiskey does not agree with her and nearly all the nourishment she has taken has been lemonade—and at times a few raw oysters—and now and then a kind of lemon jelly that she has made—she goes down-stairs once a day—generally abt 6oclk in the evening to dinner and when she gets to her room again she feels very tired and has to go to bed   Lately the Dr has had to give her some medicines to make her sleep and since she has been taking that her cough has got better a little—I feel in hopes however if we do not have too hard a winter that she may get along till spring and then I shall get her up into the mountains in Colorado   She speaks very often about you all and has been much disappointed that you did not feel able to come out and see her—she sends lots of love to you all

Hattie and Jess are well and growing to be quite big girls they act pretty good and work pretty hard what with one thing and another that they have to do—

I still am running the Water Works of course—and hope to do so but like all other city affairs we are expecting a roust-a-bout from the Legislature this winter—how it will all turn out is one of them things that no feller can find out—I was sorry to hear that the Brooklyn people had dropped George—as it indicated that they (I fear) wished to get rid of him to give his place to some other party—though perhaps this is not the case—at any rate he ought to keep posted at what they are doing and when he goes to New York <u>always</u> go go over and see them in Brooklyn—tell him to write me after he sees them all and tell me who is who and who has charge of the pipe

1. WW's letters of about January 12 to Hattie and about January 10 to Mattie are not extant.

department now whether it be Adams[2] or Rhodes[3]   If Adams
I may help him to get back again when they have anything to
do

We have had the most terrible weather here this winter—
cold as could be for a few days then mild—to day has been mild
but very rainy, damp and just the most disagreeable in the
world for Mat.

Yesterday was fine and warm and clear—but so much frost
in the ground that one could not stir out with comfort

Mat and I and the children often talk about you all and
wonder if you can keep warm this winter and how you all
look—We would like to pop in on you some evening—what a
jolly time we would all have would we not

Give my love to Lu and George and Ed—and when you
write Walt tell him how we all are[4]—

All send love over and over again

affectionately Jeff

[79]

St. Louis, Feb 5th 1873

Dear Mother

I write to say that Mattie is very sick—that although yet
hopeful—I fear very much that in some of the paroxisms of
coughing she may become so weak that she will not rally
again—most of the time she continues cheerful and good—but
at times her sufferings are too much for her to bear—as good
as she always has been about such things

Of course we will all hope and pray for the best—yet you
must not be surprised to hear that it is all over with the dear

---

2. Jeff is probably referring to his old friend Colonel Julius W. Adams
who was now chief engineer of the Brooklyn Water Works; see Letter 41.

3. Probably John H. Rhodes, a water surveyor for the Brooklyn Department of City Works.

4. LVVW sent this letter on to WW after she added this postscript:
"Write to poor Mat Walter dear   i am about as usual   my cold is not much
better but it will wear off & pass   i thought i would send Jeffs letter."

soul at any time—I have written to Walt[1]—I wish Walt would come and see her—do you not think he would[2]—Love to all

affectionately Jeff

[80]

St. Louis, Feb 7th 1873

My dear Mother

I wrote you a few days ago apprising you as to Mattie's health   I do not see that there is any change since then—if any she is somewhat easier—that is these terrible fits of coughing and choking do not come so often—yet when they do come I hardly expect her to come out of them

The weather has been exceedingly pleasant here for four or five days now and I have had Mattie out in the buggy for about an hour each day—this seems to do her more good than anything else

To-day, if I can arrange it I intend to take her to a photograph gallery to have another picture taken

She speaks often and much about you—and wants to see you very, very much—I suppose you would hardly dare undertake the journey—and it would be impossible for me to leave her to come for you—of course I would arrange all the money matters if you could come—I suppose you know how the coming would be—you would take a "section" in one of the through sleeping cars—you would be abt 40 hours on the car—this car would bring you to East St. Louis—where I would meet you—here we would take a carriage that would take you to the house—Of course I can understand that you may not feel able for the journey—but I feel positive that if you once did get here you would feel better than you do[1]—

1. This letter is not extant.

2. Unfortunately, WW had suffered a paralytic stroke on January 23 and could not leave his rooms (see *Correspondence*, II, 196). LVVW wrote two letters to Jeff about the poet's stroke but neither one reached its destination (LVVW to Helen Price, February 12, 1873 [Morgan]).

1. Despite LVVW's own failing health, this letter made her seriously consider making the trip to St. Louis. She wrote Helen Price that Mattie "seems to have such a wish to see me and walt i am going to try to go if i think i can any way stand the journey" (February 12, 1873 [Morgan]).

I will write you as soon as I can again   Love to George and
Loo and Eddy—I hope you are feeling pretty well dear Mother
affectionately Jeff

[81]

St. Louis, Feb 7th 1873

Dear brother Walt

I wrote you a few days since about Mattie

The next day I saw in one of the papers here that you were
confined to your room with sickness—is this true?[1] I have
written mother again this morning—there is no particular
change in Mattie—I have been able to take her out for about an
hour's drive for the last three days—this helps her more than
anything else

In writing you I spoke to you about coming on—I also mentioned it to Mother—since then I have wondered if—
supposing you to feel pretty good—you could'nt come by way
of Philadelphia and bring Mother with you   Mat seems to
want to see you two so very very much

I will write or telegraph you if any change occurs before I
hear from you

affectionately Jeff

[82]

St. Louis, Feb 9th 1873

Dear Mother

Mattie is, I think a little improved since I last wrote you—
she passed an easier night last night—

Friday she went down to a photograph gallery in a carriage
and we took her in a chair up the stairs—I had a lady sent there

1. In the "Personal" column for February 4, 1873, the *Missouri Republican* tersely noted, "Walt Whitman is ill with paralysis." WW's sad letter of
February 8 made clear both his affection for Mattie and the serious nature of
his illness: "Dear, dear, dear, sister Matty—O how I have been thinking of
you, & shall all day—I have not now the use of my limbs to move from one
room to the other—or else I should come on immediately to St. Louis . . .
Your unhappy, sorrowful, loving brother" (*Correspondence*, II, 196).

to fix her hair and dress her and altogether I think we obtained a most excellent picture of her—though I hav'nt seen the pictures yet

I do not think she suffers so much—though yesterday she had a bad day all day—on account of the excitement

Love to all—will write again to morrow

affectionately Jeff

[83]

St Louis, Feb 11th /73

Dear Mother

Mattie is about the same—she has not failed so much within the last few days—indeed I do not know but that she feels a little better—but she is weaker—yet does not suffer so much   If the weather should prove good I hope she may still gain again—yet the Dr gives no hope—if she can keep up till Walt gets well enough to come to see her I should rejoice

I received your letter this morning dear Mother—I knew you would all feel badly—but as Mattie was failing so very rapidly I then thought she would not live even a day—I cannot say that Mattie worries much about the children—the fact is that she has been sick so long and suffered so much that I do not think she appreciates how near the end is

If there is any change I will write immediately. Love to all

affectionately Jeff

[84]

St Louis Feb 11th /73

Dear Walt

Yours received last night[1]—We were all sorry to hear that you had had such a bad turn[2]—and glad enough to hear that you were gaining—

Mattie is about the same as when I last wrote—she is not failing so badly now—last night she rested better—did not seem to have quite so much pain

1. WW's letter of about February 9 is not extant; it is also not listed among the poet's lost letters (_Correspondence_, II, 363).

2. See Letter 81.

Still I do not think that she can be said to gain any—only she is not failing so fast and that is a great comfort—The last two days have been damp and cold and rainy so that makes it bad—I do hope dear Walt you will be able to come and see her—if [*sic*] would be a great comfort to her—

She sends you love and so dear brother do I

Jeff

[85]

St. Louis, Feb 13th 1873

Dear Mother

Mattie is still about the same—for the last two days she has suffered more with her side and back—severe and cutting pain,—than before—I wish you would write to her as soon as you get this. I did not like to show her your last letter on account of fearing she would see and feel too badly that she could not live—she is cheerful and brave—no thing can make her despondent in the shape of personal suffering—and I do not allow her to suffer from any feeling that we feel mournful or despondent

The children are very well indeed and good too—I am well except a bad throat and cold

affectionately Jeff

[86]

St. Louis, Feb 15th 1873

Dear Mother

Yours received—Mattie is still about the same—her cough and choking is a little better but she has more trouble with her arm and side   last night it was terrible painful and she slept very little

This morning she was feeling a little easier

Tell George that I am exceeding grateful to him—and may call for him to come on—but not at present

Love to all

affectionately Jeff

You must excuse brevity—I have hardly time to do what business is absolutely required

[87]

St. Louis, Feb 16th 1873

Dear Mother

When I wrote you yesterday I had not had time to read your last letter but when I went home and gave it to Mattie the thought that you _might_ yet come to see her made her feel very happy It seems to be the one desire of her life to have you come and see her—she rested much better last night—her throat is better and her cough better but she has the most intense pain in her side and shoulder and arm—One side and breast is so swollen that it makes her quite one-sided and the pain most all the time is terrible severe—

What do you think about the trip? I am sure we can make you very comfortable here—and I believe you could come through without hardly knowing it—at the same time if George could he might come with you—

You would not need to make any preparation for the journey—you would find a colored porter on the car that would bring you your meals—you could have the table put up in the section and eat as if you were at home—

If Mat was well enough I would come for you—but as it is I cannot leave her—

The children are very good and as well as can be—

I will write again soon write me and tell [me] what you think about coming

Love to Loo and George

affectionately Jeff

[88]

St. Louis, Monday Feb 24th 1873

My dear dear Mother

Since Matties death I could not write you before—there were many things I had to do and as I knew you had been advised of it by telegraph on the evening of the 19th I felt as if it would be better to wait until I could feel a little like writing to you

The circumstances attending her death are quite impressive—Over two weeks before it the Dr. told me that I might

expect her death at any moment—that her lungs were in immediate liability to rupture and that each breath she drew was
a risk, that I must not leave her alone a moment   On Tuesday
she seemed to feel a little more like her old self—though suffering much pain from the fact that the right lung had been
pierced by the gathering and the air in breathing would gather
between the parts and remain—her right side and breast were
very much enlarged from this cause—the pain was intense
from the cancer and a few days before her death the old spinal
trouble came back to her[1]—yet with all this, dear Mother, did
she keep up to the last—not a murmer escaped her   she was
cheerful to a degree and at noon of the day she died sat up in
her chair and directed how my lunch should be prepared

We had been having a number of days of bad rainy and cold
weather—but Tuesday was bright and warm—but so many
called that she could not go out riding   On Wednesday, the
day being clear she thought if I could take her out that she
might feel better, as the Dr. had told her when out in the air he
thought perhaps the slight increased out-side pressure of air
from what it would be in a room might decrease the swelling of
her side. As I said I was home at lunch and she was up and
dressed—I then went to my office to attend to some business
and then took my horse and buggy arriving at the house abt
3ck—I found Mattie dressed—furs &c on—sitting awaiting
me—I took her in my arms and carried her out to the buggy
as I sat her in—she said "wait now 'till I fix my dress"—these
were the last words she spok—She then fell over on her side
I immediately took her back to the room and sat her in the
chair—she knew me yet—but could not speak—a short time
after Hattie came from school   Mattie knew her too—then
Jessie came—she took their hands and mine and laid them
with her own and so held them until she became uncon-
scious—she died at 8ock in the evening—but the Dr—who
came and sat an hour or so with us thought that she had no
pain after about 5ock.

Quite a number of ladies came in—it seemed quite singular
that they should happen to come at that time   Mrs Flad,[2] Mrs

1. See Letter 43.
2. The wife of Henry Flad, an important civil engineer and public figure
with whom Jeff frequently worked (see Letter 104 and Introduction). The
Flads and Jefferson Whitmans also visited socially (Waldron, pp. 49 and 61).

Knipper[3] and Mrs Darcy[4] all happen to come to see her without notice within 5 or 6 moments after she was taken—I sent for Mr & Mrs Bulkley[5]   the[y] came over immediately and remained till Thursday night and have come and attended to every thing for me—Mrs Bulkley took the children down town and had black made for them and Bulkley himself attended to all the funeral arrangements—The funeral was Saturday at 10½ ock. I should have mentioned in the first dispatch at what time the funeral would have been but I feared if I asked George to come on he might do so at a risk to his business—yet wished to make it so that he could come if he could without too much trouble. Not hearing from you and feeling something had to be decided I then sent the second dispatch and made it I thought so that George could get here. However it was just the same. I know and feel that George and his wife too sympathize with me deeply and I also know dear Mother that you do. Mattie spoke about you in the morning for a long time and asked with her whole heart that she might yet live to see you—she loved you very dearly and had she been with you—or had we all been together no doubt she would have been happier in her life— yet she seemed quite happy and I feel that we did all we could— though I sometimes think perhaps I was not as good to her as she deserved—that I was too jolly—you may say—when I knew from the bottom of my heart that she suffered so much—dear dear child—how brave she was—how true she was—how good she was.

The funeral was large, very large.[6] two clergymen came. they each gave an address and spoke most feelingly about her—the children behaved like angels, almost, and tried to cheer me by promises and protests that they would be good and that dear Mamma was free from suffering—and that it was for the best. To-day, Monday, Jessie has commenced her

3. The wife of Adolph Knipper, a superintendent at the waterworks.

4. Either Mary Darcy, a widow, or the wife of Henry J. D'Arcy, an attorney. The latter was temporarily a partner of one O'Reilly, perhaps Henry B. or Michael B. O'Reilly.

5. Mary Moody and Philemon C. Bulkley were former residents of New York City who had moved to St. Louis in 1867. Mr. Bulkley held an interest in an iron foundry and may have provided material for the waterworks.

6. Funeral services were held in the family dwelling at 934 Hickory Street. According to Hattie, Jeff's "office was closed so that all the commissioners came" (letter to WW, February 24, 1873 [Feinberg]).

school again, and Hattie is at home attending to the house—
our girls remain at present and I think they will, though they
say that they cannot do so without I get some one as they express it to be the "head of the house" and I am now trying to
make some arrangements for a "housekeeper" though I shall
not decide of course until I can find out and ascertain something [about] the person I propose to get

                                          2ock P.M. 24th—
We have just received your letter and also the one from Aunt
Loo to the children—I have just come from home—Hattie had
written a long letter to Uncle Walt and I shall mail it with
this—I am extremely sorry to hear that Walt is worse. I do
hope he will not have a set back of any length of time

You must write to us dear Mother as often as you can and
[tell] dear brother George and dear sister Loo that they must
write also when they can—

The children are behaving bravely—indeed more so than I
had an idea they could—they are very very good—Tell Eddy
that we often speak of him and we all believe that he feels bad
enough about his Sister Mats death

All send best love

                                          Affectionately Jeff

[89]

                                    St Louis, March 16th 73
Dear Walt,

I have been wishing to write you for some days, but I have
been away so much lately that it did seem as if I never would
get time[1]

Dear Walt, I wrote Mother a long, long letter giving as
near as I could the particulars about dear Matties death[2]—I
hope and suppose that they sent it to you and that it is not
necessary therefore for me to re-state it.

Dear Walt this has been and is a heavy blow to me   I was
so much with her and we were so in each others confidences
that it leaves me very lonly

I think Hattie has written to you about how we have

---

1. On March 9 Hattie wrote to LVVW that "Papa will never write a
letter   he makes me write all the letters" (WW Papers).
2. See Letter 88.

*Manahatta Whitman around the age of 20 (c. 1880). Courtesy of
the Missouri Historical Society.*

broken up and are now living at Mr Bulkleys[3]   It is by far the
best thing for us all—Mrs Bulkly was a particular friend of
Matties and liked her much—she likes the children and takes
good care of them—I could not very well continue to keep
house without stopping Hattie's schools and I did not wish to
do that—but I shall not sell my things but pack them away as I
best may and hope as soon as Hattie gets a couple of years older
we will try again

Well my dear Walt how is it with you—you have been and I
fear are yet—sick   I hope—sincerely hope that you are getting better now—you must take good care of yourself and not
attempt over exertion   From what I have heard it is a terrible
sickness—and one that is apt to discourage—Dear Walt I hope
you will get all right again soon

3. For the Bulkleys, see Letter 88. The specific letter Jeff refers to is not
known; however, on March 14 Hattie wrote to LVVW that the family had
moved to Bulkley's on Saturday, March 8, and that "Papa has a very nice
room but I sleep with Minnie Bulkley a young lady about sixteen years old"
(WW Papers). Hattie does not mention what arrangements were made for
Jessie.

Jessie Louisa Whitman around the age of 17 (c. 1880). Courtesy of the Missouri Historical Society.

I have had to go to Jefferson City—for some three or four days—and last week was at Kansas City[4]—. I have been engaged to make a plan of water works for Kansas City[5] and shall have to go up there again in eight or ten days

Mr Lane[6] came down from Millwaukee to the funeral—I was exceeding glad to see him as he was so kind and sympathetic

When you can Dear Walt write to me—you must not accuse me of not thinking or wondering about you—I have often

4. Jeff disliked having to leave his daughters so soon after Mattie's death. Hattie's letter to LVVW of March 14 notes that "Papa gave me a present of a most beautiful diamond ring   it is perfectly elegant   it has 4 splendid diamonds and five emeralds and he gave me a git [gilt?] necklace and cross and a black locket with six pearls and he gave Jessie a plain gold ring. I told him that I never got so many presents at once before   I dont know what he did it for but I suppose he gave them to me because he was sorry he was going away" (WW Papers).

5. Kansas City, Missouri, was planning a new waterworks at this time. Jeff may have submitted one of the two propositions the city rejected in the spring of 1873.

6. See Letter 9.

thought how I would like to see you and if I can so arrange my work shall come on to do so

For a few days before her death Mattie talked a great deal about you and Mother   She wanted to see you both once more and at one time thought she would try to do so   poor child she little knew how soon she would be free from her pains

Love to you dear brother and I hope you will be able to come out and see me soon—do you not think it would do you good.

I think I could make you enjoy yourself.

Jeff

[90]

St Louis March 26th 73

My dear Mother

I received your latest letter—I was glad indeed to hear from you—yet exceeding sorry to hear from Walt that he was feeling so badly—I hope beyond all things that he is now feeling better[1]

The children are quite well and apparently quite happy—they speak of you often—and talk only of you and their mamma

You ask a question in regard to the silence of all our letters in regard to Mrs O'Rielly.[2] in regard to this I must say to you that though I cannot tell you in a letter in regard to why the letters are silent in regard to her I can and will explain the matter to you when I see you which I sincerely hope will be before long—I do not know how soon—yet as we have made a contract with some Hartford people for a new Engine[3]—I

1. In his letters to LVVW of March 1873, WW stressed that he was slowly, gradually regaining his health. Nonetheless, he acknowledged on March 13 that "the principal trouble is yet in the head, & so easily getting fatigued—my whole body feels heavy, & sometimes my hand" (*Correspondence*, II, 205–06).

2. Unfortunately Mrs. O'Reilly remains a mysterious figure. Jeff is obviously flustered in writing about her—he repeats "in regard" five times in two sentences—and he clearly intends to hide something. This woman may have been married to the O'Reilly connected with Henry J. D'Arcy (see Letter 88), but this is conjecture. See Letter 92.

3. The Hartford Foundry and Machine Company of Hartford, Connecticut, provided the third pumping engine for the waterworks.

hope I may be sent East early in the summer—Of one thing I can assure you no one on earth loved Mattie better than she except our own family and though denied—to the public her company yet they did meet and were happy—I wrote you very fully in regard to Matties death—much I could write you about her later life—abt all she talked about was Walt and yourself—she had a great desire to see you—and I am sorry—very sorry—that you could not have met—but fate cannot be helped

I am feeling pretty well Have been away from the city [a] great deal of the time lately—am employed to make a design for water works at Kansas city, and have been up there a good deal lately[4]—shall write you again soon Love to George and Loo—and all send love to you

Affectionately Jeff

[91]

St. Louis, March 30th 1873

My dear Walt

Although I have written two or three letters to you, and Hattie one or two—yet we do not hear from you dear brother, are you too sick to write I had a letter from Mother yesterday in which she told me that you had been out a few times and once as far as the office—I hope you have not had a set back since then

If you can I wish you would write me how you are and if you have any chance of getting out here this season—I wish you could come I think you would enjoy it and I know we would enjoy it hugely

I fear from the way that Mother writes that she is not feeling very well—that she is not quite as happy as when she kept her own house—what do you think about it[1]

I shall always feel sorry that Mother could not have come out here before Mattie died—she did want to see her so

4. See Letter 89.

1. LVVW was in her final months of life, and some of her complaints undoubtedly resulted from fatigue and pain. She was also bothered by George's wife, Louisa, who talked of nothing "much but house and money" and who sent Edward Whitman on many errands but begrudged him his portion of butter. See LVVW to WW, March 24, 1873, and April 21, 1873 (Trent).

badly—for a week or two before she died she talked much about both you and Mother and longed much to see you both—but it was not [to] be that she could see either of you

I have felt quite anxious about you—as tis so long since I heard from you directly—I [hope] dear Walt you feel like writing, at least a short letter to me

Hattie and Jess keep quite well and are as good as can be Write to me Walt

Affectionately Jeff

[92]

St. Louis—Apl 24th 1873

My dear Mother—

Your letter was handed me just as I was leaving the city to go to Kansas.¹ I could not answer it then—nor did I have time to do so while there   I read it and sent it to our dear friend,² as I knew it was very much desired.

Dear Mother, I can see by your letter that you still worry and think about Mattie, dear dear Mattie, and in this you are not unlike all of us. We all remember her—we all love her—and I above all others know how good, how true how brave she was—the blow is indeed a great one—yet I try hard to bear up under it. Dear Mother you speak of dear Mat as being very near to you—as being always in sympathy with you   Yes indeed was that true—not only to you but to all of us. You speak of receiving a letter from a dear friend—yes friend indeed—and one whom Mattie most dearly and sincerely loved—one whom—if you knew—you would find as near the dear daughter you have lost as two can be alike, in all things of affection love and truth—No doubt you will hear from the same person again—only you must keep the matter to yourself for reasons that I will explain when I see you   it would be unfortunate and create mischief were it known that you were receiving these letters. Mattie had talked so much to her, about you and about Walt, that she feels as if she knew you both personally—and indeed I think you would feel the same way—When assured

1. Jeff must mean Kansas City, Missouri. See Letter 89.
2. Almost certainly the Mrs. O'Reilly mentioned in Letter 90.

positively that you alone read the letters no doubt you will hear oftener[3]

And about brother Walt—I am indeed pained to hear that he is not gaining as fast as he thought he would[4]—Walt is generally so patient too, under these things—I do so hope he is better—I wish you would write me whenever you hear from him—as he writes me but seldom—and I presume I do not write to him as often as I ought. I will endeavor to do better— Aand [*sic*] George and Loo and Ed I hope they are well—I suppose George is interested a good deal in his new house[5]—if I remember rightly the locality it will be a beautiful place in summer to live.

And your own health, dear Mother I hope, now that the cold winter is over, that you may have some rest from the pains of your old complaint—the last I heard of you, before this last letter was that your hand and arm were troubling you again— does it yet continue? My health, and that of the Children continues first-rate we get along nicely at Mrs Bulkley['s][6] and have everything that we can wish I have been up to Kansas City for a few days doing some work the pay for which will come in very nicely just now.—nothing particularly new in regard to our own works in this city—matters go on about as usual—Mr Bulkley, I think, will go to New York, within a week or so—or within a month—he told me the other day that he should come back by way of Washington and try and bring Walt out to St. Louis with him—I hope he may and hope that

3. Given Jeff's discomfiture in writing about his "friend," his attempts to keep his mother quiet about her, his conviction that gossip about her would cause mischief, and his mysterious ways of alluding to her, it seems within bounds to infer that Jeff had a romantic relationship with Mrs. O'Reilly. LVVW had probably already told WW that she had received a letter from Jeff's "friend," for on April 20 (?), 1873, she wrote: "i got a letter the other day that frightened me it was from St louis i opened it and the first words i saw was dear madam dont be surprised at being addressed by a stranger the first thought i had was that Jeff or the children had been attacked by that desease that has been so fatal in St louis the spinal disease but it proved to be a letter from one of matties dear friends" (Trent).

4. On April 19, 1873, WW wrote LVVW that with shocks of electricity applied to his leg he progressed steadily but "very slowly, (& with an occasional bad spell)" (*Correspondence*, II, 215).

5. George was building another, larger house on a corner lot at 431 Stevens Street, Camden (Loving, p. 30).

6. See Letter 88.

Walt will be well enough and able to come—I feel quite positive that staying here awhile would do him good and perhaps bring him out all right much quicker than anything else he could do—If you write him speak to him abt it—I wish you could see the little girls—they would so like to see you—of course I suppose you are prepared to see them much larger than when you saw them last—yet I doubt if you imagine how large Hattie has grown—she is quite tall—and much stouter than she used to be—Jess of course is fat and I presume always will be—they both go to the same school and study well—they take music lessons—and have just completed their second quarter at the dancing school   but of all the great times and happy children, you should see them on a Saturday—this is their great day—for on this day—ever since their Mamma died they have been in the habit of meeting our dear friend, whom they love with an affection second only to that they gave their mamma, and I honestly believe they get as much as they give, in return. This has been the regular Saturday programme for even a long while before our dear Mattie died[7]—and of course now more dear to the children than ever—for they go over all their little troubles—what they like, what they wish, and never could they speak to one more willing to listen, more willing to sympathize, more willing to help and aid them—If nothing prevents, and they are allowed to continue this meeting—it will be one of the great favors to both me and them—that sometimes comes on the heels of the greatest of misfortunes[8]

I enclose a small amount and let me say just here, that I am ashamed that I have not been more thoughtful in this respect—but what with Mat's sickness and my trouble with the works I have just about as much to think about as I can hold—I often and often promised Mattie that I would send [money] to you—but failed—not so much for want of means as for want of thought and care—and thus the more to be regretted   Do not fail to write me—and if you feel like it send a note to our friend, enclosed in the one to me—

7. Mrs. O'Reilly had been involved with the family for at least a year. On May 5, 1872, Hattie and Jessie had written to their mother, who was away on a trip with Jeff, that "Mrs O'Reilly is getting Mrs. Noland to make our dresses   she is going to make polonaise of it and an under dress" (WW Papers).

8. Possibly Jeff is contemplating remarriage at this point.

Good bye, dear Mother and write me—Love to George Loo
and all—

Affectionately Jeff

[93]

St Louis May 9th 1873

My dear Walt

I received your letter and I do not think you can form an
idea how very badly I feel to hear that you are not recovering
faster.[1] I do so sincerely hope that you are right in your theory
that the slow recovery indicates permanency—I hope to God,
my dear Brother that you may permanently recover—

Not much new with me—I have had several outside jobs
lately that will pay me I think in time but so far they are only
sources of investment

How do you get along on money matters? do not fail to let
me know if you have any prospect of being short   I read with
much regret mother's statement about the eating at George's,[2]
it does seem too bad that with every chance to make things
good and happy they should fail so completely on so small a
cause. I hope you may carry out your idea of getting a little
place in Washington and have Mother live there   It would be
happiness indeed for her, and for you too for that matter

I cannot understand how it is that Loo is so stingy nor how
it is that George does not correct it[3]—I would suppose he
would (and naturally he is so) prevent it at once

Hattie wrote you a few days ago—I hope you have it ere
this

Write me when you can and let me know if you are in want
of a little money

Affectionately Jeff

1. WW's letter of about May 8 is not extant.
2. On April 21, 1873, LVVW commented to WW that the George
Whitman household would be eating a "not very good" piece of beef every
day from Sunday "till wensday or thursday." Recognizing that her health was
failing and that her appetite was poor, she expressed a desire for something
other than "the regular fare" (May 1, 1873 [Trent]).
3. A model of thrift herself, LVVW complained frequently of the penny-
saving ways of George's wife.

Olive Street west from Fourth, St. Louis, 1874 (Emil Boehl, photos.). From 1874–77 Jeff was a consultant in Henry Flad's firm at 417 Olive. In the late 1880s Jeff located his own offices at 600 Olive. Courtesy of the Missouri Historical Society.

St. Louis, July 5th 1875

My dear Walt

Although you hear from us so seldom yet we do not forget you—I expected to get to Camden before this[1]—but business prevented—We have had lots of political trouble here this spring and summer and the end is not yet—how it will affect me I am unable to even guess now—sometimes it looks bad and then again as if it would blow over—at any rate it cannot be long before it will decide itself one way or another[2]—

Tis a long while since we have heard from you—how are you getting along   now and then we see some little thing in the papers—the last was that you were engaged in getting up another book[3]—I was glad to know that you were feeling well enough—

How is George and Loo. I hope well   Is George busy still on the pipe question   We are having very hot weather for the last few days—On Thursday next Hattie and Jessie depart for Iowa or Wisconsin for a month or two—Jess and Hat have grown quite up and begin to look like young ladies—they keep to school pretty close and study well—

Let me hear from you when you can—if matters change here I shall make you a visit for awhile—I should endeavor to get a job in Baltimore as I see they are getting ready to build works there—

Love to all—not forgetting Ed

Jeff

1. Jeff had visited WW at least twice since the last extant letter: in September 1873 and June 1874 (*Correspondence*, II, 241, 306).
2. In April 1875 a new Board of Water Commissioners was appointed. Jeff's close friend Henry Flad, a member of the board since 1867 and president since 1873, was among those replaced. Because one of the new appointees was Joseph Brown, the former mayor, Jeff may be concerned that politics is exerting too much influence over the waterworks. He may also be anxious about the vote on the new state constitution scheduled for August 1875 in which St. Louis would be granted home rule. See Letter 95.
3. In the spring of 1875, WW began work on his so-called "Centennial Edition" of *Leaves of Grass* (Allen, p. 463).

[95]

St. Louis, July 22nd 1877

Dear Walt—

I could not answer you before this as I have just returned from a trip down in South East Missouri.

On 1st of July the Bd of Water Com. abolished my office and consequently it left me out in the cold—it was a political move and done to get me out of the way on the question of re-appointment—and I am sorry to say I fear it will be successful[1]

To-morrow I go to Little Rock Ark—to look into the water works question there—shall be gone a few days, and if I succeed shall have the job of making plans &c for that place—this will take me a month or so—

Mrs Archer, the lady of the school[2] where the children are has written me saying that she thinks it would be much [the] best for them to remain with her during the vacation on account of the question of health.[3] I have just written her that I would like to have them visit you at Camden and spend also a sho[r]t visit with Mrs Gilchrist.[4]

When I returned here I found your letter and postal telling

1. From 1876 to 1877 St. Louis was in political turmoil. Under the new state constitution of August 1875, St. Louis adopted a city charter on August 22, 1876, which abolished the independent state Board of Water Commissioners and replaced it with a city Board of Public Improvements, a change similar to that made in Brooklyn in 1872 (see Letter 76). Because of a series of legal challenges, the charter did not go into effect until April 1877, and the new Board was not appointed until August. The discredited political appointees of 1875 were apparently striking a final vindictive blow against Jeff before they were replaced under the new law. Nonetheless, the city council appointed Jeff as water commissioner on August 21 (*Journal of the City Council*, August 10–30, 1877).

2. Mrs. Archer's Patapsco Seminary, located in Ellicott City, Maryland (*Correspondence*, III, 99).

3. On September 21, WW reported that Hattie, who was then visiting him, suffered from "a sort of *Cholera morbus* & fever" (*Correspondence*, III, 97).

4. The widow Anne Gilchrist (1828–86), mother of four children and author of "A Woman's Estimate of Walt Whitman" (1870), left her home in England in 1876 to offer herself, body and soul, to the man she had envisioned from reading *Leaves of Grass*. In the poetry the Whitman persona spoke boldly of begetting "far more arrogant republics" ("Song of Myself"), but in dealing with Mrs. Gilchrist's passion WW was timid and evasive.

about Lou.[5] I am sincerely glad that she is getting well again   It is sad to think of how she must have suffered   My love to her and to George also. I hope ere this she has recovered her health again

Everything in this section is very quiet   I have just made an arrangement about the right to operate some lead mines[6] which if I can carry through will return a fortune to the party investing and will also be an excellent thing for me. I may likely come East this fall or latter part of the summer to see about getting the money to start the work. It is a most favorable thing and it seems to me I ought to have no difficulty in putting the matter into working shape   I would like to have you drop me a line as to how Lou and all of you are—

Affectionately Jeff

[96]

St. Louis, Oct 27th 1878

My dear Walt

Tis a long time since I have heard from any of you—but I suppose all goes about the same as ever. I suppose you have had all sorts of newspaper rumors in regard to the yellow fever in St Louis[1]—but the truth is that the stories are nearly entirely fabrications   Altogether there has been, probably, some 35 to 40 deaths by yellow fever during the season—out of this number some 6 or 8 were St Louis people who had been in some capacity about those that had come from the South—or had been connected with the hospital boat that carries the sick people from the city to the fever hospital. I have no doubt but that had the weather continued warm for a couple or three weeks longer we should have had quite a touch of the trouble. From what I can observe I judge the spread of this disease is simply a question of time   That it always commences in the

5. WW's letter of about July 21 is not extant. The poet undoubtedly informed Jeff that Louisa's baby had died before it was delivered (see *Correspondence*, III, 90).

6. During this period the lead trade was among the fastest-growing and most profitable segments of the St. Louis economy.

1. Only ten "local cases" of yellow fever were reported in St. Louis this season; the other individuals came up from New Orleans.

south (so far as the West is concerned at any rate) is a fact—
that it will progress with quite a certain rate of travel—now if
the time between its first breaking out and where it meets a
heavy frost is long enough I do not see why it should not spread
to the lakes. This season it broke out in New Orleans abt 6
weeks earlier than usual—we have had rather a backward season as regards frost and cool weather—the disease was quite
bad within abt 150 miles of us—I think more favorable conditions would undoubtedly have produced it here—Steamboats
seem to be the home of the disease—let one of them be in the
locality where the sickness is bad and it is pretty sure death to
have anything to do with it—this does not seem to be the case
with R. R. Cars—Another thing seems sure and that is that
with proper sanitary laws—with good energetic health officers—no city that is kept decently clean but what can stamp
out the disease by taking prompt action

I do not know that you are interested in all this, but I have
been pretty well exercised about the matter, knowing that if it
did come here I should have to stop and face the music no
matter how bad it became—We have had several cool nights—
and to-day the weather is what might be called cold—I think
we will have a decided show of ice to-night—and so the question of fever for this season is certainly disposed of.

I am getting on reasonably well have pretty good health—
indeed just now it is extremely good—at one time—near the
latter part of July I got poisoned by the bad air of the numerous
sewers, bone boiling and fat rendering establishments that I
had to visit[2] and was badly off for a couple of weeks—and
indeed did not feel well until we had a "cold wave" about two
weeks ago—since that time I have felt the very best—and too
my work has let up very much

How are you all getting on   How is George and Lou and
Ed and yourself—I hope you continue to gain—I judge from
what Hattie writes that you made quite headway this last
summer   I hope so and am very glad. What is new with
you   are you doing anything in the way of books—I dont see
anything in the papers[3]—but then the papers I see would not

2. Because of the rapid growth of the city, the Bissell's Point Water
Works was increasingly vulnerable to pollution from slaughterhouse waste
and sewage.
3. WW was not working on a book at this time, but he frequently published poems and essays in periodicals. Around October 26, 1878, he sent Jeff

be apt to say much anyhow—except in a mean way. Has George got through his foundry work—and if so I suppose is mostly on his farm[4]—will you make a winter trip to your New York friends   if so you must call and see Worthen[5]   I have just had a letter from Hattie in which I learn that she is a little sick—has been laid off from study—I hope she is not sick to any extent—indeed I sincerely hope she is all right now—I have just written her to-night to let the study go and get well as quick as she can—I hope to hear in a day or two that she is all well again

Give my love to all—write me when you feel like it and give me all the news.

Jeff

[97]

On September 10, 1879, Walt departed from Camden on a western jaunt to participate in the Old Settlers' Quarter Centennial Celebration near Lawrence, Kansas. The poet travelled in the company of the Philadelphia publisher John W. Forney and newspapermen J. M. W. Geist, E. K. Martin, and W. W. Reitzel. By September 12 the group had reached St. Louis, where Jeff guided them on a tour of the city. According to Geist, "nothing interested us more than an inspection of the Water Works . . . . As we went down the winding stairs with the great deep pit below the bed of the river, and viewed the herculean workings of these ponderous machines, we felt like taking off our hats in reverence to the engineering and mechanical skill which were personified in those masses of immovable stone and animated iron and steel." Geist judged

"Gathering the Corn"; on November 25, 1878, "Thou who has Slept all Night upon the Storm" (later titled "To the Man-of-War Bird"); at the end of January 1879, "Winter Sunshine: A Trip from Camden to the Coast"; on August 9, 1879, an account of the lecture on the death of Abraham Lincoln (*DN*, pp. 118, 122, 35, 152). WW sent Jeff similar items in the following years. It seems unlikely that the poet would have sent materials to Jeff this often if he really believed that no family member sympathized with his work (see Introduction).

4. Probably the farm in Burlington, New Jersey, where George would eventually build a permanent home in 1884.

5. See Letter 43.

*Jeff's water tower to be "the only beautiful . . . standpipe
. . . I have ever seen. It is a perfect copy of the classic Corinthian column on a collosal* [sic] *scale"* (Daily New Era [*Lancas-
ter, Pennsylvania*], *September 17, 1879*).

*Although Geist's paean may today sound excessive, he was
giving voice to the widespread nineteenth-century excitement
about the advances of science. Walt, too, marvelled at the engineering achievements of St. Louis, particularly the Eads
Bridge: "I dont believe there can be a grander thing of the kind
on earth"* (Correspondence, III, 172); *"It is indeed a structure
of perfection and beauty unsurpassable, and I never tire of it"*
(Prose Works 1892, I, 229). *Surprisingly, the poet left no record of his reaction to Jeff's waterworks, an omission which
seems especially odd when compared with Geist's enthusiasm.*

*After his one-day stop in St. Louis, Walt travelled as far
west as the Rockies and then returned to St. Louis, tired and ill,
on September 27. He recuperated during a three-month visit
with Jeff and the girls, but there were some difficulties: he was
irritated by Hattie's piano playing and troubled by a shortage
of money (see Jessie Whitman's interview with Garrett Newkirk, Fansler Collection, Northwestern Univ., and Allen, p.
489). Nonetheless, Walt and Jeff seem to have enjoyed their
first extended visit in over a decade.*

St. Louis, Oct 29 1882

Dear brother Walt

I append [a] slip from the Evening paper of last Thursday
that frightened us all so.[1] I telegraphed Thursday evening and
again Friday—and was on my way to the telegraph office yesterday afternoon when I was handed your dispatch.[2] We were
all glad to know that the statement was wrong although as the
time passed and I had an opportunity to reason it over I felt
pretty well assured that there was a mistake in the statement[3]—The morning papers of Friday, however, all repeated
the statement and gave as authority the press reports

1. Jeff enclosed a clipping from the *St. Louis Post-Dispatch* of October
26, 1882, stating that "Walt Whitman is so seriously ill of Bright's disease
that few if any hopes for his recovery are entertained."
2. WW's telegram of October 28, 1882, is not extant.
3. False reports about the poet's health seem to have been innumerable.
Two of the more colorful rumors were the belief in 1871 that WW had been
killed in a train crash and in 1877 that the poet was starving (*Correspondence*, II, 123, and IV, 72).

Standpipe No. 1, the "White Tower" or "Corinthian Column," St. Louis, 1870s. Jeff built this water tower, the first of its kind in the city, in 1871. It still stands just north of downtown St. Louis at the foot of Grand Boulevard, where it is a notable fixture in the city skyline. Courtesy of the Missouri Historical Society.

I hope you are all o.k. again and able to get around as usual. If you are tied down to the house I imagine you feel pretty sick. In my own case when sick I find that the fact that I cannot get out makes me feel as badly as anything else

We are all well and getting on quite nicely. The girls have been busy "putting up" large quantities of all sorts of stuff in the pickle &c line—as much to practice I presume as with any idea that it would be needed

I have had considerable to do this summer[4]—have only been away once (to St Joseph) since I was East   I expect to go to St Jo the last of this week—and toward the middle or last of Nov hope to come East—at least as far as Camden—so dont be surprised to see me pop in at any time

All send love to George and Lou and to yourself—by-the-way I must be considerable behind in regard to Ed's board[5]—when George or Lou write ask them to please state how far and I will square up—

We are having splendid fall weather—never so delight-ful—I have just finished a seven days out door survey—putting up at the nearest place where night found us—the country was new to me and very beautiful—the weather perfect   it was like going back 25 years. Let me hear from you soon—again love to all

Affectionately Jeff

4. There was some interest at this time in expanding the waterworks. On October 5, 1882, Sarah L. Glasgow, wife of the public school commis-sioner William Glasgow, Jr. and daughter of the first mayor of St. Louis, wrote to her family in Paris: "The news from the Water Works is not encour-aging. . . . They say Flad and Whitman are making an exhaustive search, strange to say the Chain [of Rocks] is not mentioned but a spot one mile above the Chain and Music's Ferry near St Charles are spoken of . . . . I am persuaded it only wants a thousand or so dollars to decide Flad, but he will have to decide without any such reminder from any of us" (William Carr Lane Collection, Missouri Historical Society). Interestingly, Mrs. Glasgow thinks that Flad can be bribed but not, apparently, Jeff. When the water-works was finally extended to the Chain of Rocks in 1890, the city paid William Glasgow, Jr., $39,000 for his land near the site.

5. Edward had been boarding for some years with various families and WW generally made the monthly payments, which at this time were sixteen dollars. Here Jeff implies that he too is obligated to support his feeble-minded brother and wants to even up on back payments.

St. Louis, Feb 23rd 1885

My dear Walt

I have had such hard work for the last six weeks that I have hardly had time to answer the regular business letters but to day thought I would "drop you a line" at any rate—

Just now I am having rather a bad time in keeping up the water—so large a portion of the people let the water run to prevent freezing of the pipes—and our city—being so hilly that I cannot keep the water on the high points—still unless we have more than another week of this extremely cold weather we shall get through all right.[1]

We talk of you often and wonder how you get on if you have anything like as bad a winter as we have   I hope you take it easy and get on without much trouble. I have not been able to get out as much this season as usual—we have had the cold so long and so bad that I was forced to keep in doors to a great extent.

I saw by yesterday's paper that Kingsley,[2] of Brooklyn, had given up—poor fellow, all his keen striving and jobbing and talk is over forever   He would have been happier, I think had he remained more like he was when he first came to Brooklyn—

I mail you to-day a little picture of a new stand pipe tower that I am going to build this next year[3]—we have let the work and shall commence on it as soon as the weather will let us.

1. Jeff had been concerned with the recurring problem of water waste since 1876. From January 8 to 13, 1884, the city suffered a five-day water shortage because of open faucets. To stop the practice, Jeff instituted house-to-house inspections and advocated universal metering.
2. See Letter 44. William C. Kingsley died in Brooklyn on February 21. He had worked with Jeff in Brooklyn, and later, in partnership with Colonel Abner C. Keeney, supervised the construction of the East River or Brooklyn Bridge. This engineering feat required fourteen years of work (1869–83) and was completed only after some loss of life, much political bickering, and enormous expenditures of capital and labor. Jeff echoes the popular view that this project exhausted Kingsley and perhaps destroyed him.
3. Standpipe No. 2, the "Red Tower" at Blair and Bissell streets, was authorized by the city council on June 10, 1884. Construction began in June 1885 and was substantially completed by March 1886. Jeff probably refers to a drawing of the water tower by its designer, William S. Eames, at that time deputy commissioner of public buildings.

Standpipe No. 2, the "Red Tower," at Blair and Bissell streets, St. Louis, about 1890. Jeff completed this water tower in 1886, near the end of his term of service to the city. He was proud enough of this structure to send a picture of it to Walt. Courtesy of the Missouri Historical Society.

The design has been cut and changed—and re-made, till I got it
to look as I thought it ought. The young man that made it has
good taste and I think when finished it will look as well as
anything of the kind in the country. The total cost will be about
eighty thousand dollars complete. Let me know Walt how it
looks to you please—All the lower part is to be of granite—and
above that brick work—of the best bricks and workmanship.
There will be nothing particularly grand about it except its
proportions—That is I hav'nt attempted to make any wonderfully fine carving or anything of that kind   I shall be terribly
disappointed if it fails to look well when built as I have carried
out several things in opposition to the opinions of fellows who
have the reputation of knowing all about such things—Well in
a year from now, if we all live, we will know how it will be

Walt, if you have a copy of your "Author's Edition" of your
book that you can send me I would esteem it a great favor if you
will write in it "A. J. Chaphe,[4] from the Author" and send it to
me. Chaphe intends to get all your books as soon as he can get a
little money ahead—but I would like to give him this one
He has read all my copies—and is interested in them to a great
extent.

Hat and Jess keep pretty well and we all get on in the regular old way

A few weeks ago Willard Arnold[5] called at my office—he
was in St Louis a week—with one of the dramatic Companies
I saw him often—did'nt go to the play but had him down to the
house. Willard is in many respects the same as when a boy—he
asked all about you—and well remembered many of the walks
we all used to take on Sundays years and years ago.

A few days ago I had a letter from Bill DeVoe,[6] who is now
located at Springfield, this state. Bill sent me a young mocking
bird—his home is at a small town on the red-river in La. but he
is running a surveyor's office at Springfield

I dont know whether I shall be able to get East this spring
or not but I intend to make the effort. I feel the need of a
vacation badly. I note what a terrible disaster you had in Phila-

4. Andrew J. Chaphe was the chief engineer of the pumping department
at the St. Louis Water Works. Twice Jeff singled him out for praise in the
official reports to the Board of Water Commissioners (1875 and 1876).
    5. Unidentified.
    6. See Letter 2.

delphia a few days since[7]—in some way it seemed to me the most heart rending of anything of the kind I ever read about. I suppose because it was a family dwelling perhaps. All send love to you dear Walt.

Aff., Jeff

[99]

St. Louis, July 31st 1885

My dear Walt—

I enclose a check for ten dollars payable to your order—the money comes from Chaphe[1] who wants you to send him copies of your various books so far as it will pay for them—particularly he desires to get Dr [Bosch's?][2] book—You will remember that you sent him a copy of the "Author's Edition" of Leaves of Grass—so I suppose that may be left out—If you express the books (which I suppose would be the best way) direct them to me and we will pay the express charges at this end.

There is no particular hurry for this; you of course will leave it till you are feeling all right[3]—and the hot weather has lifted a little. In depositing this check or getting the money for it you will just write your name on the back below mine

We are all well   have had a terrible seige of hot weather—yesterday—they say the heat was greater on the street level than it has been since 1838—it was 102 in the shade at my office

We were all very glad to hear from you—the telegram came all right—as did the postal[4]—I hope you are having cool weather now—and that you will have no more of the bad spells—We had a fine shower last night—and to-day it has

7. The *St. Louis Post-Dispatch* carried the following headline on February 21: "*An entire Philadelphia family perishes in a burning dwelling.*" The fire began in the home of John A. King, 1539 Pine Street, and eventually destroyed three houses and killed five people, including a nine-year-old boy.

1. See Letter 98.

2. Unidentified. Jeff's chirography is so unclear that this name may be Basch, Bascelles, or something else.

3. From July 20 to July 23 WW suffered from "bad vertigo fits" (*DN*, p. 362).

4. Neither communication from WW is extant.

dropped some 18 degrees—so that we are comparatively comfortable—I dont want another day like yesterday

All send love—and sincerely hope you are all right. I am trying to arrange to get on and pay you a visit some time this fall—if I can make it, I want to do it

Affectionately Jeff

[100]

St. Louis, Sept. 11th 1885

My dear Walt

Enclosed please find check for $10—payable to your order This check is sent by Mr Chaphe[1]   he is so much pleased with his books.

We are getting on about in the usual manner—all well—I am pretty busy—but still hope to get away long enough to make you all a visit

Weather here just perfect for the last few days—Hat and Jess doing the "Exposition" which has just opened[2]—they say tis first class

Glad to see that you are all right again—saw a little notice in last evenings paper stating this fact[3]—

Have just received a telegram from Horace Tarr of New York (Mr Lane's nephew)[4] stating that he would call on me to-day—shall be glad to see him—

All send love

Jeff

1. See Letter 98.
2. The second annual St. Louis Exposition opened on September 9, 1885, in a downtown block called Missouri Park. It featured music, amusements, art galleries, and commercial displays, and attracted 750,000 people.
3. "Walt Whitman writes to his London friends as follows: 'Fortunately, I have a good, faithful young Jersey woman and friend, Mary Davis, who cooks for me and vigilantly sees to me' " (*St. Louis Post-Dispatch*, September 10, 1885). This item is quoted from a letter of WW's to Herbert Gilchrist, August 1, 1885 (*Correspondence*, III, 399).
4. See Letter 26. Tarr was now a journalist. He and Jeff evidently maintained a close association during Jeff's last four or five years of life (Tarr to WW, December 1, 1890 [Feinberg]). For Lane, see Letter 9.

[101]

St. Louis, Nov 9th 1886

My dear Walt

Two or three times within the last half dozen days we have seen (and felt badly about) squibs in the papers saying you were "sick"—"not well" "confined to his room" etc etc—Each day I have been hoping to get something from you—but as the days pass and I do not I am beginning to fear that it is possible that you are not getting on as well as usual[1]—and that there may be some foundation for the newspaper stuff—more than usual with you

Dear Walt we all hope and pray that it is not so—yet fear that you may not be as well as usual—and hope you will let us know just how you are getting on. The last time we heard from you, you said you did not feel quite as well as usual—but that you had been out on a long drive and that you were able to get out every day or two—is there anything different

We are jogging along as best we may[2]   I manage to be at home and with Jess considerable of the time—and often I take her with me when I visit the works—and the places where they are building—I find both for her and myself there is nothing like the open air—the out doors. As good luck would have it we have had a splendid fall as regards weather—and too my work has been of such a kind that I could be out much of the time—and this way we manage, after a fashion, to put in the days—yet there are times when it does seem as if it was impossible to keep up.

It is pretty hard on Jess to leave her alone (with servants of course) in the house yet at times (for a short time) this does occur, and of course she gives way to her feelings, poor child, but I am doing my best to counteract it all I can do

Dear Walt write upon the receipt of this and let us know how you are   We always like to hear from you   it seems to help—Love of both

affectionately Jeff

1. On November 5, [1886?], WW reported to John Burroughs that he "had a bad week . . . [of] gastric & head troubles" (*Correspondence*, IV, 53).

2. Hattie had died suddenly from enteritis on September 3. She was only twenty-six. In response, WW wrote Jeff six letters in nine days. Jeff's an-

Milwaukee, Dec 11th 1887

My dear Walt

I received your letter[1] the other day—also the papers with the enclosures—and glad I was to hear from you again   Probably as Jess has told you I am poking around from place to place spending about 1/3 of my time on Rail Road trains[2]—and although it is not as bad as it might be yet I cannot say that I enjoy it much—suppose I would if I was fifteen years younger—but it is as it is[3]

We are having a bad snow storm here to-day—and I hav'nt been out yet—but I think I will walk over and look at the lake which I suppose is kicking up considerable of a bobbery just about now   The Milwaukee bay is a first rate place to see the waves dash on the shore it being about this shape A∿⌒B[4] and when the wind is blowing stiff from the East you can see a wave start in at A̲ and follow it for two or three miles as it passes B—that is except at the points at the mouth of the river or where the projecting piers are. When a fellow feels good it is lots of fun to see them—but just to day I dont feel first class Kinder lonely—been in too much I suppose—

guish is recorded in WW's letter of September 8: "I hope & trust you both bear up under it, & that the 'God help us' of your telegraphic message will be fulfilled" (*Correspondence*, IV, 47).

1. WW's letter of about December 9 is not extant.

2. Jessie may have given WW this information when she visited him in Camden in October 1887 (*DN*, p. 439).

3. In May 1887 M. L. Holman succeeded Jeff as water commissioner. Jeff's authority may have been weakened by the resolution adopted on February 18, 1887, by the lower house of the city assembly: "Resolved by the House of Delegates, the Council concurring therein, that the Water Commissioner be informed that the continued practice of furnishing the consumers of water with a filthy, unsettled substance for the purpose of extracting influence in support of an ordinance to extend the present water system, the the [*sic*] said extension having for its purpose the perpetuation in office of barnacles whose places can be better filled by just as practical men, who will be glad to do their duty—should they be appointed—is discountenanced by the Municipal Assembly, and the Water Commissioner is hereby respectfully requested to serve his purpose by means other than those calculated to inconvenience the taxpayers of the city" (*Journal of the City Council*, February 23, 1887).

4. Jeff's diagram is reproduced about one-quarter size.

I am up here engaged in the almost hopeless task of trying to determine what can be done with the sewage of the town. Just now it is all emptied into the river that flows through the city and the deposit has become so great that in the summer it is terribly offensive to those who live along the edge of the river

I shall be here, off and on probably, five or six months— that is if the infernal thing dont worry me to death

I judge from your letter that you are holding your own fairly well—of course we are all getting older and as you say the machine will show wear, never so well may we patch it up. But I feel very much like our old friend Ruggles[5] used to say, "we must make the best of it"

I hope, dear Walt, that you will keep in good spirits during the bad weather—I find in my own case that it is the hardest thing I have to combat—I often think that the only fellow that knows how to live is the wild-goose   He makes the world his own and follows the climate he likes—and no question of business can keep him either   Well good by Walt—write me whenever you feel like it   I always want to know how you are

affectionately Jeff

[103]

St. Louis, Mo., Jan. 26th, 1888

My dear Jessie

<u>My darling girl</u>, I enclose you a check for $50, hoping it will reach you before you leave Burlington[1]

I got home from Ark yesterday, after a pretty hard time—I had to abandon my Texas trip for the reason that I had some bids here to be opened on Monday   I did not get here till Wednesday—but that was owing to the weather and the Rail Roads   I shall go out to the cemetery on Sunday and leave Sunday night for Texas. I suppose I shall be gone about a week   Mr Smith[2] of Leavenworth was at my office on Monday last and came for the express purpose of carrying me off to

5. See Letter 18.

1. Jessie had probably been visiting George and Louisa Whitman at their farmhouse in Burlington, New Jersey.
2. Unidentified.

New York all expenses paid—but of course I could not go—
much as I wanted to—No I must make the best of what is
wanted now—I presume I shall have lots of time after
awhile—

Well my dear girl I wish you would go and do just what
gives you the most fun—and I do hope you will make fast
friends of the New York and the Hartford people—they are
good folk to know

I shall write Horace[3] that you are at Worthens[4] after the
1st for ten days—I think he will call and ask you to go to his
place—and if he does I would like to have you go

Nothing new with me—I am feeling fairly well—except I
have my old terrible cough—it is pulling me down some—but
I shall get out all right when the spring comes

Wish you would go and see Walt as often as you can

Love to all

affectionately Papa

[104]

Milwaukee, July 14th 1888

My dear Walt

I was very very glad to get a letter from you yesterday.[1] I
have been quite worried about you, wondering how things
were going   I am more than glad to hear that you are holding
your own

I am up here on a question of the disposal of the sewage of
the city   Davis and Flad[2] are associated with me and we have
been confabing about a week—Yesterday they went away—
leaving me here to make surveys etc

---

3. Horace Tarr (see Letters 26 and 100).
4. See Letter 43.

1. WW's letter of about July 12 is not extant.
2. For Davis, see Letter 36. Henry Flad (1824–98) graduated from the
University of Munich in 1846. Sentenced to death after serving as captain of
engineers in the Parliamentary Army during the revolution of 1848, he fled
to New York City in 1849 and embarked on a distinguished career in civil
engineering. He worked on several railroad projects, including one which
brought him to Missouri in 1854. He joined the Union army in 1861 and
eventually became colonel of the First Regiment of Engineers, Missouri Volunteers. In 1865 he became the chief assistant engineer under James P.

I am going down to Chicago in the morning to meet some people—will be back here on Wednesday

I hope dear Walt that you are gaining again—I was very sorry that I could not get back to Camden—but I had to go with my Committee to Louisville

Yours affectionately Jeff

[105]

Milwaukee, Dec. 23 1888

My dear Jessie

A Merry Christmas to you—

I enclose a little momento as I could not let the day go by without reminding you that I thought of you

I hope you will like the muffler—I did not know but I thought perhaps this would suit your ideas—

Again a Merry, Merry Christmas—and I feel sad that I cannot be with you

Papa
Thos. J. Whitman

[106]

St. Louis, May 31, 1889[1]

To Walt Whitman—

Congratulations on reaching the seventy notch. Hope you will complete another score.

Kirkwood on the St. Louis Water Works and served continuously on the Board of Water Commissioners from 1867 to 1875. During this period he was also the assistant engineer on the Eads Bridge, a pioneering achievement in bridge construction. He was a cofounder of the Engineers' Club of St. Louis and served as its president from 1868 to 1880. He was president of the St. Louis Board of Public Improvements from 1877 to 1890 and was elected president of the American Society of Civil Engineers in 1886.

1. Jeff sent WW this telegram on the occasion of the poet's seventieth birthday. It is reprinted from *Camden's Compliment to Walt Whitman: May 31, 1889: Notes, Addresses, Letters, Telegrams,* ed. Horace L. Traubel (Philadelphia: David McKay), p. 71, and is the last known message between the brothers.

Appendix A

E. D. Meier's Obituary of Jeff Whitman

At least seven obituaries of Jeff were published, one in the St. Louis Republican, *November 29, 1890, one in the* Post [*Camden, New Jersey*], *January 20, 1891, and five in national engineering periodicals:* Engineering News, *December 6, 1890;* The Engineering Record, *December 6 and 13, 1890; Robert Moore and Henry Flad's memoir in the* Proceedings of the American Society of Civil Engineers, *April 1892; and E. D. Meier's eulogy in the* Journal of the Association of Engineering Societies, *January 1891. Meier, president of the Engineers' Club of St. Louis, based his remarks on information he received from Walt on December 10, 1890, and sent the poet a copy of the typed draft (December 19, 1890 [Feinberg]). Because Walt's letter to Meier is not extant, we reprint Meier's memorial with annotations from the TS in Special Collections, University Libraries, Washington University in St. Louis.*

Our club is again called upon to mourn the loss of one of our charter members, called away so suddenly that some of his oldest friends, hurrying to his bedside on learning of his illness, found crape on the door to tell them they were too late to clasp that kindly hand again.

Thomas Jefferson Whitman was born in Brooklyn, N.Y., on July 18th, 1833, the eighth of a family of nine children. His father was a carpenter and builder, of extraordinary ability, a natural mechanic, noted for the strength and symmetry of his work. From him our friend, no doubt, inherited that straightforward honesty, and that intuitive mechanical insight which marked his professional life. His mother, descended from the early Dutch settlers of New Amsterdam, was a woman of sympathetic and poetical temperament, in whose kindly face could be traced those pleasant lines indicative of quick wit and humor. From her he must have drawn that fund of geniality, which smoothed over many a rugged path his sterling integrity compelled him to choose.

His elder brother, "the good gray poet," had large part in his early education, and in 1848 carried "Jeff," then a lad of 15, with him on a leisurely journey through all the Middle states, and down the Ohio and Mississippi; no doubt this training enhanced his natural tendency for the poetical in life. Returned to Brooklyn, he was at 16 apprenticed to the printers' trade, but soon left that for land surveying, and when about 20 years old took professional service with an engineering firm largely interested in harbor improvements in New York City. At 23 he became an assistant engineer under James P. Kirkwood in the location and construction of the Brooklyn water works. Under this celebrated engineer he also did duty in the Bergen, N.J., tunnel, and in the construction of the Newburg branch of the Erie railroad. In 1860 and 1861 respectively he was an assistant engineer in the sewer departments of Brooklyn and New York. In 1863 he became chief assistant engineer, under Moses Lane, of the Consolidated Sewer & Water Departments of Brooklyn. In May, 1867, he accepted the position of chief engineer of our St. Louis Water Works, which were constructed under his skillful supervision, his old friend and former chief, James P. Kirkwood, being consulting engineer.

The works were completed and put into service in June, 1871, and with occasional additions to machinery and plant, have served our city for nearly 20 years, and stand today possibly the best designed, best constructed, and most practical system of water works of any large city west of the Alleghenies. There is his monument.

We may not believe that the political "pull" was any weaker, the desire of city contractors for profits less ardent in the 70's than in the 90's; nor were there wanting then, beardless youths, ambitious of journalistic honors, with whom a sensation at the expense of city officials out weighed the ninth commandment. But we rejoice in the thought that here was an engineer able, skillful, thorough and conscientious, who built these works according to true rules, who saw that the city got its full rights under the contracts, whose conduct throughout all obeyed the same plumb and level which he applied to engine and reservoir.

On the adoption of the "Scheme & Charter," Capt. Whitman became the water commissioner of the city, continuing as such by reappointment under successive administrations until three years ago. Since then he has been engaged in an extensive and important practice as consulting engineer. Such works as the Kansas City, Leavenworth, Minneapolis, and

Memphis water works have had the benefit of his talents; and the design for a comprehensive sewer system in Milwaukee was among his works during this period.

Like most of the older generation of engineers, Whitman depended less on formulae and mathematical deductions than on native talent sharpened and instructed by the hard experiences of a life spent in actual construction, and trained to quick action in the face of novel difficulties. One of our former members, whose genial face looks down upon us from its place of honor, himself skilled to chase the elusive "x" through the mazes of a cubic equation, was wont to illustrate this by an anecdote. He had been levelling and cross-sectioning patiently for some days to prove up the best location for a reservoir for a growing southern city—Whitman came up, looked quizzically at the well filled field books, and sauntered leisurely off across the country; in an hour he came back with the positive statement that he had found a better location for the basin. A few measurements by the surveyors proved him correct, and the reservoir was built on the new site for half the estimated cost of the first location.

Who could soothe the overwrought nerves of an expert testing party on constant strain for twenty-four hours, at the concluding breakfast or supper, by a well-told and well-turned story, better than this genial friend? Who better than he could shorten and cap off a long argument by a witty speech which convinced even more than it amused?[1] As an engineer and a public officer his escutcheon is spotless. This is what he made of himself, and this the memory we will cherish.

To his only surviving daughter, the brightener of his lonely hearth and faithful nurse in his last hours of pain and waning, we extend a sympathy as heartfelt as it is powerless to assuage her grief.

To the poet-brother the assurance that his fame is safe with those who worked with him will suffice.

---

1. On the TS, "answered" is lined out and "amused" is inserted by hand above it. Immediately following is this partially erased sentence: "We do not deny that as a man he had his faults and his weaknesses; but we were wont to forget them in the kind humor which spiced his conversation." Perhaps Meier erased this sentence before he read the eulogy to the Engineers' Club on December 17, 1890.

Appendix B

Horace Traubel's Obituary of Jeff Whitman

The following obituary appeared in the Post *[Camden, New Jersey], January 20, 1891. Probably basing his remarks on conversations with Walt, Traubel connects the poet's relationship with Jeff to the "gospel of 'Calamus.'" The poet preserved a copy of this obituary in his private papers (Feinberg).*

Walt Whitman has written tenderly of his brother "Jeff" in one of the engineering journals. There are things known about this strong man, now dead, which disclose family traits, and always family virtues, of a high order. It is told of him, for instance, that he was a good counsellor. Called in to sit upon great engineering questions, his opinion, always the last, was waited for and almost inevitably and universally adopted. Then we are informed of his calm demeanor in trial, of his happy view of life, of his clean tendencies, corporeal and spiritual. I hit upon these, not from Walt himself (though from him, too), but from contact with engineers who either knew "Jeff" personally or are intimates of others who did know him. A deep inter-working thread of comradship bound and knit Jeff and Walt closer than ordinary tie of family or clan. Their intercourse was palpably affectionate, in a series of years linked from the youthful journey South, to these later serious and sometimes pathetic experiences belonging to Walt's consistent and increasing sickness. There is nothing more beautiful and rare than this undemonstrative and yet frank love of strong men; it gives a majesty to personal virtue and prepares and announces new characters and sounder national and world forces. Walt alway [*sic*] lives the gospel of "Calamus," and in his relations with Jeff subsisted one great signal illustration. Great qualities active and now immortal in Walt and his work were not wanting in the more concrete life of the lesser, and yet large, brother. Attention belongs to the faith, skill, cheer, self-containedness, emotionality of the splendid man gone, and with these to the subtle resemblances which in some respects would make the Whitman's [*sic*] a marked group without the prestige that Walt's extra-mundane spirituality brings. These big bodies and big souls, enclosing the healthiest hope, belief, integrity, courage, of our generation—based upon an absolute immunity from the faint final suspicions of the introspective morbidity that disfigures and unnerves literature and life—command respect, reverence, emulation.

Index

Kirkwood, James P., xxv, xxvi, xxix, 121; contributes to Walt Whitman's hospital work, 16, 62, 76, 77, 78, 88, 92; designs St. Louis waterworks, xxvii, xxxi, 117, 120; recommends Jeff Whitman for St. Louis job, xxvii, 119
Kisselbrack, Peter, 89
Knipper, Mrs. Adolph, 159–60

Lane, Kate, 112 n
Lane, Moses: attends Mattie Whitman's funeral, 163; contributes to Walt Whitman's hospital work, 22, 24, 25, 28, 33–34, 42–43, 44, 53, 54, 57–58, 71, 75, 78, 93, 118; engineering career of, 56, 141, 149, 150; letters of introduction for Walt Whitman, 26, 30–31 (quoted); letters to Walt Whitman, 22, 57–58, 112 (quoted); receives engineering book from Walt Whitman, 45; recommends Walt Whitman for job, 60; supports George Whitman's military career, 110, 116; supports Jeff Whitman's career, 51, 67, 82; mentioned, xxvi, 23, 48, 49, 55, 63, 79, 91, 94–96, 128, 129, 132, 183
Lee, Robert E., 56, 63, 64
Lees, Henry A., xvii, 15
Lewis, David J., 118
Lincoln, Abraham, 64, 71, 107; Jeff's opinion of, 59, 61, 106
Lippincott's Magazine, 130
Lucas, J. W., 100

McAlpine plan, xviii
McClellan, George Brinton, 62
McClure, J. E. ("Sam"), 3, 11
McElroy, Samuel, 16
McEvoy, Thomas, 70
[McMear?], Johny M., 129
McNamee, [John or Robert], 118, 129; letter to Jeff Whitman, 130
Martin, E. K., 175
Martin, John D., 26, 29, 62, 68, 78, 92
Mason, Gordon F., 123
Mason, Julius W., 27, 126; supports George Whitman, 102, 105, 109–10
Mazzoleni, Francesco, 32, 39
Meade, George Gordon, 62, 64
Medori, Josephine, 37, 39
Meier, E. D.: letter to Walt Whitman,

quoted, xxxii n; writes obituary of Jeff Whitman, xxxiv
Memphis Water Works, xxix
Merian, Henry W., 90–91
Milwaukee (Wisconsin), 185, 187, 188
Milwaukee Water Works, xxviii–xxix, 185–86
Moore, [E. D. or John], 16
Mount Sterling (Kentucky), 48
Mullan, John, xxvii, 47, 49

Nelson, Camp (Kentucky), 94
New Bern (North Carolina), 58, 60
New Orleans (Louisiana), 3–13; description, 6, 7, 9, 11, 12; parades, 6, 7; yellow fever, 8
New Orleans Daily Crescent, xvi, 3
New York Evening Post, 97, 98 n, 103, 104
New York Herald, 67
New York Times, 69, 101, 122; publishes Walt Whitman's hospital letter, 79
New York Tribune, 102
Ninth Army Corps, 29, 67, 69
Noah (son of Mordecai M. Noah), 127

O'Connor, Ellen (Mrs. William Douglas), 61 n, 122, 123, 136, 139
O'Connor, William Douglas, 61 n, 113 n, 119, 122, 123, 127, 136; and Jeff Whitman's career, 107–08, 119; letter to Jeff Whitman, 107; sends engineering reports to Jeff Whitman, xxvii, 120, 137, 139–42
Old Settlers' Quarter Centennial Celebration, 175
Olmstead (landlord?), 120
Opdyke, George, 64, 65
O'Reilly, Mrs.: Jeff Whitman's close personal relationship with, 164–65, 166, 168

Pacific Railroad: Jeff Whitman's possible job on, xxvii; "Excursions," 126, 135, 139
Pacific Railroad Reports (*Reports of Explorations . . .*), xxvi, 41, 45–46, 82
"Papers on Practical Engineering," 141
Patapsco Seminary (Ellicott City, Maryland), 172 n
Pfaff's (New York City), 90